GU00032108

HARRAP'S

German
Business Management
Terms

English-German
German-English

HARRAP'S

German Business Management Terms

James Coveney
Emeritus Professor of Modern Languages
University of Bath

David Head
Lecturer in German
School of Modern Languages and International Studies
University of Bath

HARRAP
Edinburgh • Paris • New York

This edition first published in Great Britain 1993
by Harrap, 43-45 Annandale Street, Edinburgh EH7 4AZ.

© W & R Chambers Ltd, 1993

ISBN 0 245-60357-3
German Business Management Terms

Printed in Great Britain by
Clays Ltd, St Ives plc

Contents

Introduction

The rapid growth of the management sciences has resulted in the coining of many terms to describe new techniques and concepts, terms which are not easily found in current English-German and German-English dictionaries. A comprehensive glossary of business management terms is therefore urgently needed both by business practitioners and by students of business administration.

Our glossary is an attempt to fill this gap. The terms included have been drawn from the main areas of business management interest: business policy and corporate planning, finance, information technology, marketing, operational research, personnel management, and production.

We have tried to keep a proper balance by not overemphasizing any one area. Moreover, since the scope of the subject is very wide, we have selected only those terms in most frequent use.

We wish to thank Agnes Scheuermann and the Düsseldorf office of McKinsey & Company, Inc. for their invaluable advice on the German terms and Professor G. P. Butler of the School of Modern Languages and International Studies, University of Bath, for providing some crucial published examples of recent business German. Finally, we wish to express our gratitude to the McKinsey Foundation for Management Research, which some years ago made possible the publication of a smaller work which has provided the basis for our glossary - its updated and considerably enlarged successor.

James Coveney
David Head

Notes for the User

Where there are alternative translations of a particular term, they are listed in alphabetical order. That is to say terms have been alphabetized according to the initial letter of their main lexical components. Abbreviations and acronyms have also been incorporated in the alphabetical listings for each letter.

In certain instances we have come up against the untranslatable, where a direct German equivalent does not exist for a particular English term. In such cases, an approximate translation has been given in italics.

English orthography

It should be noted that for words with the alternatives *-ise* or *-ize* and *-isation* or *-ization* the forms *-ize* and *-ization* have been adopted, as English usage is about equally divided between the two, and American practice favours the *-ize*, *-ization*.

In general, however, British English spelling has been used throughout, except in cases connected with computing such as *analog*, *disk* and *program*, where the American English variant appears to have gained general acceptance as the norm.

The attention of the reader is therefore drawn to a few salient differences between British English and American orthography:

(a) The British English use of *-our* (as in lab*our*) where American usage is *-or* (lab*or*)

(b) The British English use of the final *-re* (as in cent*re*) where American usage is *-er* (cent*er*)

(c) The doubling of certain intervocalic consonants in British English (as in programmer) where American usage favours a single consonant (programer).

Finally, the hyphenation of compound terms has proved to be a difficult matter in a book that contains so many new coinages. Compound headwords that are used only as attributive adjectives (such as *stand-alone*) have been hyphenated. Noun compounds have generally been left unhyphenated except in cases where established usage has indicated the need for a hyphen.

German job titles

For technical reasons and also for reasons of space, most German job titles have been given only in the masculine form.

To form the feminine equivalents, add the suffix *-in* to nouns ending in *-ent*, *-ist*, *-er* and *-or* and change the *-er* ending of any preceding adjective to *-e* (e.g. *Direktionsassistentin*, *Computerspezialistin*, *Computerberaterin*, *Generaldirektorin*, *stellvertretende Direktorin*). In the case of adjectival nouns, the customary *-er* masculine ending is replaced by the feminine ending *-e* (e.g. *EDV-Sachverständige*, *ganztägig Beschäftigte*, *Vorstandsvorsitzende*).

ENGLISH-GERMAN

A

abandonment: product ...	Produktaufgabe *(f)*
	Produkteliminierung *(f)*
above par	über dem Nennwert *(m)*
	über pari
absenteeism	Krankfeiern *(n)*
absorption	Zurechnung *(f)* von Kosten *(pl)* auf die Kostenträger *(mpl)*
	Kostenübernahme *(f)*
absorption costing	Kostenaufteilungsverfahren *(n)*
acceptance: brand ...	Markenakzeptanz *(f)*
acceptance: consumer ...	Akzeptanz *(f)* durch die Verbraucher *(mpl)*
	Kaufbereitschaft *(f)* des Konsumenten *(m)*
access (to)	zugreifen auf
	Zugriff *(m)* haben auf
access: multi-...	mehrfacher Zugang *(m)*
access: random ...	wahlfreier Zugriff *(m)*
accountability	Rechenschaftspflicht *(f)*
	Verantwortlichkeit *(f)*
accountant: chief ...	Hauptbuchhalter *(m)*
accounting	Buchhaltung *(f)*
accounting department	Buchhaltungsabteilung *(f)*
accounting model	Buchhaltungsmodell *(n)*
	Kostenrechnungsart *(f)*
accounting period	Abrechnungszeitraum *(m)*
	Rechnungsperiode *(f)*
accounting ratio	Betriebskennziffer *(f)*
accounting: cost ...	Kostenrechnung *(f)*
accounting: creative ...	Bilanzfrisur *(f)*
accounting: electronic ... system	elektronisches Buchführungssystem *(n)*
accounting: management ...	Betriebsrechnungswesen *(n)*
	Kosten- und Leistungsrechnung *(f)*
accounting: profit centre ...	Profit-Center-Ergebnisrechnung *(f)*
accounting: responsibility ...	Verantwortungsrechnung *(f)*
accounts department	Buchhaltungsabteilung *(f)*

accounts: consolidated ...	konsolidierter Geschäftsabschluß *(m)*
	Konzernabschluß *(m)*
	Konzernrechnung *(f)*
accounts: group ...	Konzernabschluß *(m)*
acquisition	Akquisition *(f)*
	Erwerb *(m)*
	Kauf *(m)*
acquisition profile	Akquisitionsprofil *(n)*
acquisition: data ...	Datenbeschaffung *(f)*
acquisitions: mergers and ...	Fusionen *(fpl)* und Übernahmen *(fpl)*
(M & A)	Mergers und Acquisitions *(pl)*
across-the-board increase	genereller Lohnanstieg *(m)*
	genereller Preisanstieg *(m)*
action plan	Aktionsplan *(m)*
	Durchführungsplan *(m)*
action: industrial ...	Arbeitskampfmaßnahmen *(fpl)*
	Streikmaßnahmen *(fpl)*
action: unofficial ...	von einer Gewerkschaft *(f)* nicht genehmigter Streik *(m)*
	wilder Streik *(m)*
actionable	belangbar
	einklagbar
	klagbar
activate (to)	aktivieren
activity chart	Tätigkeitsdiagramm *(n)*
activity sampling	Arbeitsstichproben *(fpl)*
activity: support ...	Stützung *(f)*
actualization: self-...	Eigendynamik *(f)*
adaptive control	adaptive Kontrolle *(f)*
	Anpassungskontrolle *(f)*
add-on equipment	diskretes Bauelement *(n)*
	Zusatzgeräte *(npl)*
added: value ...	Mehrwert *(m)*
	Wertschöpfung *(f)*
added: value ... tax (VAT)	Mehrwertsteuer *(f)*
administration	Verwaltung *(f)*
administration-production ratio	Verhältnis *(n)* von Verwaltung *(f)* zu Produktion *(f)*
administration: financial ...	Finanzverwaltung *(f)*

administrative control procedure	administratives Kontrollverfahren *(n)*
	verwaltungstechnisches Kontrollverfahren *(n)*
administrative expenses	Verwaltungskosten *(pl)*
administrative overheads	Verwaltungsgemeinkosten *(pl)*
administrative theory	Verwaltungstheorie *(f)*
ADP (automatic data processing)	automatische Datenverarbeitung *(f)*
advancement	Beförderung *(f)*
	Förderung *(f)*
advancement: executive ...	Aufstieg *(m)* der Führungskräfte *(fpl)*
	Beförderung *(f)* der Führungskräfte *(fpl)*
advantage: competitive ...	Wettbewerbsvorteil *(m)*
advertising agent	Werbeagent *(m)*
	Werbemittler *(m)*
advertising appropriation	bewilligter Werbeetat *(m)*
	bewilligtes Werbebudget *(n)*
advertising budget	Werbebudget *(n)*
	Werbeetat *(m)*
advertising campaign	Werbekampagne *(f)*
advertising drive	Werbefeldzug *(m)*
advertising effectiveness	Werbeerfolg *(m)*
	Werbewirksamkeit *(f)*
advertising manager	Werbeleiter *(m)*
	Werbemanager *(m)*
advertising media	Werbemedien *(npl)*
	Werbeträger *(mpl)*
advertising message	Werbeaussage *(f)*
	Werbebotschaft *(f)*
advertising research	Werbeforschung *(f)*
advertising theme	Werbethema *(n)*
advertising: corporate ...	Unternehmenswerbung *(f)*
advertising: point-of-sale ... (POS)	POS-Werbung *(f)*
advertising: product ...	Produktwerbung *(f)*
advertising: subliminal ...	unterschwellige Werbung *(f)*
advisory services	Beratungsdienste *(mpl)*
affiliate company	Konzerngesellschaft *(f)*
	Schwestergesellschaft *(f)*
	verbundene Gesellschaft *(f)*

after-sales service	Kundenbetreuung *(f)*
	Kundendienst *(m)*
agenda: hidden ...	unerwähnte Ziele *(npl)*
agenda: to be on the ...	auf der Tagesordnung *(f)* stehen
agent: advertising ...	Werbeagent *(m)*
	Werbemittler *(m)*
agent: forwarding ...	Spediteur *(m)*
agent: sole ...	Alleinvertreter *(m)*
	Exklusivvertreter *(m)*
agreement (*written*)	schriftliche Vereinbarung *(f)*
agreement: collective bargaining ...	Tarifvertrag *(m)*
agreement: gentleman's ...	Gentleman's Agreement *(n)*
	Gentlemen's Agreement *(n)*
agreement: productivity ...	Produktivitätsabkommen *(n)*
	Produktivitätsvereinbarung *(f)*
algorithm	Algorithmus *(m)*
alliance: strategic ...	strategische Allianz *(f)*
allocate (to)	verteilen
	zuteilen
	zuweisen
allocation of costs	Kostenumlage *(f)*
	Verteilung *(f)* von Kosten *(pl)* auf Kostenstellen *(fpl)*
allocation of responsibilities	Zuweisung *(f)* von Aufgabengebieten *(npl)*
	Zuweisung *(f)* von Zuständigkeitsbereichen *(mpl)*
allocation: resource ...	Bereitstellung *(f)* von Ressourcen *(fpl)*
	Planung *(f)* und Bereitstellung *(f)* von Produktionsmitteln *(npl)*
allotment: budget ...	Etatszuweisung *(f)*
allowance: capital ...	Abschreibung *(f)*
allowance: depreciation ...	Abschreibungsbetrag *(m)*
	Wertberichtigung *(f)*
amalgamate (to)	fusionieren
	sich zusammenschließen
amalgamation	Fusion *(f)*
	Zusammenschluß *(m)*

analog computer	Analogrechner *(m)*
analog(ue) representation	Analogdarstellung *(f)*
analysis: break-even ...	Break-Even-Analyse *(f)*
	Deckungspunktanalyse *(f)*
	Gewinnschwellenanalyse *(f)*
analysis: competitor ...	Konkurrenzanalyse *(f)*
analysis: contribution ...	Analyse *(f)* des Deckungsbeitrag(e)s *(m)*
analysis: cost ...	Kostenanalyse *(f)*
analysis: cost-volume-profit ...	Kosten-/Umsatz-/Gewinnanalyse *(f)*
analysis: cost-benefit ... (CBA)	Kosten-Nutzen-Analyse *(f)*
analysis: critical path ... (CPA)	Analyse *(f)* der kritischen Ablaufstufen *(fpl)*
	Analyse *(f)* des kritischen Pfades *(m)*
analysis: decision ...	Entscheidungsanalyse *(f)*
analysis: depth ...	Tiefenanalyse *(f)*
analysis: environmental ...	Umfeldanalyse *(f)*
analysis: financial ...	Finanzanalyse *(f)*
analysis: functional ...	funktionale Analyse *(f)*
analysis: input-output ...	Input-Output-Analyse *(f)*
analysis: investment ...	Investitionsanalyse *(f)*
analysis: job ...	Stellenanalyse *(f)*
analysis: marginal ...	Marginalanalyse *(f)*
analysis: media ...	Media-Analyse *(f)*
	Medienanalyse *(f)*
analysis: morphological ...	morphologische Analyse *(f)*
analysis: multiple regression ... (MRA)	Mehrfach-Regressionsanalyse *(f)*
analysis: needs ...	Bedarfsanalyse *(f)*
analysis: network ...	Analyse *(f)* des kritischen Pfades *(m)*
	Netzplantechnik *(f)*
analysis: operations ...	Arbeitsanalyse *(f)*
	Betriebsanalyse *(f)*
analysis: part-... training	Ausbildung *(f)* in Teilanalysen *(fpl)*
analysis: problem ...	Problemanalyse *(f)*
analysis: product ...	Produktanalyse *(f)*
analysis: profit-factor ...	Analyse *(f)* der Gewinnfaktoren *(mpl)*
	Gewinnfaktoranalyse *(f)*
analysis: profitability ...	Rentabilitätsanalyse *(f)*
analysis: project ...	Projektanalyse *(f)*
analysis: quantitative ...	quantitative Analyse *(f)*

analysis: regression ...	Regressionsanalyse *(f)*
analysis: risk ...	Risikoanalyse *(f)*
analysis: sales ...	Absatzanalyse *(f)*
analysis: sensitivity ...	Sensitivitätsanalyse *(f)*
analysis: sequential ...	Sequenzanalyse *(f)*
	Verlaufsanalyse *(f)*
analysis: skills ...	Analyse *(f)* der Fähigkeiten *(fpl)*
	Fähigkeitsanalyse *(f)*
analysis: social ...	Sozialdiagnose *(f)*
analysis: systems ...	Systemanalyse *(f)*
analysis: training needs ...	Analyse *(f)* des Ausbildungsbedarfs *(m)*
analysis: transactional ... (TA)	Transaktionsanalyse *(f)*
analysis: value ... (VA)	Wertanalyse *(f)*
analysis: variance ...	Abweichungsanalyse *(f)*
analytic accounting	analytische Buchführung *(f)*
	analytische Buchhaltung *(f)*
analytical training	analytische Ausbildung *(f)*
	Ausbildung *(f)* im analytischen Denken *(n)*
ancillary operations	Hilfsoperationen *(fpl)*
	Nebenoperationen *(fpl)*
answerback code	*Rückmeldung (f) beim Telexen (n)*
	Bestätigung (f) von erfolgreicher Übermittlung (f) eines Fernschreibens (n)
answerphone	Anrufbeantworter *(m)*
anticipatory response	Vorwegnahme *(f)*
appeal: sales ...	Verkaufsappeal *(m)*
application: software ...	Softwareanwendung *(f)*
	Softwareanwendungsmöglichkeit *(f)*
apportion (to)	verteilen
	zuteilen
	zuweisen
apportionment	Verteilung *(f)*
	Zuteilung *(f)*
	Zuweisung *(f)*
apportionment: cost ...	Kostenumlage *(f)*
	Kostenzurechnung *(f)*

appraisal	Abschätzung *(f)*
	Beurteilung *(f)*
	Bewertung *(f)*
	Schätzung *(f)*
appraisal: capital expenditure ...	Investitionsbeurteilung *(f)*
	Investitionsbewertung *(f)*
appraisal: financial ...	Bewertung *(f)* der Finanzmittel *(fpl)*
	Finanzbewertung *(f)*
appraisal: investment ...	Investitionsbewertung *(f)*
appraisal: market ...	Marktbeurteilung *(f)*
appraisal: performance ...	Leistungsbeurteilung *(f)*
appraisal: resource ...	Bewertung *(f)* von Ressourcen *(fpl)*
appraisal: self-...	Selbsteinschätzung *(f)*
appraisal: staff ...	Personalbeurteilung *(f)*
appraise (to)	abschätzen
	beurteilen
	bewerten
	schätzen
appreciate (to)	an Wert *(m)* gewinnen
	im Wert *(m)* steigen
appreciation: capital ...	Kapitalwertsteigerung *(f)*
	Wertzuwachs *(m)*
approach: functional ...	funktionale Methode *(f)*
approach: systems ...	Systemverfahren *(n)*
	Systemvorgehen *(n)*
approach: top management ...	Verfahrensweise *(f)* des Top-Managements *(n)*
appropriate (to)	bewilligen
appropriation: advertising ...	bewilligter Werbeetat *(m)*
	bewilligtes Werbebudget *(n)*
appropriation: budget ...	Bewilligung *(f)* von Haushaltsmitteln *(npl)*
appropriation: marketing ...	bewilligte Marketing-Mittel *(npl)*
aptitude test	Eignungsprüfung *(f)*
	Eignungstest *(m)*
arbitrage	Arbitrage *(f)*
arbitrageur	Arbitrageur *(m)*
arbitration	Schiedsverfahren *(n)*
	Schlichtungsverfahren *(n)*
area manager	Gebietsleiter *(m)*
area network: wide ... ... (WAN)	Weitbereichsnetz *(n)*

area: growth ...	Wachstumsbereich *(m)*
	Wachstumsgebiet *(n)*
area: problem ...	Problembereich *(m)*
area: product ...	Produktbereich *(m)*
area: sales ...	Absatzgebiet *(n)*
	Verkaufsgebiet *(n)*
area: trading ...	Absatzgebiet *(n)*
	Einkaufsgebiet *(n)*
arm's length	auf Armeslänge *(f)*
	Prinzip (n) der rechtlichen Selbständigkeit (f) einer Tochtergesellschaft (f)
artificial intelligence	künstliche Intelligenz *(f)*
assembly line	Montagebahn *(f)*
	Montageband *(n)*
assess (to)	beurteilen
	bewerten
	einschätzen
assessment	Beurteilung *(f)*
	Bewertung *(f)*
	Einschätzung *(f)*
assessment centre	Assessment-Center *(n)*
assessment: demand ...	Nachfragebewertung *(f)*
assessment: problem ...	Problembeurteilung *(f)*
assessment: project ...	Projektbewertung *(f)*
assessment: quality ...	Qualitätsbeurteilung *(f)*
	Qualitätsbewertung *(f)*
	Qualitätseinschätzung *(f)*
assessment: risk ...	Risikoeinschätzung *(f)*
	Risikobewertung *(f)*
asset liability management	Aktiva- und Passivamanagement *(n)*
asset management	Anlagenwirtschaft *(f)*
asset portfolio	Kreditportfolio *(n)*
	Kreditvolumen *(n)*
asset-stripping	Anlagenausschlachtung *(f)*
	Ausschlachtung *(f)* einer Unternehmung *(f)*
asset turnover	Verhältnis *(n)* von Umsatz *(m)* zu Anlagen *(fpl)*
asset value	Substanzwert *(m)*
	Vermögenswert *(m)*

assets	Aktiva *(pl)*
	Vermögenswerte *(mpl)*
assets: capital ...	Kapitalvermögen *(n)*
	Wirtschaftsgüter *(npl)*
assets: current ...	Umlaufvermögen *(n)*
assets: earnings on ...	Vermögensertrag *(m)*
assets: fixed ...	Anlagevermögen *(n)*
assets: hidden ...	stille Reserven *(fpl)*
	versteckte Vermögenswerte *(mpl)*
assets: intangible ...	immaterielle Anlagewerte *(mpl)*
assets: liquid ...	flüssige Mittel *(npl)*
	liquide Mittel *(npl)*
assets: net ...	Nettovermögen *(n)*
	Reinvermögen *(n)*
assets: net current ...	Nettoumlaufvermögen *(n)*
assets: quick ...	leicht realisierbare Aktiva *(pl)*
assets: return on ...	Anlagenrendite *(f)*
	Verzinsung *(f)* der Aktiva *(pl)*
assets: revaluation of ...	Neubewertung *(f)* von Vermögenswerten *(mpl)*
assets: tangible ...	materielle Vermögenswerte *(mpl)*
	Sachvermögen *(n)*
assets: wasting ...	kurzlebige Vermögenswerte *(mpl)*
assignment of expenditure	Kostenaufgliederung *(f)*
	Kostenaufschlüsselung *(f)*
	Kostenaufteilung *(f)*
assignment: job ...	Aufgabenzuteilung *(f)*
assistant director	stellvertretender Direktor *(m)*
assistant manager	stellvertretender Direktor *(m)*
assistant to manager	Direktionsassistent *(m)*
assistant: line ...	Linienassistent *(m)*
assistant: staff ...	Stabsassistent *(m)*
associate company	Beteiligungsgesellschaft *(f)*
	verbundenes Unternehmen *(n)*
association: trade ...	Berufsverband *(m)*
assurance: quality ...	Qualitätssicherung *(f)*
at par	al pari
	zum Nennwert *(m)*
attitude survey	Einstellungsuntersuchung *(f)*
attitude: user ...	Verbrauchereinstellung *(f)*

audiovisual aids	audiovisuelle Unterrichtsmittel *(npl)*
audit (to)	prüfen
audit	Buchprüfung *(f)*
	Rechnungsprüfung *(f)*
	Revision *(f)*
audit: efficency ...	Produktivitätsanalyse *(f)*
audit: internal ...	betriebsinterne Revision *(f)*
	Innenrevision *(f)*
audit: management ...	Prüfung *(f)* der Ablaufsysteme *(npl)* einer Unternehmung *(f)*
	Prüfung *(f)* und Bewertung *(f)* der Manager-Leistung *(f)*
audit: manpower ...	Personalbestandsanalyse *(f)*
audit: operations ...	Prüfung *(f)* der Ablaufsysteme *(npl)* einer Unternehmung *(f)*
audit: staff ...	Personalbestandsanalyse *(f)*
auditing: balance sheet ...	Bilanzprüfung *(f)*
auditor	Buchprüfer *(m)*
	Rechnungsprüfer *(m)*
	Revisor *(m)*
authority structure	Aufteilung *(f)* der Weisungsgewalt *(f)*
authority: contraction of ...	Beschränkung *(f)* der Befugnisse *(fpl)*
authority: line ...	Leitungsbefugnis *(f)*
	Leitungskompetenz *(f)*
authorized capital	autorisiertes Kapital *(n)*
automate (to)	automatisieren
	vollautomatisch machen
automatic data processing (ADP)	automatische Datenverarbeitung *(f)*
automation	Automation *(f)*
	Automatisierung *(f)*
automation: office ...	Büroautomation *(f)*
average	Durchschnitt *(m)*
average costs	durchschnittliche Kosten *(pl)*
	Durchschnittskosten *(pl)*
average revenue	Durchschnittseinkünfte *(fpl)*
	Durchschnittseinnahmen *(fpl)*
average yield	Durchschnittsertrag *(m)*
	Durchschnittsrendite *(f)*
average: weighted ...	gewogener Durchschnitt *(m)*

awareness level	Bekanntheitsgrad *(m)*
	Bewußtheitsgrad *(m)*
awareness: brand ...	Bekanntheit *(f)* einer Marke *(f)*
	Markenbewußtsein *(n)*
awareness: cost ...	Kostenbewußtsein *(n)*
awareness: market ...	Marktbewußtsein *(n)*
	Marktkenntnisse *(fpl)*

B

back burner: put on the	verschieben
... ... (to)	vorläufig nicht weiter bearbeiten
backlog	Rückstand *(m)*
back-up facility	Sicherungseinrichtung *(f)*
bad-debt losses	*aus zweifelhaften Forderungen (fpl)*
	herrührende Verluste (mpl)
bad debts	zweifelhafte Forderungen *(fpl)*
balance sheet	Bilanz *(f)*
balance sheet auditing	Bilanzprüfung *(f)*
balanced portfolio	ausgeglichenes Portfolio *(n)*
ball game: different ...	eine ganz andere Chose *(f)*
	etwas ganz anderes *(n)*
ballpark figure	ungefährer Betrag *(m)*
bank rate	Darlehenszinssatz *(m)*
	Diskontsatz *(m)*
bank: commercial ...	Clearingbank *(f)*
	Geschäftsbank *(f)*
bank: computer ...	Computer-Bank *(f)*
bank: data ...	Datenbank *(f)*
bank: investment ...	Effekten- und Emissionsbank *(f)*
	Emissionsbank *(f)*
	Investmentbank *(f)*
bank: merchant ...	Handelsbank *(f)*
	Merchant Bank *(f)*
bar chart	Balkendiagramm *(n)*
bargaining: collective ...	Tarifverhandlungen *(fpl)*
bargaining: collective ... agreement	Tarifvertrag *(m)*
bargaining: plant ...	innerbetriebliche Tarifverhandlung *(f)*

bargaining: productivity ...	Tarifverhandlungen *(fpl)* über Produktivitätszulagen *(fpl)*
barrier: non-tariff ... (NTB)	Zollfreigrenze *(f)*
barrier: tariff ...	Zollschranke *(f)*
barter trade	Tauschhandel *(m)*
base rate	Eckzins *(m)* für Ausleihungen *(fpl)*
base year	Vergleichsjahr *(n)*
base: data ...	Data Base *(f)*
	Datenbasis *(f)*
batch control	Stapelkontrolle *(f)*
batch processing	Stapelverarbeitung *(f)*
batch production	Sortenfertigung *(f)*
	Sortenproduktion *(f)*
batch: economic ... quantity	wirtschaftliche Fertigproduktmenge *(f)*
bear	Baissespekulant *(m)*
	Baissier *(m)*
bear market	Baisse *(f)*
behaviour: buying ...	Einkaufsverhalten *(n)*
	Kaufverhalten *(n)*
behaviour: consumer ...	Konsumentenverhalten *(n)*
behaviour: organizational ...	Verhalten *(n)* in der Organisation *(f)*
behavioural science	Verhaltensforschung *(f)*
below par	unter dem Nennwert *(m)*
	unter pari
benchmark	Maßstab *(m)*
	Richtzahl *(f)*
benefit: cost-... analysis	Kosten-Nutzen-Analyse *(f)*
benefits: fringe ...	Sozialleistungen *(fpl)*
	Vergütung *(f)* neben Gehalt *(n)* oder Lohn *(m)*
best-case scenario	Best-Case-Szenario *(n)*
	optimistischstes Szenario *(n)*
bid: leveraged ...	*von Fremdkapital (n) unterstütztes Übernahmeangebot (n)*
bid: pre-emptive ...	*mögliche Mitbieter (mpl) abschreckendes Übernahmeangebot (n)*
bid: take-over ... (TOB)	Übernahmeangebot *(n)*

blackleg	Streikbrecher *(m)*
blue-chip stock	Aktienspitzenwerte *(mpl)*
	erstklassige Standardwerte *(mpl)*
	erstklassiges Wertpapier *(n)*
blue-collar worker	Arbeiter *(m)*
	Handarbeiter *(m)*
blueprint	Entwurf *(m)*
	Plan *(m)*
blue-sky research	zweckfreie Forschung *(f)*
board control	Aufsichtsratskontrolle *(f)*
	Verwaltungsratskontrolle *(f)*
board meeting	Aufsichtsratssitzung *(f)*
	Verwaltungsratssitzung *(f)*
	Vorstandssitzung *(f)*
board of directors	Board *(m)*
	Aufsichtsrat *(m)*
	Verwaltungsrat *(m)*
board: executive ...	Vorstand *(m)*
boardroom	Sitzungssaal *(m)*
body language	Körpersprache *(f)*
bond: junk ...	Junk Bond *(m)*
bonus	Bonus *(m)*
	Gratifikation *(f)*
	Zulage *(f)*
bonus scheme	Prämienlohnsystem *(n)*
	Prämienregelungsplan *(m)*
bonus: group ...	Gruppenbonus *(m)*
bonus: premium ...	Prämienlohn *(m)*
book value	Buchwert *(m)*
boom	Aufschwung *(m)*
	Boom *(m)*
	Hausse *(f)*
	Hochkonjunktur *(f)*
booster training	zusätzliche Schulung *(f)*
	zusätzliches Training *(n)*
borrowing facility	Kreditfazilität *(f)*
bottleneck	Engpaß *(m)*
bottom line	Saldo *(m)*
bottom out (to)	die Talsohle *(f)* verlassen

bottom-up	dezentralisiert und partizipativ
	von unten nach oben
brains trust	Brain-Trust *(m)*
brainstorming	Brainstorming *(n)*
	gemeinsame Problembewältigung *(f)*
branch office	Filiale *(f)*
	Niederlassung *(f)*
	Zweigstelle *(f)*
brand	Marke *(f)*
brand acceptance	Markenakzeptanz *(f)*
brand awareness	Bekanntheit *(f)* einer Marke *(f)*
	Markenbewußtsein *(n)*
brand image	Markenbild *(n)*
	Markenimage *(n)*
	Markenprofil *(n)*
brand loyalty	Markentreue *(f)*
brand manager	Markenmanager *(m)*
	Markenbetreuer *(m)*
brand name	Markenname *(m)*
brand portfolio	Markenpalette *(f)*
	Markenportfolio *(n)*
brand positioning	Markenpositionierung *(f)*
brand recognition	Markenwiedererkennung *(f)*
brand strategy	Markenstrategie *(f)*
breakdown: operations ...	Aufgliederung *(f)* des
	Stelleninhaltes *(m)*
break even (to)	die Gewinnschwelle *(f)* erreichen
	die Rentabilitätsschwelle *(f)* erreichen
break-even analysis	Break-Even-Analyse *(f)*
	Deckungspunktanalyse *(f)*
	Gewinnschwellenanalyse *(f)*
break-even point	Break-Even-Punkt *(m)*
	Deckungspunkt *(m)*
	Gewinnschwelle *(f)*
	Nutzschwelle *(f)*
break-even quantity	Break-Even-Umsatz *(m)*
breakthrough	Durchbruch *(m)*
break-up value	Ausschlachtungswert *(m)*
	Liquidationswert *(m)*

brief (to)	beauftragen und Instruktionen *(fpl)* geben
	einweisen
	instruieren
briefing	Einweisung *(f)*
	Informationsbesprechung *(f)*
	Unterrichtung *(f)*
broker	Makler *(m)*
broker: software ...	Zwischenhändler *(m)* für Software-Vertrieb *(m)*
brokerage	Courtage *(f)*
	Maklergebühr *(f)*
	Maklerprovision *(f)*
brokerage fees	Maklergebühr *(f)*
brown goods	*holzverkleidete elektrische Gebrauchsgüter (npl)*
budget (to)	budgetieren
	etatisieren
	im Haushaltsplan *(m)* unterbringen
budget	Budget *(n)*
	Etat *(m)*
	Haushalt *(m)*
budget allotment	Etatszuweisung *(f)*
budget appropriation	Bewilligung *(f)* von Haushaltsmitteln *(npl)*
budget constraint	Budgetbeschränkung *(f)*
budget forecast	Haushaltsvoranschlag *(m)*
budget forecasting	Budgetprognose *(f)*
budget standard	Budgetnorm *(f)*
budget: advertising ...	Werbebudget *(n)*
	Werbeetat *(m)*
budget: capital ...	Kapitalbudget *(n)*
budget: cash ...	Kassenbudget *(n)*
	Kassenplan *(m)*
	Liquiditätsplan *(m)*
budget: flexible ...	elastisches Budget *(n)*
budget: investment ...	Investitionsbudget *(n)*
budget: marketing ...	Marketing-Budget *(n)*
budget: sales ...	Verkaufsbudget *(n)*
budget: zero-base ...	Finanzplanung *(f)* von Anfang *(m)* Null *(f)*
budgetary control	Budgetkontrolle *(f)*

budgetary variance	Etatsabweichung (f)
budgeting	Budgetierung (f)
budgeting control	Budgetierungskontrolle (f)
budgeting: capital ...	Kapitalbudgetierung (f)
budgeting: cash ...	Finanzplanung (f)
	Liquiditätsplanung (f)
budgeting: output ...	Produktionsplanung (f)
budgeting: performance ...	Leistungsplanung (f)
budgeting: planning, programming, ... system (PPBS)	Planungs-, Programmierungs- (und) Budgetierungssystem (n)
budgeting: programme ...	Aufstellung des Ist-Budgets (n)
	Programmbudgetierung (f)
buffer stock	Puffervorrat (m)
bug	Programmfehler (m)
	Störung (f)
building: team-...	Team-Bildung (f)
built-in	eingebaut
	eingeplant
built-in obsolescence	eingeplanter Verschleiß (m)
bull	Haussespekulant (m)
	Haussier (m)
bull market	Hausse (f)
bulletin board	computerunterstützte Nachrichtenvermittlung (f)
bundling	Bündelung (f)
bureau: computer services ...	Computer-Dienststelle (f)
bureau: employment ...	Arbeitsnachweis (m)
	Arbeitsvermittlung (f)
	Stellennachweis (m)
	Stellenvermittlung (f)
business corporation	Erwerbsgesellschaft (f)
	Geschäftsunternehmen (n)
	Kapitalgesellschaft (f)
business cycle	Konjunkturzyklus (m)
business economist	Betriebsökonom (m)
	Betriebswirt(schaftler) (m)
business forecasting	Geschäftsprognose (f)
	Konjunkturvoraussage (f)

business game	Planspiel *(n)*
	Unternehmensspiel *(n)*
business management	Betriebsführung *(f)*
	Betriebswirtschaft *(f)*
	Management *(n)*
	Unternehmensführung *(f)*
business outlook	Geschäftslage *(f)*
	Konjunkturaussichten *(fpl)*
business policy	Geschäftspolitik *(f)*
business portfolio	Geschäftsportfolio *(n)*
business proposition	geschäftlicher Vorschlag *(m)*
business relations	Geschäftsbeziehungen *(fpl)*
business strategy	Geschäftsstrategie *(f)*
business stream	Geschäftsgang *(m)*
	Geschäftsverkehr *(m)*
business system	Geschäftsbetrieb *(m)*
	Organisation *(f)* eines Unternehmens *(n)*
business unit: strategic ...	strategische Unternehmenseinheit *(f)*
buy in (to)	einkaufen
buy out (to)	auszahlen
	übernehmen
buyer: chief ...	Chefeinkäufer *(m)*
	Zentraleinkäufer *(m)*
buyer: potential ...	potentieller Käufer *(m)*
buyers' market	Käufermarkt *(m)*
buying behaviour	Einkaufsverhalten *(n)*
	Kaufverhalten *(n)*
buying: impulse ...	Impulskaufen *(n)*
	Spontankaufen *(n)*
buyout	Übernahme *(f)*
buyout: employee ...	Mitarbeiter-Buyout *(m,n)*
buyout: leveraged ... (LBO)	*von Fremdkapital (n) unterstützte Übernahme (f)*
buyout: management ... (MBO)	Management-Buyout *(m,n)* (MBO)
buyout: worker ...	Mitarbeiter-Buyout *(m,n)*
buzz-word	*modische sprachliche Neuprägung (f)*
bypass (to)	umgehen
	vermeiden

by-product	Nebenprodukt *(n)*
byte	Byte *(n)*

C

CAD (computer-aided design)	computerunterstützte Entwicklung *(f)*
	computerunterstützte Konstruktion *(f)*
CAL (computer-aided learning)	computerunterstütztes Lernen *(n)*
CAM (computer-aided manufacturing)	computerunterstützte Fertigung *(f)*
campaign: advertising ...	Werbekampagne *(f)*
campaign: productivity ...	Produktivitätskampagne *(f)*
canvass (to)	durch Kundenbesuch *(m)* werben
	werben (um)
capability	Fähigkeit *(f)*
	Kompetenz *(f)*
capacity utilization	Kapazitätsauslastung *(f)*
capacity: excess ...	Überkapazität *(f)*
capacity: full ...	volle Kapazitätsausnützung *(f)*
capacity: idle ...	ungenutzte Kapazität *(f)*
capacity: manufacturing ...	Fertigungskapazität *(f)*
	Produktionskapazität *(f)*
capacity: plant ...	Anlagenkapazität *(f)*
	Betriebskapazität *(f)*
capacity: spare ...	freie Kapazität *(f)*
capex (capital expenditure)	Investitionsaufwand *(m)*
	Investitionsausgaben *(fpl)*
capital allowance	Abschreibung *(f)*
capital appreciation	Kapitalwertsteigerung *(f)*
	Wertzuwachs *(m)*
capital assets	Kapitalvermögen *(n)*
	Wirtschaftsgüter *(npl)*
capital budget	Kapitalbudget *(n)*
capital budgeting	Kapitalbudgetierung *(f)*
capital commitment	Kapitalbindung *(f)*
capital employed	eingesetztes Kapital *(n)*
capital employed: return on ... ... (ROCE)	Rendite *(f)* des eingesetzten Kapitals *(n)*

capital expenditure (capex)	Investitionsaufwand *(m)*
	Investitionsausgaben *(fpl)*
capital expenditure appraisal	Investitionsbeurteilung *(f)*
	Investitionsbewertung *(f)*
capital formation	Kapitalbildung *(f)*
capital gain	Kapitalertrag *(m)*
	Kapitalgewinn *(m)*
capital goods	Investitionsgüter *(npl)*
	Kapitalgüter *(npl)*
capital-intensive	kapitalintensiv
capital loss	Kapitalverlust *(m)*
capital-output ratio	Kapitalkoeffizient *(m)*
capital project evaluation	Investitionsrechnungsverfahren *(n)*
capital raising	Kapitalaufnahme *(f)*
	Kapitalbeschaffung *(f)*
capital rationing	Kapitalrationierung *(f)*
capital structure	Kapitalstruktur *(f)*
capital: authorized ...	autorisiertes Kapital *(n)*
capital: circulating ...	Betriebskapital *(n)*
capital: issued ...	ausgegebenes Kapital *(n)*
capital: loan ...	Anleihekapital *(n)*
capital: return on ...	Kapitalrendite *(f)*
capital: risk ...	Risikokapital *(n)*
capital: share ...	Aktienkapital *(n)*
capital: venture ...	Risikokapital *(n)*
	Wagniskapital *(n)*
capital: working ...	Betriebskapital *(n)*
capitalist: venture ...	Risikokapitalgeber *(m)*
	Wagniskapitalgeber *(m)*
capitalization	Kapitalisierung *(f)*
capitalize (to)	kapitalisieren
care: customer ...	Service *(m)*
career planning	Laufbahnplanung *(f)*
car phone	Autotelefon *(n)*
cartel	Kartell *(n)*
case study	Fallstudie *(f)*
cash	Bargeld *(n)*
	Barmittel *(npl)*
	Geld *(n)*

cash budget	Kassenbudget *(n)*
	Kassenplan *(m)*
	Liquiditätsplan *(m)*
cash budgeting	Finanzplanung *(f)*
	Liquiditätsplanung *(f)*
cash deal	Kassageschäft *(n)*
	Kassahandel *(m)*
cash flow	Cash-flow *(m)*
cash flow: negative	negativer Cash-flow *(m)*
cash forecasting	Kassenprognose *(f)*
	Liquiditätsprognose *(f)*
	Liquiditätsvorschau *(f)*
cash management	Cash-Management *(n)*
	Kassenhaltung *(f)*
	Liquiditätssteuerung *(f)*
cash-poor	illiquid
	nicht flüssig
cash ratio	Barliquidität *(f)*
	Kassenliquidität *(f)*
cash-rich	flüssig
	liquid
cash-strapped	pleite
	sich in Liquiditätsschwierigkeiten *(fpl)* befindend
	blank
cash: discounted ... flow (DCF)	diskontierter Cash-flow *(m)*
cash: incremental ... flow	Differential *(n)* des Cash-flow *(m)*
	Zuwachs *(m)* des Cash-flow *(m)*
cash: petty ...	Portokasse *(f)*
CAT (computer-assisted teaching)	computerunterstützter Unterricht *(m)*
CBA (cost-benefit analysis)	Kosten-Nutzen-Analyse *(f)*
CBT (computer-based training)	computerunterstützte Ausbildung *(f)*
	rechnergestützte Schulung *(f)*
ceiling: wage ...	Höchstlohn *(m)*
	Lohnhöchstgrenze *(f)*
cellphone	zellulares Mobiltelefon *(n)*
central processing unit (CPU)	Zentraleinheit *(f)* (ZE)
centralization	Zentralisierung *(f)*

centralize (to)	zentralisieren
centre: assessment ...	Assessment-Center *(n)*
centre: computer ...	Datenverarbeitungszentrum *(n)*
	Rechenzentrum *(n)*
centre: cost ...	Kostenstelle *(f)*
centre: profit ...	Profit-Center *(n)*
centre: profit ... accounting	Profit-Center-Ergebnisrechnung *(f)*
centre: responsibility ...	betriebliches Verantwortungszentrum *(n)*
chain of command	Befehlsweg *(m)*
	Instanzenweg *(m)*
chain of distribution	Distributionskette *(f)*
chain of production	Produktionsgang *(m)*
	Produktionskette *(f)*
chain production	*Kettenproduktion (f)*
chain: value ...	Wertkette *(f)*
chairman	Vorsitzender *(m)*
chairman and managing director	Vorsitzender *(m)* und Generaldirektor *(m)*
	Vorsitzender *(m)* und Geschäftsführer *(m)*
chairman: deputy ...	stellvertretender Vorsitzender *(m)*
chairman: vice-...	stellvertretender Vorsitzender *(m)*
challenge: job ...	Stellenanforderung *(f)*
change management (management of change)	Innovationsmanagement *(n)* Management *(n)* des geordneten Wandels *(m)*
change: organizational ...	organisatorische Änderung *(f)*
channel: distribution ...	Absatzkanal *(m)*
	Absatzweg *(m)*
	Distributionskanal *(m)*
	Vertriebsweg *(m)*
channels of communication	Kommunikationswege *(mpl)*
characteristics: job ...	Arbeitscharakteristika *(npl)*
	Berufskennzeichen *(npl)*
	Berufsmerkmale *(npl)*
chart: activity ...	Tätigkeitsdiagramm *(n)*
chart: bar ...	Balkendiagramm *(n)*
chart: flow ...	Ablaufdiagramm *(n)*
	Flußdiagramm *(n)*
chart: flow process ...	Arbeitsablaufbogen *(m)*

chart 22

chart: management ...	Organogramm *(n)* der Unternehmensführung *(f)*
	Organogramm *(n)* der Unternehmensleitung *(f)*
chart: milestone ...	Tabelle *(f)* des kritischen Pfades *(m)*
chart: organization ...	Organisationsplan *(m)*
	Organogramm *(n)*
chart: pie ...	Kreisdiagramm *(n)*
chart: Z ...	Z-Diagramm *(n)*
chief accountant	Hauptbuchhalter *(m)*
chief buyer	Chefeinkäufer *(m)*
	Zentraleinkäufer *(m)*
chief executive	Generaldirektor *(m)*
	Vorstandsvorsitzender *(m)*
Chinese wall	*interne Abschottung (f) von Abteilungen (fpl) eines Kreditinstitut(e)s (n)*
chip	Chip *(m)*
chunk a project (to)	ein Projekt *(n)* in seine Einzelteile *(npl)* zerlegen
chunk down (to)	zerlegen
CIM (computer-integrated manufacturing)	computerintegrierte Fertigung *(f)*
	computergesteuerte Produktion *(f)*
circle: quality ...	Optimierungs-Team *(n)*
	Qualitätszirkel *(m)*
	Quality Circle *(m)*
circulating capital	Betriebskapital *(n)*
classification: job ...	Stellenklassifizierung *(f)*
clearing house	Clearinghaus *(n)*
	Clearingstelle *(f)*
	Verrechnungsstelle *(f)*
clerical work measurement (CWM)	Leistungsbeurteilung *(f)* der Büroangestellten *(f/mpl)*
	Leistungsbewertung *(f)* des Büropersonals *(n)*
clerical worker	Büroangestellter *(m)*
climate: economic ...	Wirtschaftsklima *(n)*
closed loop	geschlossene Schleife *(f)*
	geschlossener Kreislauf *(m)*
closed shop	gewerkschaftspflichtiger Betrieb *(m)*

closing-down costs	Stillegungskosten *(pl)*
co-determination	Mitbestimmung *(f)*
COINS (computerized information system)	computerisiertes Informationssystem *(m)*
collaborative	Gemeinschafts- zusammenarbeitend
collateral	Sicherungsgegenstand *(m)* Sicherungsgut *(n)* (zusätzliche) Sicherheit *(f)*
collateral security	dingliche Sicherheit *(f)*
collective bargaining	Tarifverhandlungen *(fpl)*
collective bargaining agreement	Tarifvertrag *(m)*
collusion	heimliches Einverständnis *(n)* Kollusion *(f)*
command: chain of ...	Befehlsweg *(m)* Instanzenweg *(m)*
command: line of ...	Befehlsweg *(m)* Instanzenweg *(m)*
commercial bank	Clearingbank *(f)* Geschäftsbank *(f)*
commitment: capital ...	Kapitalbindung *(f)*
commitment: staff ...	Einsatz *(m)* des Personals *(n)* Personaleinsatz *(m)*
committee: works ...	Betriebsrat *(m)*
commodity	Handelsartikel *(m)* Handelsware *(f)* Rohstoff *(m)* Ware *(f)*
commodity market	Rohstoffmarkt *(m)* Warenmarkt *(m)*
commodity: primary ...	Rohstoff *(m)*
common currency	gemeinsame Währung *(f)*
common language	gemeinsame Sprache *(f)*
Common Market	Gemeinsamer Markt *(m)*
communication: channels of ...	Kommunikationswege *(mpl)*
communication: electronic ...	elektronische Kommunikation *(f)*
communications network	Kommunikationsnetz *(n)*
communications theory	Kommunikationstheorie *(f)*
company goal	Unternehmensziel *(n)*

company logo	Firmenzeichen *(n)*
company model	Unternehmensmodell *(n)*
company objective	Unternehmensziel *(n)*
company objectives: overall	gesamte Unternehmensziele *(npl)*
company philosophy	Unternehmensphilosophie *(f)*
company planning	Unternehmensplanung *(f)*
company policy	Unternehmenspolitik *(f)*
company profile	Unternehmensprofil *(n)*
company reconstruction	Sanierung *(f)* eines Unternehmens *(n)*
	Umstrukturierung *(f)* einer Unternehmung *(f)*
company strategy	Unternehmensstrategie *(f)*
company structure	Unternehmensstruktur *(f)*
company: affiliate ...	Konzerngesellschaft *(f)*
	Schwestergesellschaft *(f)*
	verbundene Gesellschaft *(f)*
company: associate ...	Beteiligungsgesellschaft *(f)*
	verbundenes Unternehmen *(n)*
company: holding ...	Dachgesellschaft *(f)*
	Holdinggesellschaft *(f)*
company: joint-venture ...	an einem Joint Venture *(n)* beteiligte Gesellschaft *(f)*
	Gemeinschaftsfirma *(f)*
company: parent ...	Muttergesellschaft *(f)*
company: publicly listed ...	börsennotierte Gesellschaft *(f)*
company: quoted ...	börsennotiertes Unternehmen *(n)*
company: subsidiary ...	Tochtergesellschaft *(f)*
company: system-managed ...	nach System *(n)* geführtes Unternehmen *(n)*
company: unlisted ...	nicht börsennotierte Gesellschaft *(f)*
comparison: inter-firm ...	Betriebsvergleich *(m)*
compartmentalize (to)	in Sparten *(fpl)* aufteilen
	aufsplittern
compatible	kompatibel
	(zueinander) passend
	vereinbar
compensation: executive ...	Vergütung *(f)* der Führungskräfte *(fpl)*
competence: executive ...	Führungsfähigkeiten *(fpl)*
competence: job ...	Stellenqualifikationen *(fpl)*

competency	Fähigkeit *(f)*
	Kompetenz *(f)*
	Zuständigkeit *(f)*
competition	Konkurrenz *(f)*
	Wettbewerb *(m)*
competition: fair ...	fairer Wettbewerb *(m)*
competition: the ...	Konkurrenz *(f)*
competition: unfair ...	unlauterer Wettbewerb *(m)*
competitive	konkurrenzfähig
	wettbewerbsfähig
competitive advantage	Wettbewerbsvorteil *(m)*
competitive edge	Wettbewerbsvorsprung *(m)*
competitive position	Wettbewerbsposition *(f)*
	Wettbewerbsstellung *(f)*
competitive price	konkurrenzfähiger Preis *(m)*
	Konkurrenzpreis *(m)*
competitive stimulus	Wettbewerbsanreiz *(m)*
competitive strategy	Wettbewerbsstrategie *(f)*
competitive tactics	Wettbewerbstaktik *(f)*
competitive tendering	Mitabgabe *(f)* von Angeboten *(npl)*
competitive thrust	Wettbewerbsvorstoß *(m)*
competitiveness	Konkurrenzfähigkeit *(f)*
	Wettbewerbsfähigkeit *(f)*
competitor analysis	Konkurrenzanalyse *(f)*
complex: production ...	gesamte Produktionsanlagen *(fpl)*
comptroller	Controller *(m)*
	Rechnungsprüfer *(m)*
computer	Computer *(m)*
computer-aided design (CAD)	computerunterstützte Entwicklung *(f)*
	computerunterstützte Konstruktion *(f)*
computer-aided learning (CAL)	computerunterstütztes Lernen *(n)*
computer-aided manufacturing (CAM)	computerunterstützte Fertigung *(f)*
computer-assisted teaching (CAT)	computerunterstützter Unterricht *(m)*
computer bank	Computer-Bank *(f)*
computer-based training (CBT)	computerunterstützte Ausbildung *(f)*
	rechnergestützte Schulung *(f)*
computer centre	Datenverarbeitungszentrum *(n)*
	Rechenzentrum *(n)*

computer consultant	Computerberater *(m)*
computer expert	Computerspezialist *(m)*
	EDV-Sachverständiger *(m)*
computer input	Computer-Eingabe *(f)*
computer-integrated manufacturing (CIM)	computergesteuerte Produktion *(f)*
	computerintegrierte Fertigung *(f)*
computer language	Maschinensprache *(f)*
computer literate	Computer-Wissen *(n)* besitzend
	mit Computern *(mpl)* vertraut
computer memory	Speicher *(m)*
computer output	Computer-Ausgabe *(f)*
computer program	Computerprogramm *(n)*
computer programmer	Programmierer *(m)*
computer programming	maschinelle Programmierung *(f)*
computer services	Computer-Dienste *(mpl)*
computer services bureau	Computer-Dienststelle *(f)*
computer simulation	Computer-Simulation *(f)*
computer storage	Datenspeicherung *(f)*
computer terminal	Datenendgerät *(n)*
	Terminal *(n)*
computer virus	Computervirus *(n,m)*
computer: analog ...	Analogrechner *(m)*
computer: desktop ...	Desktop *(m)*
computer: digital ...	Digitalrechner *(m)*
computer: laptop ...	Laptop *(m)*
computer: personal ... (PC)	Personal-Computer *(m)* (PC)
computerize (to)	auf Computer *(mpl)* umstellen
	computerisieren
computerized information system (COINS)	computerisiertes Informationssystem *(n)*
computerized management	computergestütztes Management *(n)*
concept: value ...	Wertkonzept *(n)*
conception: product ...	Produktkonzeption *(f)*
conciliate (to)	in Einklang *(m)* bringen
	schlichten
	versöhnen
conciliation	Schlichtung *(f)*
conditions (*of a contract*)	Vertragsbedingungen *(fpl)*
	Vertragsbestimmungen *(fpl)*

conditions of employment	Arbeitsbedingungen *(fpl)*
confidentiality	Vertraulichkeit *(f)*
conglomerate	Konglomerat *(n)*
	Mischkonzern *(m)*
consciousness: cost ...	Kostenbewußtsein *(n)*
consensus	Konsens *(m)*
	Übereinstimmung *(f)*
consolidated accounts	konsolidierter Geschäftsabschluß *(m)*
	Konzernabschluß *(m)*
	Konzernrechnung *(f)*
consolidation	Konsolidierung *(f)*
consortium	Konsortium *(n)*
constraint: budget ...	Budgetbeschränkung *(f)*
consult (to)	konsultieren
	sich besprechen mit
	zu Rate *(m)* ziehen
consultancy: management ...	Management-Beratung *(f)*
	Unternehmensberatung *(f)*
consultant	Berater *(m)*
consultant: computer ...	Computerberater *(m)*
consultant: management ...	Unternehmensberater *(m)*
consultation: joint ...	gemeinsame Beratung *(f)*
consultative	beratend
	konsultativ
consumer acceptance	Akzeptanz *(f)* durch die Verbraucher *(mpl)*
	Kaufbereitschaft *(f)* des Konsumenten *(m)*
consumer behaviour	Konsumentenverhalten *(n)*
consumer durables	Gebrauchsgüter *(npl)*
	langlebige Verbrauchsgüter *(npl)*
consumer goods	Konsumgüter *(npl)*
	Verbrauchsgüter *(npl)*
consumer goods: fast-moving	Renner *(mpl)*
... ... (FMG)	Schnelldreher *(mpl)*
consumer orientation	Konsumorientierung *(f)*
consumer price index	Verbraucherpreisindex *(m)*
consumer protection	Verbraucherschutz *(m)*
consumer research	Verbraucherforschung *(f)*
consumer resistance	Käuferwiderstand *(m)*
	Verbraucherzurückhaltung *(f)*

consumer-responsive	konsumentennah
	kundennah
consumer satisfaction	Verbraucherzufriedenheit *(f)*
consumerism	Verbraucherschutzbewegung *(f)*
	Verbraucherschutzpolitik *(f)*
consumers' panel	Verbraucherpanel *(n)*
container	Container *(m)*
containerization	Containerisierung *(f)*
	Umstellung *(f)* auf Container *(mpl)*
content: work ...	Arbeitsinhalt *(m)*
	Stelleninhalt *(m)*
contingencies	Eventualfälle *(mpl)*
	Eventualverbindlichkeiten *(fpl)*
contingency planning	Notfallplanung *(f)*
contingency reserve	Reserve *(f)* für unvorhergesehene Ausgaben *(fpl)*
	Rückstellung *(f)* für Eventualverbindlichkeiten *(fpl)*
contingency theory	Kontingenztheorie *(f)*
continuous-flow production	Fließfertigung *(f)*
	Massenproduktion *(f)*
continuous stocktaking	fortlaufende Inventur *(f)*
	fortlaufende Warenbestandsaufnahme *(f)*
contract hire	Full-Service-Leasing *(n)*
contract out (to)	Unterauftrag *(m)* vergeben
contract: management ...	Anstellungsvertrag *(m)* eines Managers *(m)*
contract: work by ...	Arbeit *(f)* gemäß vertraglicher Vereinbarung *(f)*
contracting out	Vergabe *(f)* von Unteraufträgen *(mpl)*
contraction of authority	Beschränkung *(f)* der Befugnisse *(fpl)*
contribution analysis	Analyse *(f)* des Deckungsbeitrag(e)s *(m)*
control	Kontrolle *(f)*
control information	Kontrollinformationen *(fpl)*
control: adaptive ...	adaptive Kontrolle *(f)*
	Anpassungskontrolle *(f)*
control: administrative ... procedure	administratives Kontrollverfahren *(n)*
	verwaltungstechnisches Kontrollverfahren *(n)*
control: batch ...	Stapelkontrolle *(f)*

control: board ...	Aufsichtsratskontrolle *(f)*
	Verwaltungsratskontrolle *(f)*
control: budgetary ...	Budgetkontrolle *(f)*
control: budgeting ...	Budgetierungskontrolle *(f)*
control: cost ...	Kostenkontrolle *(f)*
control: financial ...	Finanz-Controlling *(n)*
	Finanzkontrolle *(f)*
control: inventory ...	Bestandskontrolle *(f)*
	Lagerkontrolle *(f)*
control: managerial ...	Führungskontrolle *(f)*
control: manufacturing ...	Fertigungskontrolle *(f)*
	Fertigungssteuerung *(f)*
control: numerical ...	numerische Kontrolle *(f)*
control: process ...	Prozeßkontrolle *(f)*
	Prozeßsteuerung *(f)*
control: production ...	Fertigungskontrolle *(f)*
	Produktionskontrolle *(f)*
control: production planning and ...	Produktionsplanung und -kontrolle *(f)*
control: progress ...	Fortschrittskontrolle *(f)*
control: quality ... **(QC)**	Qualitätskontrolle *(f)*
	Qualitätssteuerung *(f)*
control: span of ...	Kontrollspanne *(f)*
	Leitungsspanne *(f)*
control: statistical ...	statistische Kontrolle *(f)*
control: stock ...	Lagerbestandskontrolle *(f)*
control: total quality ... **(TQC)**	umfassende Qualitätskontrolle *(f)*
controller	Kontrolleur *(m)*
	Nachprüfer *(m)*
controlling interest	Aktienmehrheit *(f)*
	Mehrheitsanteil *(m)*
	Mehrheitsbeteiligung *(f)*
convenience goods	kurzlebige Konsumgüter *(npl)*
	Verbrauchsgüter *(npl)*
coordination	Koordination *(f)*
core product	Hauptprodukt *(n)*
corner	Aufkaufgruppe *(f)*
	Monopol *(n)*

corner (to)	monopolisieren
corner the market (to)	den Markt *(m)* aufkaufen
corporate advertising	Unternehmenswerbung *(f)*
corporate culture	Corporate Culture *(f)*
	Unternehmenskultur *(f)*
corporate goal	Unternehmensziel *(n)*
corporate growth	Unternehmenswachstum *(n)*
corporate image	Corporate Image *(n)*
	Unternehmensimage *(n)*
corporate mission	Unternehmensziel *(n)*
corporate model	Unternehmensmodell *(n)*
corporate objective	Unternehmensziel *(n)*
corporate planning	Unternehmensplanung *(f)*
corporate policy	Unternehmenspolitik *(f)*
corporate raider	(Corporate) Raider *(m)*
corporate strategy	Unternehmensstrategie *(f)*
corporate structure	Unternehmensstruktur *(f)*
corporation tax	Körperschaftssteuer *(f)*
corporation: business ...	Erwerbsgesellschaft *(f)*
	Geschäftsunternehmen *(n)*
	Kapitalgesellschaft *(f)*
corporatism	korporative Grundsätze *(mpl)*
correlate (to)	korrelieren
correlation	enger Zusammenhang *(m)*
	Korrelation *(f)*
	Wechselbeziehung *(f)*
cost accounting	Kostenrechnung *(f)*
cost allocation	Kostenumlage *(f)*
	Verteilung *(f)* von Kosten *(pl)* auf Kostenstellen *(fpl)*
cost analysis	Kostenanalyse *(f)*
cost apportionment	Kostenumlage *(f)*
	Kostenzurechnung *(f)*
cost awareness	Kostenbewußtsein *(n)*
cost-benefit analysis (CBA)	Kosten-Nutzen-Analyse *(f)*
cost centre	Kostenstelle *(f)*
cost consciousness	Kostenbewußtsein *(n)*
cost control	Kostenkontrolle *(f)*

cost-effective	kostengünstig
	kostenwirksam
cost-effectiveness	Kostenwirksamkeit *(f)*
cost-efficient	kosteneffizient
cost factor	Kostenfaktor *(m)*
cost of living	Lebenshaltungskosten *(pl)*
cost of production	Produktionskosten *(pl)*
cost-push inflation	Kosteninflation *(f)*
cost reduction	Kostensenkung *(f)*
	Rationalisierung *(f)*
cost-sensitive	kostenempfindlich
cost standard	Kalkulationsnorm *(f)*
cost structure	Kostenstruktur *(f)*
cost variance	Kostenabweichung *(f)*
cost-volume-profit analysis	Kosten-/Umsatz-/Gewinnanalyse *(f)*
cost: full-... method	Vollkostenprinzip *(n)*
costing	Kalkulation *(f)*
	Kostenrechnung *(f)*
costing: absorption	Kostenaufteilungsverfahren *(n)*
costing: direct ...	Grenzkostenrechnung *(f)*
	Proportionalkostenrechnung *(f)*
costing: functional ...	funktionale Kostenrechnung *(f)*
costing: marginal ...	Grenzkostenrechnung *(f)*
costing: product ...	Ermittlung *(f)* der Erzeugniskosten *(pl)*
	Produktkostenrechnung *(f)*
costing: standard ...	Plankostenrechnung *(f)*
	Standardkostenrechnung *(f)*
costs: allocation of ...	Kostenumlage *(f)*
	Verteilung *(f)* von Kosten *(pl)* auf
	Kostenstellen *(fpl)*
costs: average ...	durchschnittliche Kosten *(pl)*
	Durchschnittskosten *(pl)*
costs: closing-down ...	Stillegungskosten *(pl)*
costs: direct ...	direkte Kosten *(pl)*
costs: distribution ...	Vertriebskosten *(pl)*
costs: estimating systems ...	Systemkostenvoranschlag *(m)*
costs: fixed ...	Festkosten *(pl)*
	Fixkosten *(pl)*
costs: indirect ...	indirekte Kosten *(pl)*

costs: managed ...	kontrollierte Kosten *(pl)*
costs: marginal ...	Grenzkosten *(pl)*
costs: opportunity ...	Opportunitätskosten *(pl)*
costs: replacement ...	Wiederbeschaffungskosten *(pl)*
	Wiederbeschaffungswert *(m)*
costs: semi-variable ...	sprungfixe Kosten *(pl)*
	Sprungkosten *(pl)*
costs: set-up ...	Gründungskosten *(pl)*
	Rüstkosten *(pl)*
costs: standard ...	Sollkosten *(pl)*
	Standardkosten *(pl)*
costs: start-up ...	Anlaufkosten *(pl)*
	Gründungskosten *(pl)*
	Startkosten *(pl)*
costs: variable ...	variable Kosten *(pl)*
costs: unit labour ...	Lohnstückkosten *(pl)*
council: works ...	Betriebsrat *(m)*
counselling: employee ...	Personalberatung *(f)*
countertrade	Gegengeschäfte *(npl)*
	Tauschhandel *(m)*
cover ratio	Deckungsverhältnis *(n)*
coverage: sales ...	Abdeckung *(f)* durch den Verkauf *(m)*
	Marktabdeckung *(f)*
CPA (critical path analysis)	Analyse *(f)* der kritischen Ablaufstufen *(fpl)*
	Analyse *(f)* des kritischen Pfades *(m)*
CPM (critical path method)	Methode *(f)* des kritischen Pfades *(m)*
CPU (central processing unit)	Zentraleinheit *(f)* (ZE)
crash	Crash *(m)*
	Zusammenbruch *(m)*
crash (to) (*a program*)	ein Programm *(n)* unabsichtlich auslöschen
creative accounting	Bilanzfrisur *(f)*
creative marketing	kreatives Marketing *(n)*
creative thinking	kreatives Denken *(n)*
credit control	Kreditkontrolle *(f)*
credit management	Kreditmanagement *(n)*
credit rating	Beurteilung *(f)* der Kreditwürdigkeit *(f)*
	Bonitätsbeurteilung *(f)*
credit squeeze	Kreditdrosselung *(f)*
	Kreditrestriktion *(f)*

credit: revolving ...	revolvierender Kredit (m)
	Revolvingkredit (m)
crisis management	Krisenmanagement (n)
criteria: investment ...	Investitionskriterien (npl)
critical mass	kritische Masse (f)
critical path analysis (CPA)	Analyse (f) der kritischen Ablaufstufen (fpl)
	Analyse (f) des kritischen Pfades (m)
critical path method (CPM)	Critical Path Method (f) (CPM)
	Methode (f) des kritischen Pfades (m)
cross-licensing	Lizenzaustausch (m)
culture	Kultur (f)
culture: corporate ...	Corporate Culture (f)
	Unternehmenskultur (f)
culture: organization ...	Firmenkultur (f)
	Organisationskultur (f)
currency: common ...	gemeinsame Währung (f)
currency: parallel ...	Parallelwährung (f)
currency: single ...	einheitliche Währung (f)
current assets	Umlaufvermögen (n)
current expenditure	laufende Betriebsausgaben (fpl)
	laufende Betriebskosten (pl)
current liabilities	kurzfristige Verbindlichkeiten (fpl)
current ratio	Liquiditätsgrad (m)
	Liquiditätskennzahl (f)
current: net ... assets	Nettoumlaufvermögen (n)
cursor	Cursor (m)
	Kursor (m)
curve: learning ...	Lernkurve (f)
curve: salary progression ...	Gehaltsprogressionskurve (f)
custom and practice	Sitten (fpl) und Gebräuche (mpl)
custom-made	maßgefertigt
	spezialangefertigt
customer care	Service (m)
customer orientation	Kundenorientierung (f)
	Unterrichtung (f) der Kundschaft (f)
customer profile	Kundenprofil (n)
customer service	Kundendienst (m)
customer: prospective ...	potentieller Kunde (m)
	voraussichtlicher Kunde (m)

customized	nach Maß *(n)* hergestellt
cut one's losses (to)	rechtzeitig zu spekulieren aufhören
	Verluste *(mpl)* abschreiben
cut prices (to)	Preise *(mpl)* herabsetzen
	Preise *(mpl)* senken
cut-back: staff ...	Arbeitskräfteabbau *(m)*
cut-off point	Stichtag *(m)*
cutting edge	Innovationsführerschaft *(f)*
cutting: price-...	Preisunterbietung *(f)*
CWM (clerical work measurement)	Leistungsbeurteilung *(f)* der Büroangestellten *(flmpl)*
	Leistungsbewertung *(f)* des Büropersonals *(n)*
cybernetics	Kybernetik *(f)*
cycle: business ...	Konjunkturzyklus *(m)*
cycle: life ... *(of a product)*	Lebenszyklus *(m)* *(eines Produkt(e)s (n))*
cycle: trade ...	Konjunkturzyklus *(m)*
cycle: work ...	Arbeitszyklus *(m)*

D

daisy wheel	Typenrad *(n)*
	Typenraddrucker *(m)*
damage limitation	Schadensbegrenzung *(f)*
data acquisition	Datenbeschaffung *(f)*
data bank	Datenbank *(f)*
data base	Data Base *(f)*
	Datenbasis *(f)*
data flow chart	Datenablaufplan *(m)*
	Datenflußplan *(m)*
data gathering	Datensammlung *(f)*
data processing	Datenverarbeitung *(f)*
data protection	Datenschutz *(m)*
data retrieval	Datenwiedergewinnung *(f)*
data: automatic ... processing (ADP)	automatische Datenverarbeitung *(f)*

data: electronic ... processing (EDP)	elektronische Datenverarbeitung *(f)*
date: due ...	Fälligkeitstag *(m)*
	Fälligkeitstermin *(m)*
date: expected ...	Stichtag *(m)*
	Termin *(m)*
date: latest ...	äußerster Termin *(m)*
	letzter Tag *(m)*
date: sell-by ...	letztes Verkaufsdatum *(n)*
date: use-by ...	*haltbar bis*
	Mindesthaltbarkeitsdatum *(n)*
day shift	Tagschicht *(f)*
DCF (discounted cash flow)	diskontierter Cash-flow *(m)*
deadline	Frist *(f)*
	Termin *(m)*
deal	Deal *(m)*
	Geschäft *(n)*
deal: cash ...	Kassageschäft *(n)*
	Kassahandel *(m)*
deal: package ...	Kopplungsgeschäft *(n)*
deal: reach a ... (to)	ein Geschäft *(n)* abschließen
	ein Geschäft *(n)* machen
	einen Deal *(m)* machen
dealer	Händler *(m)*
dealing: insider ...	Insidergeschäfte *(npl)*
debenture	Schuldverschreibung *(f)*
debottleneck (to)	einen Engpaß *(m)* beseitigen
debrief (to)	Einsatz *(m)* (anschließend) besprechen
	Einsatzerfolg *(m)* analysieren
debriefing	Einsatzanalyse *(f)*
	Einsatzbesprechung *(f)*
debt financing	Finanzierung *(f)* durch die Emission *(f)* von Schuldtiteln *(mpl)*
	Finanzierung *(f)* von Verpflichtungen *(fpl)*
debt ratio	Verschuldungsgrad *(m)*
	Verschuldungskoeffizient *(m)*
debt-equity ratio	Verhältnis *(n)* von Eigen- zu Fremdkapital *(n)*
	Verschuldungsgrad *(m)*
	Verschuldungskoeffizient *(m)*

debtor	Schuldner *(m)*
debts: bad ...	zweifelhafte Forderungen *(fpl)*
debug (to)	Fehler *(mpl)* beseitigen
decentralization	Dezentralisierung *(f)*
decentralize (to)	dezentralisieren
decentralized management	dezentralisiertes Management *(n)*
decision analysis	Entscheidungsanalyse *(f)*
decision-making	Entscheidungsfindung *(f)*
decision model	Entscheidungsmodell *(n)*
decision process	Entscheidungsprozeß *(m)*
decision theory	Entscheidungstheorie *(f)*
decision tree	Entscheidungsbaum *(m)*
deductible: tax-...	steuerlich absetzbar
defensive strategy	defensive Strategie *(f)*
deficit financing	Defizitfinanzierung *(f)*
deindustrialization	De-Industrialisierung *(f)*
delegate (to)	delegieren
delegation	Delegation *(f)*
delivery time	Lieferzeit *(f)*
demand assessment	Nachfragebewertung *(f)*
demand forecasting	Nachfrageprognose *(f)*
	Nachfrageprognostizierung *(f)*
demand-pull inflation	nachfrageinduzierte Inflation *(f)*
	Nachfrageinflation *(f)*
demanning	Personalabbau *(m)*
demerger	Konzernentflechtung *(f)*
democracy: industrial ...	Mitbestimmung *(f)*
demotivate (to)	demotivieren
	entmutigen
demotivation	Demotivierung *(f)*
	Entmutigung *(f)*
department: accounting ...	Buchhaltungsabteilung *(f)*
department: engineering and design ...	technische Abteilung *(f)* und Konstruktionsbüro *(n)*
department: marketing ...	Marketingabteilung *(f)*
department: personnel ...	Personalabteilung *(f)*
department: planning ...	Planungsabteilung *(f)*
department: research ...	Forschungsabteilung *(f)*
department: sales ...	Verkaufsabteilung *(f)*

departmental head	Abteilungsvorstand *(m)*
	Abteilungsleiter *(m)*
departmental management	Abteilungsleitung *(f)*
departmental manager	Abteilungsleiter *(m)*
departmental plan	Abteilungsplan *(m)*
departmentalization	betriebliche Aufgliederung *(f)*
	Dezentralisierung *(f)*
deploy (to)	einsetzen
deployment	Einsatz *(m)*
depreciate (to)	abschreiben
	an Wert *(m)* verlieren
	entwerten
depreciation allowance	Abschreibungsbetrag *(m)*
	Wertberichtigung *(f)*
depth analysis	Tiefenanalyse *(f)*
depth interview	Tiefeninterview *(n)*
deputy chairman	stellvertretender Vorsitzender *(m)*
deputy manager	stellvertretender Direktor *(m)*
deputy managing director	stellvertretender
	Generaldirektor *(m)*
	stellvertretender Geschäftsführer *(m)*
deregulate (to)	deregulieren
deregulation	Deregulierung *(f)*
description: job ...	Stellenbeschreibung *(f)*
design engineering	Konstruktionstechnik *(f)*
design office	Konstruktionsbüro *(n)*
design: computer-aided ... (CAD)	computerunterstützte Entwicklung *(f)*
	computerunterstützte Konstruktion *(f)*
design: engineering and ... department	technische Abteilung *(f)* und Konstruktionsbüro *(n)*
design: job ...	Stellenentwurf *(m)*
design: product ...	Produktgestaltung *(f)*
design: systems ...	Systemgestaltung *(f)*
desk research	Schreibtischforschung *(f)*
desktop computer	Desktop *(m)*
desktop publish (to)	als Desktop-Veröffentlichung *(f)* herausbringen
desktop publishing	Desktop-Publishing *(n)*
determination: price ...	Preisfestsetzung *(f)*

developer	Baulöwe *(m)*
	Bauträger *(m)*
	Erschließungsgesellschaft *(f)*
development potential	Entwicklungspotential *(n)*
development programme	Entwicklungsprogramm *(n)*
development: executive ...	Management-Entwicklung *(f)*
development: human resource ...	Personalentwicklung *(f)*
(HRD)	
development: management ...	Management-Entwicklung *(f)*
development: new-product ...	Entwicklung *(f)* neuer Produkte *(npl)*
development: organizational ...	Entwicklung *(f)* der Organisation *(f)*
	organisatorische Entwicklung *(f)*
	organisatorischer Aufbau *(m)*
development: product ...	Produktentwicklung *(f)*
development: research and ...	Forschung *(f)* und Entwicklung *(f)*
(R & D)	(FE, F & E)
deviation: standard ...	Normalabweichung *(f)*
	Standardabweichung *(f)*
diagnostic routine	Beseitigung *(f)* von Fehlerquellen *(fpl)*
diagram: flow ...	Flußdiagramm *(n)*
diagram: scatter ...	Punktediagramm *(n)*
	Streubild *(n)*
	Streudiagramm *(n)*
different ball game	eine ganz andere Chose *(f)*
	etwas ganz anderes *(n)*
differential price	differenzierter Preis *(m)*
differential pricing	Differentialpreisfestsetzung *(f)*
	Preisdifferenzierung *(f)*
	unterschiedliche Preisgestaltung *(f)*
differential: earnings ...	Lohndifferenzen *(fpl)*
	Lohnunterschiede *(mpl)*
differential: price ...	Preisgefälle *(n)*
	Preisunterschied *(m)*
differential: wage ...	Lohngefälle *(n)*
differentiate (to)	differenzieren
	unterscheiden
differentiate: product ... (to)	sich deutlich von Konkurrenzprodukten *(npl)*
	unterscheiden
differentiation: product ...	Produktdifferenzierung *(f)*

digital	digital
	Digital-
digital computer	Digitalrechner *(m)*
digitize (to)	digitalisieren
	digitieren
dilution of equity	Kapitalverwässerung *(f)*
	Verwässerung *(f)* des Aktienkapitals *(n)*
dilution of labour	Einstellung *(f)* ungelernter Arbeitskräfte *(fpl)*
direct costs	direkte Kosten *(pl)*
direct costing	Grenzkostenrechnung *(f)*
	Proportionalkostenrechnung *(f)*
direct expenses	direkte Ausgaben *(fpl)*
direct labour	Fertigungslöhne *(mpl)*
	unmittelbar geleistete Arbeitszeit *(f)*
direct mail	Direktversand *(m)*
direct marketing	Direktmarketing *(n)*
direct selling	Direktverkauf *(m)*
director	Direktor *(m)*
director: assistant ...	stellvertetender Direktor *(m)*
director: deputy managing ...	stellvertetender Generaldirektor *(m)*
	stellvertetender Geschäftsführer *(m)*
director: executive ...	Board-Mitglied *(n)*
	Vorstandsmitglied *(n)*
director: financial ...	Finanzchef *(m)*
	Finanzvorstand *(m)*
director: managing ... (MD)	Generaldirektor *(m)*
	Geschäftsführer *(m)*
director: non-executive ...	Aufsichtsratsmitglied *(n)*
	Mitglied *(n)* des Verwaltungsrat(e)s *(m)*
director: outside ...	Aufsichtsratsmitglied *(n)*
	Mitglied *(n)* des Verwaltungsrat(e)s *(m)*
director: production ...	Produktionsleiter *(m)*
directorate: interlocking ...	Mandatsverflechtung *(f)*
directors: board of	Aufsichtsrat *(m)*
	Board *(m)*
	Verwaltungsrat *(m)*
disburse (to)	ausgeben
	auslegen
	auszahlen

disbursement	Auszahlung *(f)*
discounted cash flow (DCF)	diskontierter Cash-flow *(m)*
discretion: time span of ...	zulässige Zeitspanne *(f)* für unterdurchschnittliche Leistung *(f)*
discriminate (to)	diskriminieren unterschiedlich behandeln
discrimination	Diskriminierung *(f)*
discrimination: positive ...	*Bevorzugung (f) bei der Personalauslese (f) um der beruflichen Chancengleichheit (f) willen* Quotenregelung *(f)*
discrimination: price ...	Preisdiskriminierung *(f)*
diseconomy of scale	Größennachteil *(m)* Kostenprogression *(f)*
disincentive	Abschreckungsmittel *(n)* arbeitshemmender Faktor *(m)*
disintegration	Auflösung *(f)* Desintegration *(f)* Zerfall *(m)*
disinvestment	Desinvestition *(f)*
disk	Magnetplatte *(f)* Platte *(f)*
disk drive	Diskettenlaufwerk *(n)* Plattenlaufwerk *(n)*
disk: floppy ...	Diskette *(f)* Floppy-Disk *(f)*
disk: hard ...	Festplatte *(f)* Harddisk *(f)*
disk: Winchester ...	Winchesterplatte *(f)*
dismissal	Entlassung *(f)*
dismissal: summary ...	fristlose Entlassung *(f)*
dismissal: unfair ...	sozialwidrige Kündigung *(f)*
dispatching	Abfertigung *(f)*
display unit	Anzeigegerät *(n)* Bildschirmgerät *(n)* Datensichtgerät *(n)*

display unit: visual … … (VDU)	Anzeigeeinheit *(f)*
	Bildschirm *(m)*
	Bildschirmgerät *(n)*
	Bildsichtgerät *(n)*
disposable income	verfügbares Einkommen *(n)*
disposition: source and … of funds	Mittelherkunft *(f)* und -einsatz *(m)*
dispute: industrial …	Arbeitskonflikt *(m)*
	Tarifkonflikt *(m)*
dispute: labour …	Arbeitskonflikt *(m)*
dissolution	Auflösung *(f)*
	Liquidation *(f)*
distance learning	Fernstudium *(n)*
distributed profit	verteilter Gewinn *(m)*
	ausgeschüttete Gewinne *(mpl)*
distribution	Absatz *(m)*
	Distribution *(f)*
	Vertrieb *(m)*
distribution channel	Absatzkanal *(m)*
	Absatzweg *(m)*
	Distributionskanal *(m)*
	Vertriebsweg *(m)*
distribution costs	Vertriebskosten *(pl)*
distribution manager	Vertriebsleiter *(m)*
distribution network	Vertriebsnetz *(n)*
distribution planning	Vertriebsplanung *(f)*
distribution policy	Vertriebspolitik *(f)*
distribution: chain of …	Distributionskette *(f)*
distribution: frequency …	Häufigkeitsverteilung *(f)*
distribution: physical … management	Warenverteilung *(f)*
diversification	Diversifikation *(f)*
	Diversifizierung *(f)*
diversification strategy	Diversifikationsstrategie *(f)*
diversification: product …	Produktdiversifizierung *(f)*
	Produktionsbreite *(f)*
diversify (to)	diversifizieren

divestment	Entflechtung *(f)*
	Veräußerung *(f)*
	Verkauf *(m)*
dividend	Dividende *(f)*
dividend policy	Dividendenpolitik *(f)*
division: operating ...	Betriebsabteilung *(f)*
	Sparte *(f)*
	Unternehmensbereich *(m)*
divisional management	Spartenleitung *(f)*
doomwatcher	Schwarzseher *(m)*
double taxation relief	Steuernachlaß *(m)* aufgrund eines
	Doppelbesteuerungsabkommens *(n)*
down the line	auf nachgeordneten Führungsebenen *(fpl)*
down-market	für den Massenmarkt *(m)*
	weniger anspruchsvoll
downstream	in Bandlaufrichtung *(f)*
downswing	Abschwung *(m)*
	Konjunkturabschwung *(m)*
down time	Ausfallzeit *(f)*
downturn	Flaute *(f)*
	Geschäftsrückgang *(m)*
	Konjunkturabschwächung *(f)*
drift: wage ...	Lohnauftrieb *(m)*
	Lohndrift *(f)*
drip-feeding	stufenweise Finanzierung *(f)*
drive: advertising ...	Werbefeldzug *(m)*
drive: disk ...	Diskettenlaufwerk *(n)*
	Plattenlaufwerk *(n)*
drive: productivity ...	gezielte Bemühungen *(fpl)* um
	Produktivitätssteigerung *(f)*
	Produktivitätskampagne *(f)*
drive: sales ...	Verkaufskampagne *(f)*
dual sourcing	zweigleisige Beschaffung *(f)*
due date	Fälligkeitstag *(m)*
	Fälligkeitstermin *(m)*
dummy activity	Blindbefehl *(m)*
dumping	Dumping *(n)*
durables	Gebrauchsgüter *(npl)*
	langlebige Verbrauchsgüter *(fpl)*

durables: consumer ...	Gebrauchsgüter *(npl)*
	langlebige Verbrauchsgüter *(npl)*
dynamic evaluation	dynamische Bewertung *(f)*
dynamic management model	dynamisches Führungsmodell *(n)*
	dynamisches Management-Modell *(n)*
dynamic programming	dynamische Programmierung *(f)*
dynamics: group ...	Gruppendynamik *(f)*
dynamics: industrial ...	Betriebsdynamik *(f)*
	Industriedynamik *(f)*
dynamics: market ...	Marktdynamik *(f)*
dynamics: product ...	Produktdynamik *(f)*
dysfunction	Fehlfunktion *(f)*
	Funktionsstörung *(f)*

E

e-mail (electronic mail)	Electronic Mail *(f)*
	Elektronische Post *(f)*
early retirement	vorzeitige Pensionierung *(f)*
earning power	Ertragskraft *(f)*
earnings differential	Lohndifferenzen *(fpl)*
	Lohnunterschiede *(mpl)*
earnings on assets	Vermögensertrag *(m)*
earnings per share (EPS)	Gewinn *(m)* je Aktie *(f)*
earnings performance	Ertragsleistung *(f)*
earnings yield	Gewinnrendite *(f)*
earnings: price-... ratio (P/E)	Kurs-Gewinn-Verhältnis *(n)*
EC (European Community)	EG *(f)* (Europäische Gemeinschaft *(f)*)
econometric	ökonometrisch
economic batch quantity	wirtschaftliche Fertigproduktmenge *(f)*
economic climate	Wirtschaftsklima *(n)*
economic intelligence	Wirtschaftsinformation *(f)*
economic life	wirtschaftliche Nutzungsdauer *(f)*
economic manufacturing quantity	wirtschaftliche Produktionsmenge *(f)*
economic mission	wirtschaftlicher Auftrag *(m)*
economic order quantity	wirtschaftliche Losgröße *(f)*
economic research	Wirtschaftsforschung *(f)*

economic trend	Konjunkturtrend *(m)*
	Konjunkturverlauf *(m)*
	Wirtschaftstendenzen *(fpl)*
economist: business ...	Betriebsökonom *(m)*
	Betriebswirt(schaftler) *(m)*
economy of scale	Größenvorteil *(m)*
	Kostendegression *(f)*
economy: motion ...	Bewegungsökonomie *(f)*
ECU (European Currency Unit)	Ecu *(m)* (Europäische Währungseinheit *(f)*)
ecu: hard ...	harter Ecu *(m)*
edge: competitive ...	Wettbewerbsvorsprung *(m)*
edge: cutting ...	Innovationsführerschaft *(f)*
edge: leading ...	Avantgarde *(f)*
EDP (electronic data processing)	elektronische Datenverarbeitung *(f)*
effective management	wirksame Unternehmensführung *(f)*
	wirksames Management *(n)*
effective: cost-...	kostenwirksam
	kostengünstig
effectiveness	Wirksamkeit *(f)*
effectiveness: advertising ...	Werbeerfolg *(m)*
	Werbewirksamkeit *(f)*
effectiveness: cost-...	Kostenwirksamkeit *(f)*
effectiveness: managerial ...	wirksame Unternehmensführung *(f)*
	wirksame Unternehmensleitung *(f)*
	wirksames Management *(n)*
effectiveness: organizational ...	organisatorische Wirksamkeit *(f)*
efficiency	Effizienz *(f)*
	Leistungsfähigkeit *(f)*
efficiency audit	Produktivitätsanalyse *(f)*
efficient	effizient
	leistungsfähig
efficient: cost- ...	kosteneffizient
effort: sales expansion ...	Bemühungen *(fpl)* um Verkaufssteigerungen *(fpl)*
EFTPOS (electronic funds transfer at point of sale)	*elektronischer Zahlungsverkehr (m) in Verbindung (f) mit einem POS-System (n)*
elasticity	Elastizität *(f)*
electronic accounting system	elektronisches Buchführungssystem *(n)*
electronic communication	elektronische Kommunikation *(f)*

electronic data processing (EDP)	elektronische Datenverarbeitung *(f)*
electronic funds transfer at point-of-sale (EFTPOS)	*elektronischer Zahlungsverkehr (m) in Verbindung (f) mit einem POS-System (n)*
electronic mail (e-mail)	Elektronische Post *(f)*
	Electronic Mail *(f)*
electronic office	elektronisches Büro *(n)*
electronic processing	elektronische Verarbeitung *(f)*
empirical	empirisch
employed: capital ...	eingesetztes Kapital *(n)*
employed: return on capital ... (ROCE)	Rendite *(f)* des eingesetzten Kapitals *(n)*
employee buyout	Mitarbeiter-Buyout *(m,n)*
employee counselling	Personalberatung *(f)*
employee relations	Beziehungen *(fpl)* zu Arbeitnehmern *(mpl)*
employees: front-line ...	Personal *(n)* im Außendienst *(m)*
employment bureau	Arbeitsnachweis *(m)*
	Arbeitsvermittlung *(f)*
	Stellennachweis *(m)*
	Stellenvermittlung *(f)*
employment: conditions of ...	Arbeitsbedingungen *(fpl)*
employment: full-time ...	Ganztagsbeschäftigung *(f)*
employment: part-time ...	Halbtagsbeschäftigung *(f)*
	Teilzeitbeschäftigung *(f)*
EMS (European Monetary System)	EWS *(n)* (Europäisches Währungssystem *(n)*)
EMU (European Monetary Union)	Europäische Währungsunion *(f)*
engineer: sales ...	Verkaufsingenieur *(m)*
	technischer Kaufmann *(m)*
engineer: software ...	Software-Engineer *(m)*
engineer: systems ...	Systemingenieur *(m)*
engineering	Maschinenbau *(m)*
	Technik *(f)*
engineering and design department	technische Abteilung *(f)* und Konstruktionsbüro *(n)*
engineering: design ...	Konstruktionstechnik *(f)*
engineering: human ...	Arbeitsplatzgestaltung *(f)*
	Ergonomie *(f)*

engineering: industrial ...	Betriebstechnik *(f)*
	ingenieur- und arbeitswissenschaftliche Organisationsgestaltung *(f)*
engineering: methods ...	Ermittlung *(f)* von Arbeitsablaufstudien *(fpl)*
engineering: product ...	Fertigungstechnik *(f)*
engineering: production ...	Produktionstechnik *(f)*
engineering: systems ...	Systemplanung *(f)*
engineering: value ...	Konzept-Wertanalyse *(f)*
enlargement: job ...	Erweiterung *(f)* der Arbeitsaufgaben *(fpl)*
enrichment: job ...	Arbeitsbereicherung *(f)*
enterprise	Unternehmen *(n)*
	Unternehmung *(f)*
enterprise: private ...	freies Unternehmertum *(n)*
	Privatwirtschaft *(f)*
enterprise: public ...	öffentliche Wirtschaftsbetriebe *(mpl)*
	öffentlicher Sektor *(m)*
enterprising	einfallsreich
	unternehmungslustig
	unternehmerisch eingestellt
entrepreneurial spirit	Unternehmergeist *(m)*
environment	Umwelt *(f)*
environmental analysis	Umfeldanalyse *(f)*
environmental forecasting	Wirtschaftsprognose *(f)*
environmental scan	Environmental Scanning *(n)*
EPS (earnings per share)	Gewinn *(m)* je Aktie *(f)*
equal employment opportunity	berufliche Chancengleichheit *(f)*
equal opportunity	Chancengleichheit *(f)*
equal pay	gleicher Lohn *(m)*
	gleiches Entgelt *(n)*
equality	Gleichberechtigung *(f)*
	Gleichheit *(f)*
	Parität *(f)*
equipment leasing	Investitionsgüter-Leasing *(n)*
equipment: add-on ...	diskretes Bauelement *(n)*
	Zusatzgeräte *(npl)*
equipment: peripheral ...	Peripheriegeräte *(npl)*
equipment: process ... layout	Betriebsanlage *(f)* nach Werkstattprinzip *(n)*
equity	Eigenkapital *(n)*
equity market	Aktienmarkt *(m)*

equity: dilution of ...	Kapitalverwässerung *(f)*
	Verwässerung *(f)* des Aktienkapitals *(n)*
equity: return on ... (ROE)	Eigenkapitalrendite *(f)*
	Eigenkapitalrentabilität *(f)*
ergonometrics	Ergonometrik *(f)*
ergonomics	Ergonomik *(f)*
ERM (Exchange Rate Mechanism)	Wechselkursgefüge *(n)*
	Wechselkursmechanismus *(m)* im Europäischen Währungssystem *(n)*
escalation: price ...	sich gegenseitig verstärkender Preisauftrieb *(m)*
espionage: industrial ...	Industriespionage *(f)*
establishment	Betrieb *(m)*
estimate: sales ...	Absatzkalkulation *(f)*
	Absatzprognose *(f)*
estimating systems costs	Systemkostenvoranschlag *(m)*
Eurobond	Euroanleihe *(f)*
	Eurobond *(m)*
Eurocurrency	Eurowährung *(f)*
Eurodollar	Eurodollar *(m)*
Euromarket	Euromarkt *(m)*
European Community (EC)	Europäische Gemeinschaft *(f)* (EG)
European Currency Unit (ECU)	Europäische Währungseinheit *(f)* (Ecu *(m)*)
European Monetary System (EMS)	Europäisches Währungssystem *(n)* (EWS)
European Monetary Union (EMU)	Europäische Währungsunion *(f)*
evaluate (to)	beurteilen
	bewerten
evaluation: capital project ...	Investitionsrechnungsverfahren *(n)*
evaluation: dynamic ...	dynamische Bewertung *(f)*
evaluation: job ...	Arbeitsbewertung *(f)*
evaluation: performance ...	Leistungsbeurteilung *(f)*
ex gratia **payment**	freiwillige Zuwendung *(f)*
	Gratifikation *(f)*
exception: management by ...	Management *(n)* by Exception *(f)* (MbE)
excess capacity	Überkapazität *(f)*

Exchange Rate Mechanism (ERM)	Wechselkursgefüge *(n)*
	Wechselkursmechanismus *(m)* im Europäischen Währungssystem *(n)*
exchange rate: forward	Devisenterminkurs *(m)*
execution: policy ...	Durchführung *(f)* der Unternehmenspolitik *(f)*
executive	Führungskraft *(f)*
	Manager *(m)*
executive advancement	Aufstieg *(m)* der Führungskräfte *(fpl)*
	Beförderung *(f)* der Führungskräfte *(fpl)*
executive board	Vorstand *(m)*
executive compensation	Vergütung *(f)* der Führungskräfte *(fpl)*
executive competence	Führungsfähigkeiten *(fpl)*
executive development	Management-Entwicklung *(f)*
executive director	Board-Mitglied *(n)*
	Vorstandsmitglied *(n)*
executive manpower strategy	Führungskräftestrategie *(f)*
executive promotion	Beförderung *(f)* von Führungskräften *(fpl)*
executive remuneration	Vergütung *(f)* der Führungskräfte *(fpl)*
executive search	Suche *(f)* nach Führungskräften *(fpl)*
executive training	Ausbildung *(f)* von Führungskräften *(fpl)*
executive: chief ...	Generaldirektor *(m)*
	Vorstandsvorsitzender *(m)*
executive: line ...	Linienmanager *(m)*
expansion strategy	Expansionsstrategie *(f)*
	Wachstumsstrategie *(f)*
expansion: sales ... effort	Bemühungen *(fpl)* um Verkaufssteigerungen *(fpl)*
expectations: job ...	mit einer Stelle *(f)* verbundene Erwartungen *(fpl)*
expectations: sales ...	Absatzerwartungen *(fpl)*
	Verkaufserwartungen *(fpl)*
expected date	Stichtag *(m)*
	Termin *(m)*
expenditure: capital ... (capex)	Investitionsaufwand *(m)*
	Investitionsausgaben *(fpl)*
expenditure: current ...	laufende Betriebsausgaben *(fpl)*
	laufende Betriebskosten *(pl)*
expense account	Spesenkonto *(n)*
expenses: administrative ...	Verwaltungskosten *(pl)*

expenses: direct ...	direkte Ausgaben (fpl)
expenses: indirect ...	indirekte Ausgaben (fpl)
expenses: operating ...	Betriebskosten (pl)
expenses: petty ...	kleine Spesen (pl)
	kleine Unkosten (pl)
expenses: recovery of ...	Spesenerstattung (f)
expenses: running ...	laufende Ausgaben (fpl)
expert system	Expertensystem (n)
expert: computer ...	Computerspezialist (m)
	EDV-Sachverständiger (m)
exploration: market ...	Markterkundung (f)
exponential smoothing	exponentielle Glättung (f)
exponential trend	exponentieller Trend (m)
extension services	Fortbildungsangebote (npl)
external relations	Außenbeziehungen (fpl)
externalities	Äußerlichkeiten (fpl)
externalize (to)	externalisieren

F

facility: borrowing ...	Kreditfazilität (f)
facsimile	Faksimile (n)
	Faksimiledruck (m)
factor	Faktor (m)
factor: cost ...	Kostenfaktor (m)
factor: load ...	Auslastungsfaktor (m)
factor: profit-... analysis	Analyse (f) der Gewinnfaktoren (mpl)
	Gewinnfaktoranalyse (f)
factoring	Factoring (n)
factors of production	Produktionsfaktoren (mpl)
factory overheads	Fabrikgemeinkosten (pl)
	Fertigungsgemeinkosten (pl)
failure (of firm)	Unternehmenszusammenbruch (m)
fair competition	fairer Wettbewerb (m)
fair return	angemessener Gewinn (m)
	angemessene Rendite (f)
family tree	Stammbaum (m)
fast-moving consumer goods	Renner (mpl)
(FMG)	Schnelldreher (mpl)

fast-track	*Berufsweg (m) eines Highflyers (m)*
fax (to)	faxen
fax	Fax *(n)*
fax machine	Faxgerät *(n)*
	Fernkopierer *(m)*
	Telefax-Gerät *(n)*
feasibility study	Durchführbarkeitsstudie *(f)*
	Machbarkeitsstudie *(f)*
feasible	durchführbar
	machbar
	realisierbar
featherbedding	Einstellung *(f)* nicht benötigter Arbeitskräfte *(fpl)*
feedback	Feedback *(n)*
	Rückkopplung *(f)*
fiddle (to)	frisieren
field research	Feldforschung *(f)*
	Primärforschung *(f)*
field testing	Feld-Tests *(mpl)*
	Überprüfung *(f)* im Feld *(n)*
figure: ballpark ...	ungefährer Betrag *(m)*
finance (to)	finanzieren
financial administration	Finanzverwaltung *(f)*
financial analysis	Finanzanalyse *(f)*
financial appraisal	Bewertung *(f)* der Finanzmittel *(npl)*
	Finanzbewertung *(f)*
financial control	Finanz-Controlling *(n)*
	Finanzkontrolle *(f)*
financial director	Finanzchef *(m)*
	Finanzvorstand *(m)*
financial futures	Financial Futures *(pl)*
	Finanzfutures *(pl)*
	Finanzterminkontrakte *(mpl)*
financial incentive	finanzieller Anreiz *(m)*
financial involvement	finanzielle Beteiligung *(f)*
financial management	Finanzmanagement *(n)*
financial market	Markt *(m)* für Investitionspapiere *(npl)*
financial planning	Finanzplanung *(f)*

financial position	Finanzlage *(f)*
	Finanzstatus *(m)*
financial ratio	finanzielle Kennzahl *(f)*
	Finanzierungskennzahl *(f)*
financial review	Finanzüberprüfung *(f)*
	Überprüfung *(f)* der Finanzlage *(f)*
financial standard	Finanznorm *(f)*
financial statement	Bilanz *(f)*
financial strategy	Finanzstrategie *(f)*
financial year	Geschäftsjahr *(n)*
	Rechnungsjahr *(n)*
financing	Finanzierung *(f)*
financing: debt ...	Finanzierung *(f)* durch die Emission *(f)* von Schuldtiteln *(mpl)*
	Finanzierung *(f)* von Verpflichtungen *(fpl)*
financing: deficit ...	Defizitfinanzierung *(f)*
financing: self-...	Eigenfinanzierung *(f)*
	Selbstfinanzierung *(f)*
fire (to)	entlassen
	feuern
firing: hiring and ...	Hire-and-fire-Mentalität *(f)*
	Hire-and-fire-Praxis *(f)*
first-line manager	Manager *(m)* der unteren Leitung *(f)*
fiscal drag	Steuerbremse *(f)*
fiscal policy	Fiskalpolitik *(f)*
fiscal year	Geschäftsjahr *(n)*
	Rechnungsjahr *(n)*
fixed assets	Anlagevermögen *(n)*
fixed costs	Festkosten *(pl)*
	Fixkosten *(pl)*
fixed expenses	Festkosten *(pl)*
	Fixkosten *(pl)*
flexible budget	elastisches Budget *(n)*
flexible firm	flexible Firma *(f)*
flexible working hours	flexible Arbeitszeiten *(fpl)*
	gleitende Arbeitszeit *(f)*
flexitime	Gleitzeit *(f)*
floppy disk (floppy)	Diskette *(f)*
	Floppy-Disk *(f)*

flotation	Unternehmensgründung *(f)*
flow chart	Ablaufdiagramm *(n)*
	Flußdiagramm *(n)*
flow chart: data	Datenablaufplan *(m)*
	Datenflußplan *(m)*
flow diagram	Flußdiagramm *(n)*
flow line	Produktionsfluß *(m)*
flow process chart	Arbeitsablaufbogen *(m)*
flow production	Fließfertigung *(f)*
flow: cash ...	Cash-flow *(m)*
flow: continous-... production	Massenproduktion *(f)*
	Fließfertigung *(f)*
flow: discounted cash ... (DCF)	diskontierter Cash-flow *(m)*
flow: funds ...	Kapitalströme *(mpl)*
flow: incremental cash ...	Differential *(n)* des Cash-flow *(m)*
	Zuwachs *(m)* des Cash-flow *(m)*
flow: information ...	Informationsfluß *(m)*
FMG (fast-moving consumer goods)	Renner *(mpl)*
	Schnelldreher *(mpl)*
focus (to)	sich konzentrieren auf
focus	Schwerpunkt *(m)*
follow up (to)	nachgehen
	weiterverfolgen
follow-up	Nachfassen *(n)*
	Weiterverfolgen *(n)*
force: sales ...	Außendienstmitarbeiter *(mpl)*
	Verkaufsaußendienst *(m)*
force: task ...	Projektgruppe *(f)*
forces: market ...	Marktkräfte *(fpl)*
forecast	Prognose *(f)*
forecast: budget ...	Haushaltsvoranschlag *(m)*
forecast: market ...	Marktprognose *(f)*
forecast: sales ...	Absatzprognose *(f)*
	Verkaufsprognose *(f)*
forecasting	Prognose *(f)*
	Prognostizierung *(f)*
	Voraussage *(f)*
forecasting: budget ...	Budgetprognose *(f)*

forecasting: business ...	Geschäftsprognose *(f)*
	Konjunkturvoraussage *(f)*
forecasting: cash ...	Kassenprognose *(f)*
	Liquiditätsprognose *(f)*
	Liquiditätsvorschau *(f)*
forecasting: demand ...	Nachfrageprognose *(f)*
	Nachfrageprognostizierung *(f)*
forecasting: environmental ...	Wirtschaftsprognose *(f)*
forecasting: manpower ...	Personalprognose *(f)*
forecasting: staff ...	Personalprognose *(f)*
forecasting: technological ...	Prognose *(f)* der technologischen Entwicklung *(f)*
foreman	Meister *(m)*
	Vorarbeiter *(m)*
formation: capital ...	Kapitalbildung *(f)*
formulation: policy ...	Formulierung *(f)* der Unternehmenspolitik *(f)*
formulation: strategy ...	Formulierung *(f)* der Unternehmensstrategie *(f)*
forward exchange rate	Devisenterminkurs *(m)*
forward market	Terminmarkt *(m)*
forward planning	Zukunftsplanung *(f)*
forward rate	Devisenterminkurs *(m)*
forward swap	Termin-Swap *(m)*
forwarding	Spedition *(f)*
	Versand *(m)*
forwarding agent	Spediteur *(m)*
fractionalize (to)	fraktionieren
	in Bruchteile *(mpl)* zerlegen
franchise (to)	franchisieren
	in Franchise *(f)* vergeben
franchise	Franchise *(f)*
	Konzession *(f)*
	Konzessionsbetrieb *(m)*
franchising	Franchising *(n)*
freelance (to go)	freiberuflich tätig werden
freeze (to)	einfrieren
	sperren
freeze: wage ...	Lohnstopp *(m)*
frequency distribution	Häufigkeitsverteilung *(f)*

friendly: user-...	benutzerfreundlich
fringe benefits	Sozialleistungen *(fpl)*
	Vergütung *(f)* neben Gehalt *(n)* oder Lohn *(m)*
fringe market	Nebenmarkt *(m)*
	Randmarkt *(m)*
front-line employees	Personal *(n)* im Außendienst *(m)*
full capacity	volle Kapazitätsnützung *(f)*
full-cost method	Vollkostenprinzip *(n)*
full-time employment	Ganztagsbeschäftigung *(f)*
full-timer	ganztägig Beschäftigter *(m)*
function	Funktion *(f)*
function key	Funktionstaste *(f)*
function: managerial ...	Führungsfunktion *(f)*
functional	funktional
	funktionell
functional analysis	funktionale Analyse *(f)*
functional approach	funktionale Methode *(f)*
functional costing	funktionale Kostenrechnung *(f)*
functional layout	funktionale Aufteilung *(f)*
functional management	funktionales Management *(n)*
functional organization	funktionale Organisation *(f)*
functional relations	funktionale Beziehungen *(fpl)*
functional responsibility	funktionale Verantwortlichkeit *(f)*
fund: sinking ...	Amortisationsfonds *(m)*
	Tilgungsfonds *(m)*
fund: slush ...	Schmiergeldfonds *(m)*
funding	Finanzierung *(f)*
funds flow	Kapitalströme *(mpl)*
funds: source and disposition of ...	Mittelherkunft *(f)* und -einsatz *(m)*
futures	Termingeschäfte *(npl)*
	Terminkontrakte *(mpl)*
	Terminwaren *(fpl)*
futures market	Terminkontraktmarkt *(m)*
futures: financial ...	Financial Futures *(pl)*
	Finanzfutures *(pl)*
	Finanzterminkontrakte *(mpl)*

G

gain: capital ...	Kapitalertrag *(m)*
	Kapitalgewinn *(m)*
game theory	Spieltheorie *(f)*
game: business ...	Planspiel *(n)*
	Unternehmensspiel *(n)*
game: management ...	Führungsspiel *(n)*
	Planspiel *(n)*
game: zero-sum ...	*Spiel (n), bei dem sich Gewinne (mpl) und Verluste (mpl) ausgleichen*
gap	Abweichung *(f)*
	Marktlücke *(f)*
gap study	Abweichungsanalyse *(f)*
gateway	Gateway *(n)*
	Netzkoppler *(m)*
	Überleiteinrichtung *(f)*
gathering: data ...	Datensammlung *(f)*
GDP (gross domestic product)	BIP (Bruttoinlandsprodukt *(n)*)
gearing	Kapitalausstattung *(f)*
	Verhältnis *(n)* zwischen Fremd- und Eigenkapital *(n)*
gearing ratio	Verhältnis *(n)* zwischen Fremd- und Eigenkapital *(n)*
general management	allgemeines Management *(n)*
general manager	Generaldirektor *(m)*
generate ideas (to)	Ideen *(fpl)* erzeugen
generation: product ...	Produkterzeugung *(f)*
generic	Gattungs-
	generisch
gentleman's agreement	Gentleman's Agreement *(n)*
	Gentlemen's Agreement *(n)*
gilt	erstklassige Wertpapiere *(npl)*
gilt-edged security	erstklassige Wertpapiere *(npl)*
gilt-edged stock	erstklassige Wertpapiere *(npl)*
global image	Global Image *(n)*
global marketing	Globalmarketing *(n)*
globalization	Globalisierung *(f)*

globalize (to)	globalisieren
GM (gross margin)	Bruttogewinnspanne *(f)*
GNP (gross national product)	BSP (Bruttosozialprodukt *(n)*)
go public (to)	an der Börse *(f)* zugelassen werden
go-getter: be a ... (to)	dynamisch sein
	initiativfreudig sein
go-getting	dynamisch
	initiativfreudig
go-slow	Bummelstreik *(m)*
goal-seeking	Zielfindung *(f)*
goal-setting	Zielsetzung *(f)*
goal: company ...	Unternehmensziel *(n)*
goal: profit ...	Gewinnziel *(n)*
goal: sales ...	Absatzziel *(n)*
goals: hierarchy of ...	Zielhierarchie *(f)*
going rate	Marktkurs *(m)*
	Marktpreis *(m)*
	üblicher Satz *(m)*
golden handcuffs	*Anreiz (m) für unentbehrliche Spitzenmanager (mpl)*
golden handshake	*Abfindungszahlung (f) an einen vorzeitig zum Ausscheiden (n) aus seinem Vertrag (m) gezwungenen Spitzenmanager (m)*
	Golden Handshake *(m)*
golden hello	*Einstandszahlung (f) an einen abgeworbenen Spitzenmanager (m)*
golden parachute	*Garantie (f) einer beträchtlichen Abfindungszahlung (f) im Falle (m) der Entlassung (f)*
golden share	*Kapitalanteil (m) mit besonderen Vorrechten (npl)*
goods: brown ...	*holzverkleidete elektrische Gebrauchsgüter (npl)*
goods: capital ...	Investitionsgüter *(npl)*
	Kapitalgüter *(npl)*
goods: consumer ...	Konsumgüter *(npl)*
	Verbrauchsgüter *(npl)*
goods: convenience ...	kurzlebige Konsumgüter *(npl)*
	Verbrauchsgüter *(npl)*

goods: fast-moving consumer ... (FMG)	Renner *(mpl)*
	Schnelldreher *(mpl)*
goods: impulse ...	Impulsgüter *(npl)*
	Impulswaren *(fpl)*
goods: industrial ...	Industriegüter *(npl)*
goods: investment ...	Investitionsgüter *(npl)*
	Kapitalgüter *(npl)*
goods: non-durable ...	kurzlebige Konsumgüter *(npl)*
	Verbrauchsgüter *(npl)*
goods: white ...	weiße Gebrauchsgüter *(npl)*
goodwill	Firmenwert *(m)*
	Goodwill *(m)*
	Wohlwollen *(n)*
grade: salary ...	Gehaltsstufe *(f)*
grapevine	vom Hörensagen *(n)*
graphics	Grafik *(f)*
green issues	Umweltfragen *(fpl)*
grey market	grauer Markt *(m)*
grid structure	Gitterstruktur *(f)*
grid: managerial ...	Verhaltensgitter *(n)*, aus dem Führungsstile *(mpl)* abgeleitet werden
grievance	Beschwerde *(f)*
grievance procedure	Beschwerdeverfahren *(n)*
	Schlichtungsverfahren *(n)*
gross domestic product (GDP)	Bruttoinlandsprodukt *(n)* (BIP)
gross margin (GM)	Bruttogewinnspanne *(f)*
gross national product (GNP)	Bruttosozialprodukt *(n)* (BSP)
gross profit	Bruttogewinn *(m)*
group accounts	Konzernabschluß *(m)*
group bonus	Gruppenbonus *(m)*
group dynamics	Gruppendynamik *(f)*
group incentive	Gruppenakkord *(m)*
	Gruppenanreiz *(m)*
group training	Gruppenausbildung *(f)*
	Gruppentraining *(n)*
group: product ...	Produktgruppe *(f)*
growth area	Wachstumsbereich *(m)*
	Wachstumsgebiet *(n)*
growth index	Wachstumsindex *(m)*

growth industry	Wachstumsindustrie *(f)*
growth potential	Wachstumspotential *(n)*
growth strategy	Wachstumsstrategie *(f)*
growth: corporate ...	Unternehmenswachstum *(n)*
growth: organic ...	organisches Wachstum *(n)*
growth: personal ...	persönliche Weiterentwicklung *(f)*
guesstimate	grobe Schätzung *(f)*
guidance: vocational ...	Berufsberatung *(f)*
guideline	Richtlinie *(f)*
	Richtschnur *(f)*

H

hacker	Hacker *(m)*
hacking	Hacker-Delikt *(n)*
	Hacker-Tätigkeit *(f)*
halo effect	Ausstrahlungseffekt *(m)*
handcuffs: golden ...	*Anreiz (m) für unentbehrliche Spitzenmanager (mpl)*
handling: information ...	Informationsbearbeitung *(f)*
handling: materials ...	Materialfluß *(m)*
	Materialtransport *(m)*
hands-on	manuell
	von Hand *(f)*
hands-on training	praktische Ausbildung *(f)*
handshake: golden ...	*Abfindungszahlung (f) an einen vorzeitig zum Ausscheiden (n) aus seinem Vertrag (m) gezwungenen Spitzenmanager (m)*
	Golden Handshake *(m)*
harassment: sexual ...	sexuelle Belästigung *(f)*
hard copy	Hardcopy *(f)*
	Hardkopie *(f)*
hard disk	Festplatte *(f)*
	Harddisk *(f)*
hard ecu	harter Ecu *(m)*
hard landing	*plötzlicher Abschwung (m) nach einer Periode (f) des Wirtschaftswachstums (n)*

hard sell	aggressive Verkaufstaktik *(f)*
	aggressive Verkaufsmethoden *(fpl)*
	Hardsell *(m)*
hardware	Hardware *(f)*
harmonization	Harmonisierung *(f)*
harmonize (to)	harmonisieren
hazard: occupational ...	Berufsrisiko *(n)*
hazchem (hazardous chemicals)	gefährliche Chemikalien *(fpl)*
	Gefahrstoffe *(mpl)*
head office	Hauptbüro *(n)*
	Zentrale *(f)*
head-hunt (to)	nach Führungskräften *(fpl)* suchen
	Nachwuchskräfte *(fpl)* jagen
head-hunter	Headhunter *(m)*
	Kopfjäger *(m)*
hedge (to)	absichern
hedging	Hedgegeschäfte *(npl)*
	Hedging *(n)*
	Sicherungsgeschäfte *(npl)*
hello: golden ...	*Einstandszahlung (f) an einen abgeworbenen*
	Spitzenmanager (m)
heuristics	Heuristik *(f)*
hidden agenda	unerwähnte Ziele *(npl)*
hidden assets	stille Reserven *(fpl)*
	versteckte Vermögenswerte *(mpl)*
hierarchy of goals	Zielhierarchie *(f)*
high-flier	High Potential *(n)*
	Highflyer *(m)*
	Hochtalent *(n)*
high-tech	High-Tech-
	Hochtechnologie *(f)*
hire (to)	einstellen
hire: contract ...	Full-Service-Leasing *(n)*
hire: plant ...	Industrieanlagen-Leasing *(n)*
hiring and firing	Hire-and-fire-Mentalität *(f)*
	Hire-and-fire-Praxis *(f)*
histogram	Histogramm *(n)*
	Säulendiagramm *(n)*
hive off (to)	Teile *(mpl)* absondern

hold margins (to)	Gewinnspannen *(fpl)* halten
holding company	Dachgesellschaft *(f)*
	Holdinggesellschaft *(f)*
holidays: staggered ...	gestaffelter Urlaub *(m)*
home country	Ursprungsland *(n)*
horizontal integration	horizontale Integration *(f)*
host country	Gastland *(n)*
hot money	Fluchtgelder *(npl)*
	heißes Geld *(n)*
house style	Stil *(m)* des Hauses *(n)*
HRD (human resource development)	Personalentwicklung *(f)*
HRM (human resource management)	Personalmanagement *(n)*
HRP (human resource planning)	Personalplanung *(f)*
human engineering	Arbeitsplatzgestaltung *(f)*
	Ergonomie *(f)*
human relations	innerbetriebliche Mitarbeiterbeziehungen *(fpl)*
	zwischenmenschliche Beziehungen *(fpl)*
human resource development (HRD)	Personalentwicklung *(f)*
human resource management (HRM)	Personalmanagement *(n)*
human resource planning (HRP)	Personalplanung *(f)*
human resources	Personal *(n)*
hustle (to)	sich ins Zeug *(n)* legen
hygiene factors	*mit Arbeitsbedingungen (fpl) verbundene Motivationsfaktoren (mpl)*
hype	reißerische Werbung *(f)*

I

idle capacity	ungenutzte Kapazität *(f)*
image: brand ...	Markenbild *(n)*
	Markenimage *(n)*
	Markenprofil *(n)*
image: corporate ...	Corporate Image *(n)*
	Unternehmensimage *(n)*

image: global ...	Global Image *(n)*
image: product ...	Produktimage *(n)*
imaging	Abbildung *(f)*
imbalance: trade ...	Handelsungleichgewicht *(n)*
impact	Auswirkung *(f)*
impact: profit ...	Gewinnauswirkung *(f)*
implement (to)	ausführen
	durchführen
implementation: strategy ...	Durchführung *(f)* der Strategie *(f)*
implication: profit ...	Gewinnauswirkung *(f)*
import: parallel ...	Parallelimport *(m)*
	Paralleleinfuhr *(f)*
improvement: job ...	Stellenanhebung *(f)*
improvement: product ...	Produktverbesserung *(f)*
improvement: profit ...	Gewinnverbesserung *(f)*
impulse buying	Spontankaufen *(n)*
	Impulskaufen *(n)*
impulse goods	Impulsgüter *(npl)*
	Impulswaren *(fpl)*
impulse sale	Verkauf *(m)* von Impulswaren *(fpl)*
in-company	intern
	unternehmensintern
in-depth interview	Tiefeninterview *(n)*
in-house	Inhouse-
	intern
in-plant training	innerbetriebliche Schulung *(f)*
incentive	Anreiz *(m)*
incentive scheme	leistungsbezogenes Lohnsystem *(n)*
incentive wage	Leistungslohn *(m)*
incentive: financial ...	finanzieller Anreiz *(m)*
incentive: group ...	Gruppenakkord *(m)*
	Gruppenanreiz *(m)*
incentive: tax ...	steuerlicher Anreiz *(m)*
income tax	Einkommensteuer *(f)*
income tax: negative	negative Einkommensteuer *(f)*
income: disposable ...	verfügbares Einkommen *(n)*
income: real ...	Realeinkommen *(n)*
	Reallohn *(m)*
increase: price ...	Preiserhöhung *(f)*

incremental	Inkremental- inkrementell
incremental analysis	Inkrementalanalyse *(f)* inkrementelle Analyse *(f)*
incremental cash flow	Differential *(n)* des Cash-flow *(m)* Zuwachs *(m)* des Cash-flow *(m)*
index number	Indexzahl *(f)* Indexziffer *(f)* Kennziffer *(f)*
index: consumer price ...	Verbraucherpreisindex *(m)*
index: growth ...	Wachstumsindex *(m)*
index: retail price ... (RPI)	Einzelhandelspreisindex *(m)*
indicator: performance ...	Leistungsbarometer *(n)* Leistungskennzahl *(f)*
indirect costs	indirekte Kosten *(pl)*
indirect expenses	indirekte Ausgaben *(fpl)*
indirect labour	Gemeinkostenlöhne *(mpl)*
induction	Einführung *(f)* neuer Mitarbeiter *(mpl)* in das Unternehmen *(n)*
industrial action	Arbeitskampfmaßnahmen *(fpl)* Streikmaßnahmen *(fpl)*
industrial democracy	Mitbestimmung *(f)*
industrial dispute	Arbeitskonflikt *(m)* Tarifkonflikt *(m)*
industrial dynamics	Betriebsdynamik *(f)* Industriedynamik *(f)*
industrial engineering	Betriebstechnik *(f)* ingenieur- und arbeitswissenschaftliche Organisationsgestaltung *(f)*
industrial espionage	Industriespionage *(f)*
industrial goods	Industriegüter *(npl)*
industrial injury	Arbeitsunfall *(m)* Betriebsunfall *(m)*
industrial psychology	Betriebspsychologie *(f)*
industrial relations	Arbeitgeber-Arbeitnehmer-Beziehungen *(fpl)*
industrial safety	Arbeitssicherheit *(f)* Betriebssicherheit *(f)*
industrial security	Betriebssicherheit *(f)*
industrial waste	Industriemüll *(m)*

industry: growth ...	Wachstumsindustrie *(f)*
industry: sunrise ...	junge Wachstumindustrie *(f)*
industry: sunset ...	absterbender Industriezweig *(m)*
industry: training within ... (TWI)	innerbetriebliche Ausbildung *(f)*
inflation: cost-push ...	Kosteninflation *(f)*
inflation: demand-pull ...	nachfrageinduzierte Inflation *(f)*
	Nachfrageinflation *(f)*
inflationary pressure	inflationärer Druck *(m)*
	Inflationsdruck *(m)*
informal organization	informelle Organisation *(f)*
informatics	Informatik *(f)*
information flow	Informationsfluß *(m)*
information handling	Informationsbearbeitung *(f)*
information network	Informationsnetz *(n)*
information processing	Informationsverarbeitung *(f)*
information retrieval	Informationsrückgewinnung *(f)*
	Informationswiedergewinnung *(f)*
information system	Informationssystem *(n)*
information technology	Informationstechnologie *(f)*
information theory	Informationstheorie *(f)*
information: computerized ... system (COINS)	computerisiertes Informationssystem *(n)*
information: control ...	Kontrollinformationen *(fpl)*
information: management ...	Management-Informationen *(fpl)*
information: management ... system (MIS)	Management-Informationssystem *(n)*
infrastructure	Infrastruktur *(f)*
injury: industrial ...	Arbeitsunfall *(m)*
	Betriebsunfall *(m)*
innovate (to)	innovieren
	neu einführen
innovative	innovativ
	innovatorisch
input	Input *(m)*
input (data)	Input *(m)*
input-output analysis	Input-Output-Analyse *(f)*
input-output table	Input-Output-Tabelle *(f)*
input: computer ...	Computer-Eingabe *(f)*

insider dealing	Insidergeschäfte *(npl)*
insider trading	Insiderhandel *(m)*
instruction: programmed ...	Programmbefehl *(m)*
	Programminstruktion *(f)*
intangible assets	immaterielle Anlagewerte *(mpl)*
integrate (to)	eingliedern
	integrieren
integrated management system	integriertes Management-System *(n)*
integrated project management (IPM)	integriertes Projekt-Management *(n)*
integrated: computer-... manufacturing (CIM)	computerintegrierte Fertigung *(f)*
integration	Integration *(f)*
intensive production	intensive Produktion *(f)*
intensive: labour-...	arbeitsintensiv
interactive	interaktiv
interest: controlling ...	Aktienmehrheit *(f)*
	Mehrheitsanteil *(m)*
	Mehrheitsbeteiligung *(f)*
interest: job ...	Interesse *(n)* an der Arbeit *(f)*
	Interesse *(n)* an der Stelle *(f)*
interest: majority ...	Mehrheitsbeteiligung *(f)*
interest: minority ...	Minderheitsbeteiligung *(f)*
interest: vested ...	finanzielle Beteiligung *(f)*
	persönliches Interesse *(n)*
interface (to)	anschließen
	koppeln
interface	Interface *(n)*
	Nahtstelle *(f)*
	Schnittstelle *(f)*
inter-firm comparison	Betriebsvergleich *(m)*
interlocking directorate	Mandatsverflechtung *(f)*
internal audit	betriebsinterne Revision *(f)*
	Innenrevision *(f)*
internal rate of return (IRR)	interner Zinsfuß *(m)*
internalize (to)	internalisieren
internationalize (to)	internationalisieren
interview: in-depth ...	Tiefeninterview *(n)*
intuitive management	intuitive Unternehmensführung *(f)*

inventory control	Bestandskontrolle *(f)*
	Lagerkontrolle *(f)*
inventory management	Lagerhaltung *(f)*
inventory turnover	Lagerumschlag *(m)*
inventory: perpetual ...	permanente Inventur *(f)*
investment analysis	Investitionsanalyse *(f)*
investment appraisal	Investitionsbewertung *(f)*
investment bank	Effekten- und Emissionsbank *(f)*
	Emissionsbank *(f)*
	Investmentbank *(f)*
investment budget	Investitionsbudget *(n)*
investment criteria	Investitionskriterien *(npl)*
investment goods	Investitionsgüter *(npl)*
	Kapitalgüter *(npl)*
investment management	Verwaltung *(f)* von
	Kapitalanlagen *(fpl)*
investment mix	Wertpapierportfolio *(n)*
investment policy	Investitionspolitik *(f)*
investment programme	Investitionsprogramm *(n)*
investment: offshore ...	Offshore-Investmentfonds *(m)*
investment: return on ... (ROI)	Anlagenrentabilität *(f)*
	Rentabilität *(f)* des Kapitaleinsatzes *(m)*
invisibles	unsichtbare Ein- und Ausfuhren *(fpl)*
involvement: financial ...	finanzielle Beteiligung *(f)*
IPM (integrated project management)	integriertes Projekt-Management *(n)*
IRR (internal rate of return)	interner Zinsfuß *(m)*
issue	Ausgabe *(f)*
	Ausstellung *(f)*
	Emission *(f)*
issue: rights ...	Bezugsrechtsemission *(f)*
issued capital	ausgegebenes Kapital *(n)*
IT (information technology)	Informationstechnologie *(f)*
iterative	iterativ
iterative process	Iteration *(f)*
	iterativer Prozeß *(m)*
	iteratives Verfahren *(n)*

J

JIT (just in time)	Jit- (Just-in-time-)
job analysis	Stellenanalyse *(f)*
job assignment	Aufgabenzuteilung *(f)*
job breakdown	berufliche Aufschlüsselung *(f)*
	Stellenaufschlüsselung *(f)*
job challenge	Stellenanforderung *(f)*
job characteristics	Arbeitscharakeristika *(npl)*
	Berufskennzeichen *(npl)*
	Berufsmerkmale *(npl)*
job classification	Stellenklassifizierung *(f)*
job competence	Stellenqualifikationen *(fpl)*
job content	Arbeitsinhalt *(m)*
	Stelleninhalt *(m)*
job description	Stellenbeschreibung *(f)*
job design	Stellenentwurf *(m)*
job enlargement	Erweiterung *(f)* der Arbeitsaufgaben *(fpl)*
job enrichment	Arbeitsbereicherung *(f)*
job evaluation	Arbeitsbewertung *(f)*
job expectations	mit einer Stelle *(f)* verbundene Erwartungen *(fpl)*
job improvement	Stellenanhebung *(f)*
job interest	Interesse *(n)* an der Arbeit *(f)*
	Interesse *(n)* an der Stelle *(f)*
job performance	Arbeitsergebnis *(n)*
	Arbeitsleistung *(f)*
job profile	Arbeitsplatzbeschreibung *(f)*
	Stellenbeschreibung *(f)*
job requirements	Stellenanforderungen *(fpl)*
job rotation	Jobrotation *(f)*
	systematischer Stellenwechsel *(m)*
job satisfaction	Arbeitszufriedenheit *(f)*
	Zufriedenheit *(f)* am Arbeitsplatz *(m)*
job security	Arbeitsplatzsicherheit *(f)*
job security agreement	Arbeitsplatzsicherheitsvereinbarung *(f)*
job-sharing	Job-Sharing *(n)*
job simplification	Stellenvereinfachung *(f)*

job specification	Stellenanforderungsprofil *(n)*
	Stellenbeschreibung *(f)*
job title	Stellenbezeichnung *(f)*
	Berufsbezeichnung *(f)*
job: off-the-… training	außerbetriebliche Ausbildung *(f)*
job: on-the-… training	innerbetriebliche Ausbildung *(f)*
jobbing	Effektenhandel *(m)*
	Börsenspekulation *(f)*
joint consultation	gemeinsame Beratung *(f)*
joint negotiation	gemeinsame Verhandlung *(f)*
joint representation	gemeinsame Vertretung *(f)*
joint venture	Gemeinschaftsunternehmen *(n)*
	Joint Venture *(n)*
joint-venture company	an einem Joint Venture *(n)* beteiligte Gesellschaft *(f)*
	Gemeinschaftsfirma *(f)*
junk bond	Junk Bond *(m)*
jurisdiction	Gerichtsbarkeit *(f)*
	Zuständigkeit *(f)*
just in time (JIT)	Just-in-time- (Jit-)
	Just-in-time-System *(n)* (Jit-)

K

key buying factor	wichtigster Kauffaktor *(m)*
key success factor	wichtigster Erfolgsfaktor *(m)*
know-how	Knowhow *(n)*

L

labour costs: unit … …	Lohnstückkosten *(pl)*
labour dispute	Arbeitskonflikt *(m)*
labour-intensive	arbeitsintensiv
labour mobility	Arbeitskräftemobilität *(f)*
	Arbeitsmobilität *(f)*
labour relations	Arbeitgeber-Arbeitnehmer-Beziehungen *(fpl)*
labour turnover	Personalfluktuation *(f)*

labour: direct ...	Fertigungslöhne *(mpl)*
	unmittelbar geleistete Arbeitszeit *(f)*
labour: indirect ...	Gemeinkostenlöhne *(mpl)*
labour: semi-skilled ...	angelernte Arbeiter *(mpl)*
labour: skilled ...	Facharbeiter *(mpl)*
	gelernte Arbeiter *(mpl)*
labour: unit ... costs	Lohnstückkosten *(pl)*
labour: unskilled ...	ungelernte Arbeiter *(mpl)*
lag	Verzögerung *(f)*
	Zeitabstand *(m)*
lag response	verspätete Reaktion *(f)*
lag: time ...	Zeitverzögerung *(f)*
LAN (local area network)	LAN *(n)* (Inhouse-Netz *(n)*)
landing: hard ...	*plötzlicher Abschwung (m) nach einer Periode (f) des Wirtschaftswachstums (n)*
landing: soft ...	*Aufschwungphase (f) nach einer Periode (f) restriktiver Wirtschaftspolitik (f)*
language: common ...	gemeinsame Sprache *(f)*
language: computer ...	Maschinensprache *(f)*
language: machine ...	Maschinensprache *(f)*
laptop computer	Laptop *(m)*
laser printer	Laserdrucker *(m)*
lateral thinking	laterales Denken *(n)*
latest date	äußerster Termin *(m)*
	letzter Tag *(m)*
launch: product ...	Produkteinführung *(f)*
launching	Einführung *(f)*
launder (to)	waschen
laundering	Geldwäsche *(f)*
lay off (to)	(vorübergehend) entlassen
lay-off	(vorübergehende) Entlassung *(f)*
layout: functional ...	funktionale Aufteilung *(f)*
layout: plant ... study	Untersuchung *(f)* der Betriebsanlagen *(fpl)*
layout: process equipment ...	Betriebsanlage *(f)* nach Werkstattprinzip *(n)*
LBO (leveraged buyout)	*von Fremdkapital (n) unterstützte Übernahme (f)*
lead time	Beschaffungszeit *(f)*
	Lieferzeit *(f)*
	Vorlaufzeit *(f)*

leader merchandising	Kundenwerbung *(f)* durch Sonderangebote *(npl)*
leader: loss-...	Lock(vogel)angebot *(n)*
	Lockartikel *(m)*
leader: market ...	Marktführer *(m)*
leader: price ...	Preisführer *(m)*
leader: team ...	Gruppenleiter *(m)*
	Teamchef *(m)*
leadership	Führung *(f)*
	Führungsqualitäten *(fpl)*
leading edge	Avantgarde *(f)*
leak: security ...	Sicherheitslücke *(f)*
leapfrog (to)	andere Lohnerhöhungen *(fpl)* mit den eigenen Lohnforderungen *(fpl)* übersteigen
learning curve	Lernkurve *(f)*
learning: computer-aided ... (CAL)	computerunterstütztes Lernen *(n)*
learning: distance ...	Fernstudium *(n)*
learning: programmed ...	programmierter Lernprozeß *(m)*
	programmiertes Lernen *(n)*
lease (to)	leasen
	mieten
	verleasen
	vermieten
lease or buy (to)	mieten oder kaufen
lease-lend	auf Pacht- und Leihbasis *(f)*
	Pacht- und Leihvertrag *(m)*
leasing	Leasing *(n)*
leasing: equipment ...	Investitionsgüter-Leasing *(n)*
least-cost	kostenminimal
	Minimalkosten-
level playing-field	faire (zwischenstaatliche) Handelspraktiken *(fpl)*
level: wage ...	Lohnhöhe *(f)*
	Lohnniveau *(n)*
leverage	Hebelwirkung *(f)*
	Verhältnis *(n)* von Eigen- zu Fremdkapital *(n)*
	Verschuldungskoeffizient *(m)*

leveraged bid	*von Fremdkapital (n) unterstütztes Übernahmeangebot (n)*
leveraged buyout (LBO)	*von Fremdkapital (n) unterstützte Übernahme (f)*
liabilities	Verbindlichkeiten *(fpl)*
liabilities: current ...	kurzfristige Verbindlichkeiten *(fpl)*
liability: asset ... management	Aktiva- und Passivamanagement *(n)*
liberalization	Liberalisierung *(f)*
licence	Erlaubnis *(f)*
	Genehmigung *(f)*
	Lizenz *(f)*
licence: under ...	in Lizenz *(f)*
licensing: cross- ...	Lizenzaustausch *(m)*
life cycle (*of a product*)	Lebenszyklus *(m) (eines Produkt(e)s (n))*
life: economic ...	wirtschaftliche Nutzungsdauer *(f)*
life: product ...	wirtschaftliche Lebensdauer *(f)* eines Produktes *(n)*
life: product ... expectancy	Lebenserwartung *(f)* eines Produktes *(n)*
life: shelf-...	Haltbarkeit *(f)*
lifestyle	Lebensstil *(m)*
	Lifestyle *(m)*
limitation: damage ...	Schadensbegrenzung *(f)*
line and staff	Linie *(f)* und Stab *(m)*
line and staff organization	Stablinienorganisation *(f)*
line assistant	Linienassistent *(m)*
line authority	Leitungsbefugnis *(f)*
	Leitungskompetenz *(f)*
line executive	Linienmanager *(m)*
line management	Linienmanagement *(n)*
line manager	Linienmanager *(m)*
line of command	Befehlsweg *(m)*
	Instanzenweg *(m)*
line organization	Linienorganisation *(f)*
line production	Fließbandproduktion *(f)*
line relations	instanzielle Rang- und Weisungsbeziehungen *(fpl)*
line responsibility	*instanzielle Zuständigkeit (f)*

line: assembly …	Montagebahn *(f)*
	Montageband *(n)*
line: down the …	auf nachgeordneten
	Führungsebenen *(fpl)*
line: flow …	Produktionsfluß *(m)*
line: on …	direktgekoppelt
	Online-
	prozeßgekoppelt
line: product …	Produktgruppe *(f)*
	Produktkategorie *(f)*
	Produktlinie *(f)*
line: production …	Fließband *(n)*
	Fertigungsstraße *(f)*
line: up the …	auf höheren Führungsebenen *(fpl)*
linear programming	lineare Programmierung *(f)*
	Linearplanung *(f)*
linear responsibility	lineare Verantwortung *(f)*
liquid assets	flüssige Mittel *(npl)*
	liquide Mittel *(npl)*
liquidate (to)	abwickeln
	auflösen
	liquidieren
liquidating: self-…	sich selbst abdeckend
liquidation	Liquidation *(f)*
	Liquidierung *(f)*
liquidity ratio	Liquiditätsgrad *(m)*
	Liquiditätskennziffer *(f)*
listing	Auflistung *(f)*
	Börsennotierung *(f)*
literate: computer …	Computer-Wissen *(n)* besitzend
	mit Computern *(mpl)* vertraut
load factor	Auslastungsfaktor *(m)*
load: work …	Arbeitsbelastung *(f)*
	Arbeitspensum *(n)*
loan capital	Anleihekapital *(n)*
loan stock	festverzinsliche Schuldtitel *(mpl)*
	Schuldverschreibungen *(fpl)*
loan: parallel …	Parallelanleihe *(f)*
	Parallelkredit *(m)*

local area network (LAN)	Inhouse-Netz *(n)* (LAN)
local content rules	Regeln *(fpl)* zur Bestimmung *(f)* vom Mindestanteil *(m)* einheimischer Komponenten *(fpl)*
localization	Lokalisierung *(f)*
location: plant ...	Unternehmensstandort *(m)*
lock-out	Aussperrung *(f)*
logistic process	logistisches Verfahren *(n)*
logistical	logistisch
logistics	Logistik *(f)*
logo	Logo *(n)*
logo: company ...	Firmenzeichen *(n)*
long-range planning	langfristige Planung *(f)*
long-term planning	langfristige Planung *(f)*
loop: closed ...	geschlossene Schleife *(f)*
	geschlossener Kreislauf *(m)*
loss-leader	Lock(vogel)angebot *(n)*
	Lockartikel *(m)*
loss-maker	verlustbringendes Produkt *(n)*
loss: capital ...	Kapitalverlust *(m)*
losses: bad-debt ...	*aus zweifelhaften Forderungen (fpl) herrührende Verluste (mpl)*
low-flier	*talentloser, nicht aufstrebender Mitarbeiter (m)*
low-tech	Low-Tech-
loyalty: brand ...	Markentreue *(f)*
lump sum	Pauschalbetrag *(m)*
	Pauschalsumme *(f)*

M

M & A (mergers and acquisitions)	Fusionen *(fpl)* und Übernahmen *(fpl)*
	Mergers und Acquisitions *(pl)*
machine language	Maschinensprache *(f)*
macro	Makroeinrichtung *(f)*
mailbox	Briefkasten *(m)*
	Mailbox *(f)*

mail merge	*Programm (n) zum Drucken (n) persönlich adressierter Serienbriefe (mpl)*
mail order	Mail-order *(f)*
	Postbestellung *(f)*
	Postversand *(m)*
mail: direct ...	Direktversand *(m)*
mail: electronic ... (e-mail)	Electronic Mail *(f)*
	Elektronische Post *(f)*
mailing	Mailing *(n)*
	Versand *(m)*
mainframe	Großcomputer *(m)*
	Großrechner *(m)*
	Mainframe-System *(n)*
maintenance: planned ...	geplante Instandhaltung *(f)*
	geplante Wartung *(f)*
maintenance: preventive ...	vorbeugende Instandhaltung *(f)*
maintenance: productive ...	Produktionswartung *(f)*
	Produktivwartung *(f)*
maintenance: resale price ... (RPM)	Preisbindung *(f)* der zweiten Hand *(f)*
maintenance: total plant ...	umfassende Betriebsinstandhaltung *(f)*
majority interest	Mehrheitsbeteiligung *(f)*
make-or-buy decision	Wahl *(f)* zwischen Eigenfertigung *(f)* und Kauf *(m)*
maker: market ...	Marktmacher *(m)*
malfunction	Fehlfunktion *(f)*
	Funktionsstörung *(f)*
manage (to)	führen
	leiten
	managen
managed costs	kontrollierte Kosten *(pl)*
managed: system-... company	nach Systemen *(npl)* geführtes Unternehmen *(n)*
management	Management *(n)*
	Unternehmensführung *(f)*
	Unternehmensleitung *(f)*
management accounting	Betriebsrechnungswesen *(n)*
	Kosten- und Leistungsrechnung *(f)*

management audit	Prüfung *(f)* der Ablaufsysteme *(npl)* einer Unternehmung *(f)*
	Prüfung *(f)* und Bewertung *(f)* der Manager-Leistung *(f)*
management buyout (MBO)	Management-Buyout *(m,n)* (MBO)
management by exception	Management *(n)* by Exception (MbE *(n)*)
management by objectives (MBO)	Führung *(f)* durch Zielvereinbarung *(f)*
	Management *(n)* by Objectives (MbO *(n)*)
management by walking around	*interventionistische Betriebsführung (f)*
management chart	Organogramm *(n)* der Unternehmensführung *(f)*
	Organogramm *(n)* der Unternehmensleitung *(f)*
management competence	Führungsfähigkeiten *(fpl)*
management consultancy	Management-Beratung *(f)*
	Unternehmensberatung *(f)*
management consultant	Unternehmensberater *(m)*
management contract	Anstellungsvertrag *(m)* eines Managers *(m)*
management development	Management-Entwicklung *(f)*
management game	Führungsspiel *(n)*
	Planspiel *(n)*
management information	Management-Informationen *(fpl)*
management information system (MIS)	Management-Informationssystem *(n)*
management potential	Führungspotential *(n)*
	Management-Potential *(n)*
management practices	Management-Prinzipien *(npl)*
	Verhaltensnormen *(fpl)* im Management *(n)*
management ratio	betriebswirtschaftliche Kennzahl *(f)*
management science	Management-Lehre *(f)*
management services	Management-Dienste *(mpl)*
management staff	Führungspersonal *(n)*
management style	Führungsstil *(m)*
management succession planning	Führungsnachfolgeplanung *(f)*
management system	Management-System *(n)*
management team	Führungsteam *(n)*
management technique	Führungstechnik *(f)*
	Managementtechnik *(f)*
management theory	Management-Theorie *(f)*

management training	Ausbildung *(f)* der Führungskräfte *(fpl)*
	Manager-Ausbildung *(f)*
management: asset ...	Anlagenwirtschaft *(f)*
management: asset liability ...	Aktiva- und Passivamanagement *(n)*
management: business ...	Betriebsführung *(f)*
	Betriebswirtschaft *(f)*
	Management *(n)*
	Unternehmensführung *(f)*
management: cash ...	Cash-Management *(n)*
	Kassenhaltung *(f)*
	Liquiditätssteuerung *(f)*
management: change ...	Innovationsmanagement *(n)*
(management of change)	Management *(n)* des geordneten Wandels *(m)*
management: computerized ...	computergestütztes Management *(n)*
management: credit ...	Kreditmanagement *(n)*
management: crisis ...	Krisenmanagement *(n)*
management: decentralized ...	dezentralisiertes Management *(n)*
management: departmental ...	Abteilungsleitung *(f)*
management: divisional ...	Spartenleitung *(f)*
management: dynamic ... model	dynamisches Führungsmodell *(n)*
	dynamisches Management-Modell *(n)*
management: effective ...	wirksame Unternehmensführung *(f)*
	wirksames Management *(n)*
management: financial ...	Finanzmanagement *(n)*
management: functional ...	funktionales Management *(n)*
management: general ...	allgemeines Management *(n)*
management: human resource ...	Personalmanagement *(n)*
(HRM)	
management: integrated ... system	integriertes Management-System *(n)*
management: integrated project ... (IPM)	integriertes Projekt-Management *(n)*
management: intuitive ...	intuitive Unternehmensführung *(f)*
management: investment ...	Verwaltung *(f)* von Kapitalanlagen *(fpl)*
management: line ...	Linienmanagement *(n)*
management: manpower ...	Personalführung *(f)*
management: market ...	Marktleitung *(f)*
management: matrix ...	Matrix-Organisation *(f)*

management: middle ...	Middle-Management (n)
	mittleres Management (n)
management: multiple ...	Unternehmensführung (f) unter Beteiligung (f) nachgeordneter Führungsebenen (fpl)
management: office ...	Büroleitung (f)
management: operating ...	Betriebsleitung (f)
management: operations ...	Betriebsleitung (f)
management: participative ...	kooperativer Führungsstil (m)
management: personnel ...	Personalleitung (f)
	Personalmanagement (n)
management: physical distribution ...	Warenverteilung (f)
management: portfolio ...	Portfolio-Management (n)
management: product ...	Produkt-Management (n)
management: production ...	Produktionsmanagement (n)
management: programmed ...	Führung (f) durch Vorgabe (f) von Programmen (n)
	programmiertes Management (n)
management: project ...	Projekt-Management (n)
management: quality ...	Qualitätsmanagement (n)
management: resource ...	Betriebsmittelverwaltung (f)
	Ressourcenmanagement (n)
management: safety ...	Sicherheitsmanagement (n)
management: sales ...	Verkaufsleitung (f)
	Verkaufsmanagement (n)
management: scientific ...	wissenschaftliche Unternehmensführung (f)
	wissenschaftliches Management (n)
management: staff ...	Personalleitung (f)
	Personalmanagement (n)
management: supervisory ...	Kontrollfunktionen (fpl) der Unternehmensleitung (f)
	Kontrollfunktionen (fpl) des Managements (n)
management: systems ...	System-Management (n)
	Systemverwaltung (f)
management: time ...	Zeitmanagement (n)
management: top ...	Spitzenmanagement (n)
	Top-Management (n)
management: top ... approach	Verfahrensweise (f) des Top-Managements (n)

management: total quality ... (TQM)	Total Quality Management *(n)* (TQM)
management: venture ...	risikobereite Unternehmensführung *(f)*
	risikobereite Unternehmensleitung *(f)*
manager	Führungskraft *(f)*
	Manager *(m)*
manager: advertising ...	Werbeleiter *(m)*
	Werbemanager *(m)*
manager: area ...	Gebietsleiter *(m)*
manager: assistant ...	stellvertretender Direktor *(m)*
manager: assistant to ...	Direktionsassistent *(m)*
manager: brand ...	Markenbetreuer *(m)*
	Markenmanager *(m)*
manager: departmental ...	Abteilungsleiter *(m)*
manager: deputy ...	stellvertretender Direktor *(m)*
manager: distribution ...	Vertriebsleiter *(m)*
manager: first-line ...	Manager *(m)* der unteren Leitung *(f)*
manager: general ...	Generaldirektor *(m)*
manager: line ...	Linienmanager *(m)*
manager: marketing ...	Marketing-Leiter *(m)*
manager: operations ...	Betriebsleiter *(m)*
manager: owner-...	Eigentümer-Unternehmer *(m)*
manager: personnel ...	Personalleiter *(m)*
manager: plant ...	Betriebsleiter *(m)*
	Werksleiter *(m)*
manager: procurement ...	Beschaffungsmanager *(m)*
	Einkaufsmanager *(m)*
manager: product ...	Produkt-Manager *(m)*
manager: production ...	Produktionsmanager *(m)*
manager: project ...	Projektmanager *(m)*
manager: purchasing ...	Einkaufsleiter *(m)*
manager: sales ...	Verkaufsleiter *(m)*
manager: works ...	Betriebsleiter *(m)*
	Werksleiter *(m)*
managerial	Führungs-
	Management-
	Manager-

managerial control	Führungskontrolle *(f)*
managerial effectiveness	wirksame Unternehmensführung *(f)*
	wirksame Unternehmensleitung *(f)*
	wirksames Management *(n)*
managerial function	Führungsfunktion *(f)*
managerial grid	Verhaltensgitter *(n)*, aus dem
	Führungsstile *(mpl)* abgeleitet
	werden
managerial structure	Führungsstruktur *(f)*
managerial style	Führungsstil *(m)*
managing director (MD)	Generaldirektor *(m)*
	Geschäftsführer *(m)*
managing director: deputy	stellvertretender
	Generaldirektor *(m)*
	stellvertretender Geschäftsführer *(m)*
manning	Beschäftigten-
	Personal-
manpower	Arbeitskräfte *(fpl)*
	Personal *(n)*
	Personal-
manpower audit	Personalbestandsanalyse *(f)*
manpower forecast	Personalprognose *(f)*
manpower forecasting	Personalprognose *(f)*
manpower management	Personalführung *(f)*
manpower planning	Personalplanung *(f)*
manpower resourcing	Personalbeschaffung *(f)*
manpower: executive ... strategy	Führungskräftestrategie *(f)*
manufacturing capacity	Fertigungskapazität *(f)*
	Produktivitätskapazität *(f)*
manufacturing control	Fertigungskontrolle *(f)*
	Fertigungssteuerung *(f)*
manufacturing: computer-aided ... (CAM)	computerunterstützte Fertigung *(f)*
manufacturing: computer-integrated ... (CIM)	computerintegrierte Fertigung *(f)*
	computergesteuerte Produktion *(f)*
manufacturing: economic ... quantity	wirtschaftliche Produktionsmenge *(f)*
margin of safety	Sicherheitsmarge *(f)*
margin: gross ... (GM)	Bruttogewinnspanne *(f)*

margin: net ...	Nettogewinnspanne *(f)*
	Reingewinn *(m)*
margin: profit ...	Gewinnspanne *(f)*
marginal analysis	Marginalanalyse *(f)*
marginal costs	Grenzkosten *(pl)*
marginal costing	Grenzkostenrechnung *(f)*
marginal pricing	marginale Preisfestsetzung *(f)*
marginalize (to)	machtlos machen
	Mitbestimmung *(f)* entziehen
margins: hold ... (to)	Gewinnspannen *(fpl)* halten
mark-up	Aufschlag *(m)*
	Gewinnzuschlag *(m)*
	Preisaufschlag *(m)*
market (to)	absetzen
	auf den Markt *(m)* bringen
	verkaufen
	vermarkten
	vertreiben
market appraisal	Marktbeurteilung *(f)*
market awareness	Marktbewußtsein *(n)*
	Marktkenntnisse *(fpl)*
market dynamics	Marktdynamik *(f)*
market exploration	Markterkundung *(f)*
market forces	Marktkräfte *(fpl)*
market forecast	Marktprognose *(f)*
market intelligence	Marktinformationen *(fpl)*
market leader	Marktführer *(m)*
market maker	Marktmacher *(m)*
market management	Marktleitung *(f)*
market opportunity	Marktchance *(f)*
market penetration	Marktdurchdringung *(f)*
market plan	Absatzplan *(m)*
	Marktplan *(m)*
market planning	Marktplanung *(f)*
market potential	Absatzpotential *(n)*
	Marktpotential *(n)*
market price	Marktpreis *(m)*
market profile	Marktprofil *(n)*
market prospects	Marktaussichten *(fpl)*

market rating	Marktbewertung *(f)*
	Markteinschätzung *(f)*
	Marktstellung *(f)*
market research	Marktforschung *(f)*
market saturation	Marktsättigung *(f)*
market segment	Marktsegment *(n)*
market segmentation	Marktsegmentierung *(f)*
market-sensitive	markttempfindlich
market share	Marktanteil *(m)*
market structure	Marktstruktur *(f)*
market study	Marktstudie *(f)*
	Marktuntersuchung *(f)*
market survey	Marktbefragung *(f)*
	Marktumfrage *(f)*
market test	Markttest *(m)*
market thrust	Markttrend *(m)*
market trend	Markttendenzen *(fpl)*
	Markttrend *(m)*
market value	Kurswert *(m)*
	Marktwert *(m)*
market: bear ...	Baisse *(f)*
market: bull ...	Hausse *(f)*
market: buyers' ...	Käufermarkt *(m)*
market: commodity ...	Rohstoffmarkt *(m)*
	Warenmarkt *(m)*
market: down-...	für den Massenmarkt *(m)*
	weniger anspruchsvoll
market: equity ...	Aktienmarkt *(m)*
market: financial ...	Markt *(f)* für Investitionspapiere
	(npl)
market: forward ...	Terminmarkt *(m)*
market: fringe ...	Nebenmarkt *(m)*
	Randmarkt *(m)*
market: grey ...	grauer Mark *(m)*
market: mature ...	etablierter Markt *(m)*
market: sellers' ...	Verkäufermarkt *(m)*
market: single ... *(of the EC)*	europäischer Binnenmarkt *(m)*
market: stock ...	Aktienbörse *(f)*
	Aktienmarkt *(m)*

market: target ...	Zielmarkt *(m)*
	Zielgruppe *(f)*
market: up-...	anspruchsvoll
	hochwertig
marketable	absatzfähig
	marktbar
	marktfähig
	marktgängig
marketing	Marketing *(n)*
marketing appropriation	bewilligte Marketing-Mittel *(npl)*
marketing budget	Marketing-Budget *(n)*
marketing department	Marketingabteilung *(f)*
marketing manager	Marketing-Leiter *(m)*
marketing mix	Marketing-Mix *(n)*
marketing research	Marketing-Forschung *(f)*
marketing strategy	Marketingstrategie *(f)*
marketing: creative ...	kreatives Marketing *(n)*
marketing: direct ...	Direktmarketing *(n)*
marketing: global ...	Globalmarketing *(n)*
marketing: test ...	Test-Marketing *(n)*
mass production	Massenproduktion *(f)*
mass: critical	kritische Masse *(f)*
massage the figures (to)	Zahlen *(fpl)* frisieren
material: point-of-sale ...	Point-of-sale-Material *(n)*
materials handling	Materialfluß *(m)*
	Materialtransport *(m)*
mathematical programming	mathematische Programmierung *(f)*
matrix management	Matrix-Organisation *(f)*
matrix organization	Matrix-Organisation *(f)*
mature market	etablierter Markt *(m)*
maximization: profit ...	Gewinnmaximierung *(f)*
maximize (to)	maximieren
MBO (management buyout)	MBO *(m,n)* (Management-Buyout *(m,n)*)
MBO (management by objectives)	Führung *(f)* durch Zielvereinbarung *(f)*
	MbO *(n)* (Management *(n)* by Objectives)
MD (managing director)	Generaldirektor *(m)*
	Geschäftsführer *(m)*
mean	Durchschnitt *(m)*
	Mittelwert *(m)*

meaningful	bedeutungsvoll
	sinnvoll
measurement: clerical work... (CWM)	Leistungsbeurteilung (f) der Büroangestellten (f/mpl)
	Leistungsbewertung (f) des Büropersonals (n)
measurement: performance ...	Leistungsmessung (f)
measurement: productivity ...	Produktivitätsmessung (f)
measurement: work ...	(Arbeits-)Zeitermittlung (f)
media	Kommunikationsmedien (npl)
	Medien (npl)
	Werbeträger (mpl)
media analysis	Media-Analyse (f)
	Medienanalyse (f)
media selection	Medienauswahl (f)
	Medienselektion (f)
	Medienwahl (f)
media: advertising ...	Werbemedien (npl)
	Werbeträger (mpl)
median	Zentralwert (m)
mediate (to)	vermitteln
mediation	Schlichtung (f)
	Vermittlung (f)
meeting: board ...	Aufsichtsratssitzung (f)
	Verwaltungsratssitzung (f)
	Vorstandssitzung (f)
memory	Speicher (m)
memory: computer ...	Speicher (m)
memory: random-access ... (RAM)	Schreiblesespeicher (m)
	Direktzugriffsspeicher (m)
memory: read-only ... (ROM)	Fest(wert)speicher (m)
	Nurlesespeicher (m)
merchandising	Merchandising (n)
merchandising: leader ...	Kundenwerbung (f) durch Sonderangebote (npl)
merchant bank	Handelsbank (f)
	Merchant Bank (f)
merge (to)	fusionieren
merger	Fusion (f)

mergers and acquisitions (M & A)	Fusionen *(fpl)* und Übernahmen *(fpl)* Mergers und Acquisitions *(pl)*
merit rating	Leistungsbeurteilung *(f)* Personalbeurteilung *(f)*
message: advertising ...	Werbeaussage *(f)* Werbebotschaft *(f)*
methectics	Gruppendynamik *(f)*
method: critical path ... (CPM)	Critical Path Method *(f)* (CPM) Methode *(f)* des kritischen Pfades *(m)*
method: full-cost ...	Vollkostenprinzip *(n)*
method: points-rating ...	Punktbewertung *(f)* Punktsystem *(n)*
method: present value ...	Barwertsmethode *(f)* Methode *(f)* des Gegenwartswertes *(m)*
method: random observation ...	Methode *(f)* der Arbeitsstichproben *(fpl)*
method: simplex ...	Simplex-Methode *(f)*
methods engineering	Ermittlung *(f)* von Arbeitsablaufstudien *(fpl)*
methods study	Arbeitsmethodenuntersuchung *(f)* Bewegungsstudie *(f)*
methods study department	Bewegungsstudienabteilung *(f)*
methods: organization and ... (O & M)	Organisation *(f)* und Methoden *(fpl)*
methods: time and ... study	Refa-Studie *(f)* Zeit- und Bewegungsstudie *(f)*
micro	Mikrocomputer *(m)*
microchip	Mikrochip *(m)*
middle management	Middle-Management *(n)* mittleres Management *(n)*
milestone chart	Tabelle *(f)* des kritischen Pfades *(m)*
minimize risks (to)	Risiken *(npl)* minimieren
minimum wage	Mindestlohn *(m)*
minority interest	Minderheitsbeteiligung *(f)*
MIS (management information system)	Management-Informationssystem *(n)*
mission statement	Erklärung *(f)* der Unternehmensgrundsätze *(mpl)*
mission: corporate ...	Unternehmensziel *(n)*
mission: economic ...	wirtschaftlicher Auftrag *(m)*
mix: investment ...	Wertpapierportfolio *(n)*

mix: marketing ...	Marketing-Mix *(n)*
mix: product ...	Produkt-Mix *(n)*
	Produktprogramm *(n)*
	Produktpalette *(f)*
mix: promotional ...	Absatzförderungsmix *(n)*
	Verkaufsförderungsmix *(n)*
mix: sales ...	Absatzprogramm *(n)*
mobile phone	Mobilfunk *(m)*
mobile: upwardly ...	karrierebewußt
mobility: labour ...	Arbeitskräftemobilität *(f)*
	Arbeitsmobilität *(f)*
mobility: staff ...	Mobilität *(f)* des Personals *(n)*
mode	Mode *(f)*
	Modus *(m)*
model	Modell *(n)*
model: accounting ...	Buchhaltungsmodell *(n)*
	Kostenrechnungsart *(f)*
model: corporate ...	Unternehmensmodell *(n)*
model: decision ...	Entscheidungsmodell *(n)*
model: dynamic management ...	dynamisches Führungsmodell *(n)*
	dynamisches Management-Modell *(n)*
modem	Modem *(n)*
modular production	Produktion *(f)* nach dem Baukastenprinzip *(n)*
modularity	Modularität *(f)*
monetarism	Monetarismus *(m)*
monetary policy	Geldpolitik *(f)*
money supply	Geldmenge *(f)*
monitor (to)	kontrollieren
	überwachen
monitor performance (to)	Leistung *(f)* kontrollieren
monitoring: performance ...	Leistungskontrolle *(f)*
moonlighting	Schwarzarbeit *(f)*
morphological analysis	morphologische Analyse *(f)*
motion economy	Bewegungsökonomie *(f)*
motion study	Bewegungsstudie *(f)*
motion: predetermined ... time system (PMTS)	System *(n)* vorbestimmter Zeiten *(fpl)*
motion: time and ... study	Refa-Studie *(f)*
	Zeit- und Bewegungsstudie *(f)*

motivate (to)	motivieren
motivation	Motivation *(f)*
motivation: self-...	Selbstmotivierung *(f)*
motivational	Motivations-
motivational research	Motivationsforschung *(f)*
motivator	Motivationsfaktor *(m)*
motivator: purchasing ...	Kaufanreiz *(m)*
	Kaufmotiv *(n)*
motive: profit ...	Gewinnmotiv *(n)*
	Gewinnstreben *(n)*
mouse	Maus *(f)*
MRA (multiple regression analysis)	Mehrfach-Regressionsanalyse *(f)*
multi-access	mehrfacher Zugang *(m)*
multimedia training	multimediale Ausbildung *(f)*
multiple management	Unternehmensführung *(f)* unter Beteiligung *(f)* nachgeordneter Führungsebenen *(fpl)*
multiple regression analysis (MRA)	Mehrfach-Regressionsanalyse *(f)*
mutual recognition	gegenseitige Anerkennung *(f)*

N

name of the game	*darum geht es*
	ausschlaggebendes Moment *(n)*
natural wastage	Fluktuation *(f)*
need-to-know basis	nur für unmittelbar Betroffene *(f/mpl)*
needs analysis	Bedarfsanalyse *(f)*
needs analysis: training	Analyse *(f)* des Ausbildungsbedarfs *(m)*
negative cash flow	negativer Cash-flow *(m)*
negative income tax	negative Einkommensteuer *(f)*
negotiate (to)	verhandeln
negotiation strategy	Verhandlungsstrategie *(f)*
negotiation: joint ...	gemeinsame Verhandlung *(f)*
net assets	Nettovermögen *(n)*
	Reinvermögen *(n)*
net current assets	Nettoumlaufvermögen *(n)*

net margin	Nettogewinnspanne *(f)*
	Reingewinn *(m)*
net present value (NPV)	Barwert *(m)*
	Kapitalwert *(m)*
net profit	Nettogewinn *(m)*
net worth	Eigenkapital *(n)*
	Gesellschaftsvermögen *(n)*
network (to)	mit einem Netz *(n)* verbinden
network analysis	Analyse *(f)* des kritischen Pfades *(m)*
	Netzplantechnik *(f)*
network: communications ...	Kommunikationsnetz *(n)*
network: distribution ...	Vertriebsnetz *(n)*
network: information ...	Informationsnetz *(n)*
network: wide area ... (WAN)	Weitbereichsnetz *(n)*
networking	Netzwerkbetrieb *(m)*
new-product development	Entwicklung *(f)* neuer Produkte *(npl)*
new-product launching	Produkteinführung *(f)*
niche	Marktlücke *(f)*
	Marktnische *(f)*
night shift	Nachtschicht *(f)*
non-durable goods	kurzlebige Konsumgüter *(npl)*
	Verbrauchsgüter *(npl)*
non-executive director	Aufsichtsratsmitglied *(n)*
	Mitglied *(n)* des Verwaltungsrat(e)s *(m)*
non-linear programming	nichtlineare Optimierung *(f)*
	nichtlineare Programmierung *(f)*
non-profit-making	gemeinnützig
non-tariff barrier (NTB)	Zollfreigrenze *(f)*
non-verbal communication	nichtverbale Kommunikation *(f)*
NPV (net present value)	Barwert *(m)*
	Kapitalwert *(m)*
NTB (non-tariff barrier)	Zollfreigrenze *(f)*
number-crunching	Rechnen *(n)*
	Rechnerei *(f)*
numerical control	numerische Kontrolle *(f)*

O

O & M (organization and methods)	Organisation *(f)* und Methoden *(fpl)*
objective	Ziel *(n)*
	Zielsetzung *(f)*
objective-setting	Zielsetzung *(f)*
objective: company ...	Unternehmensziel *(n)*
objectives: management by ... (MBO)	Führung *(f)* durch Zielvereinbarung *(f)*
	Management *(n)* by Objectives (MbO *(n)*)
objectives: overall company ...	gesamte Unternehmensziele *(npl)*
objectives: performance against ...	Soll-/Ist-Vergleich *(m)*
observation: random ... method	Methode *(f)* der Arbeitsstichproben *(fpl)*
obsolescence	Überalterung *(f)*
	Veralten *(n)*
obsolescence: built-in ...	eingeplanter Verschleiß *(m)*
obsolescence: planned ...	geplanter Verschleiß *(m)*
occupational hazard	Berufsrisiko *(n)*
off line	Offline-
	systemunabhängig
	indirekt prozeßgekoppelt
off-the-job training	außerbetriebliche Ausbildung *(f)*
office automation	Büroautomation *(f)*
office management	Büroleitung *(f)*
office planning	Bürogestaltung *(f)*
office: branch ...	Filiale *(f)*
	Niederlassung *(f)*
	Zweigstelle *(f)*
office: electronic ...	elektronisches Büro *(n)*
office: head ...	Hauptbüro *(n)*
	Zentrale *(f)*
officer: training ...	Ausbildungsleiter *(m)*
official strike	offizieller Streik *(m)*
offshore	Offshore-
	exterritorial
offshore investment	Offshore-Investmentfonds *(m)*
on line	direktgekoppelt
	Online-
	prozeßgekoppelt

on stream	in Betrieb *(m)*
on-the-job training	innerbetriebliche Ausbildung *(f)*
one-off	einmalig
ongoing	fortlaufend
	laufend
open-ended	alles offen lassend
	offen
open-plan	Großraum-
open shop	nicht gewerkschaftspflichtiger Betrieb *(m)*
operating division	Betriebsabteilung *(f)*
	Sparte *(f)*
	Unternehmensbereich *(m)*
operating expenses	Betriebskosten *(pl)*
operating management	Betriebsleitung *(f)*
operational	Arbeits-
	betrieblich
	Betriebs-
operational planning	kurz- bis mittelfristige Planung *(f)*
operational research (OR)	Operationsforschung *(f)*
	Operations Research *(n)* (OR)
	Unternehmensforschung *(f)*
operations	Arbeitsvorgänge *(mpl)*
	Geschäfte *(npl)*
	Geschäftstätigkeit *(f)*
operations analysis	Arbeitsanalyse *(f)*
	Betriebsanalyse *(f)*
operations audit	Prüfung *(f)* der Ablaufsysteme *(npl)* einer Unternehmung *(f)*
operations breakdown	Aufgliederung *(f)* des Stelleninhalt(e)s *(m)*
operations management	Betriebsleitung *(f)*
operations manager	Betriebsleiter *(m)*
operations research (OR)	Operationsforschung *(f)*
	Operations Research *(n)* (OR)
	Unternehmensforschung *(f)*
operations: ancillary ...	Hilfsoperationen *(fpl)*
	Nebenoperationen *(fpl)*

operations: hedging ...	Hedging *(n)*
	Hedgegeschäft *(n)*
	Sicherungsgeschäft *(n)*
opinion survey	Meinungsumfrage *(f)*
opportunity costs	Opportunitätskosten *(pl)*
opportunity: equal employment ...	berufliche Chancengleichheit *(f)*
opportunity: market ...	Marktchance *(f)*
opportunity: window of ...	günstige Gelegenheit *(f)*
	günstiger Augenblick *(m)*
optimization: profit ...	Gewinnoptimierung *(f)*
optimize (to)	optimieren
option: stock ...	Aktienbezugsrecht *(n)*
	Aktienoption *(f)*
option: stock ... plan	Aktienoptionsplan *(m)*
option: traded ...	börsengehandelte Option *(f)*
OR (operational research, operations research)	Operationsforschung *(f)*
	Operations Research *(n)* (OR)
	Unternehmensforschung *(f)*
order: economic ... quantity	wirtschaftliche Losgröße *(f)*
organic growth	organisches Wachstum *(n)*
organization and methods (O & M)	Organisation *(f)* und Methoden *(fpl)*
organization chart	Organisationsplan *(m)*
	Organogramm *(n)*
organization culture	Firmenkultur *(f)*
	Organisationskultur *(f)*
organization planning	Organisationsplanung *(f)*
organization structure	Organisationsstruktur *(f)*
organization theory	Organisationstheorie *(f)*
organization: functional ...	funktionale Organisation *(f)*
organization: informal ...	informelle Organisation *(f)*
organization: line ...	Linienorganisation *(f)*
organization: line and staff ...	Stablinienorganisation *(f)*
organization: matrix ...	Matrix-Organisation *(f)*
organization: staff ...	Stabsorganisation *(f)*
organizational behaviour	Verhalten *(n)* in der Organisation *(f)*
organizational change	organisatorische Änderung *(f)*

organizational development	Entwicklung (f) der Organisation (f)
	organisatorische Entwicklung (f)
	organisatorischer Aufbau (m)
organizational effectiveness	organisatorische Wirksamkeit (f)
organogram	Organogramm (n)
orientation: consumer ...	Konsumorientierung (f)
orientation: customer ...	Kundenorientierung (f)
	Unterrichtung (f) der Kundschaft (f)
out of stock	nicht vorrätig
out-house	außerhäuslich
	extern
outlook: business ...	Geschäftslage (f)
	Konjunkturaussichten (fpl)
outlook: profit ...	Gewinnaussichten (fpl)
outplacement	*Berufsberatung (f) von Aufsteigern (mpl) und arbeitslos gewordenen Führungskräften (fpl)*
	Outplacement (n)
output	Output (m)
	Produktion (f)
output budgeting	Produktionsplanung (f)
output: capital-... ratio	Kapitalkoeffizient (m)
output: input-... analysis	Input-Output-Analyse (f)
output: input-... table	Input-Output-Tabelle (f)
outside director	Aufsichtsratsmitglied (n)
	Mitglied (n) des Verwaltungsrat(e)s (m)
outsourcing	Auswärtsvergabe (f)
overall company objectives	gesamte Unternehmensziele (npl)
overcapacity	Überkapazität (f)
overcapitalized	überkapitalisiert
overextended	überschuldet
	ungenügend gedeckt
overheads	Gemeinkosten (pl)
overheads recovery	Aufteilungsverfahren (n) für Gemeinkosten (pl)
overheads: administrative ...	Verwaltungsgemeinkosten (pl)
overheads: factory ...	Fabrikgemeinkosten (pl)
	Fertigungsgemeinkosten (pl)
overmanned	überbesetzt

overmanning	Überbesetzung (f)
	zu große Belegschaft (f)
overprice (to)	einen zu hohen Preis (m) verlangen
	einen zu hohen Preis (m) ansetzen
overstaffed	personell überbesetzt
overstaffing	personelle Überbesetzung (f)
overtime	Überstunden (fpl)
owner-manager	Eigentümer-Unternehmer (m)

P

P/E (price-earnings ratio)	Kurs-Gewinn-Verhältnis (n)
P/V (profit-volume ratio)	Umsatzrentabilität (f)
package deal	Kopplungsgeschäft (n)
package: software ...	Softwarepaket (n)
packaging	Verpackung (f)
palletization	Palettierung (f)
panel: consumers' ...	Verbraucherpanel (n)
par	Nennwert (m)
	Pari (m)
par: above ...	über dem Nennwert (m)
	über pari
par: at ...	al pari
	zum Nennwert (m)
par: below ...	unter dem Nennwert (m)
	unter pari
parachute: golden ...	*Garantie (f) einer beträchtlichen*
	Abfindungszahlung im Falle (m) der
	Entlassung (f)
parallel currency	Parallelwährung (f)
parallel import	Paralleleinfuhr (f)
	Parallelimport (m)
parallel loan	Parallelanleihe (f)
	Parallelkredit (m)
parameter	Parameter (m)
parametric programming	parametrische Programmierung (f)
parent company	Muttergesellschaft (f)
part-analysis training	Ausbildung (f) in Teilanalysen (fpl)

part-time employment	Halbtagsbeschäftigung *(f)*
	Teilzeitbeschäftigung *(f)*
part-timer	Aushilfsarbeiter *(m)*
	Halbtagskraft *(f)*
	Kurzarbeiter *(m)*
participation	Beteiligung *(f)*
	Mitwirkung *(f)*
participation: worker ...	Mitbestimmung *(f)*
participative management	kooperativer Führungsstil *(m)*
partner	Gesellschafter *(m)*
	Partner *(m)*
	Teilhaber *(m)*
partnership	Offene Handelsgesellschaft *(f)*
	Partnerschaft *(f)*
	Personengesellschaft *(f)*
party: working ...	Arbeitsgruppe *(f)*
patent trading	Patenthandel *(m)*
pay-as-you-earn (PAYE)	Lohnsteuerabzug *(m)*
	Quellenabzugsverfahren *(n)*
pay-as-you-go	Lohnsteuerabzug *(m)*
	Quellenabzugsverfahren *(n)*
pay-off	Amortisation *(f)*
	Gewinn *(m)*
pay pause	Lohn- und Gehaltsstopp *(m)*
	Lohnpause *(f)*
pay talks	Lohnverhandlungen *(fpl)*
	Tarifverhandlungen *(fpl)*
pay: equal ...	gleicher Lohn *(m)*
	gleiches Entgelt *(n)*
pay: profit-related ...	gewinnabhängige Lohn- und Gehaltszahlung *(f)*
pay: severance ...	Entlassungsabfindung *(f)*
pay: take-home ...	Nettogehalt *(n)*
	Nettolohn *(m)*
payback	Amortisation *(f)*
	Kapitalrückfluß *(m)*
payback period	Amortisationsdauer *(f)*
	Kapitalrückflußfrist *(f)*
	Wiedergewinnungszeit *(f)*

PAYE (pay-as-you-earn)	Lohnsteuerabzug *(m)*
	Quellenabzugsverfahren *(n)*
payment by results	Akkordlohnsystem *(n)*
payment: *ex gratia ...*	freiwillige Zuwendung *(f)*
	Gratifikation *(f)*
payroll	Gehaltsliste *(f)*
	Lohn- und Gehaltssumme *(f)*
	Lohnliste *(f)*
PC (personal computer)	PC *(m)* (Personal-Computer *(m)*)
penetration pricing	Penetrationspreispolitik *(f)*
penetration: market ...	Marktdurchdringung *(f)*
per-share earnings	Gewinn *(m)* je Aktie *(f)*
perform (to)	arbeiten
	funktionieren
	leisten
performance against objectives	Soll-/Ist-Vergleich *(m)*
performance appraisal	Leistungsbeurteilung *(f)*
performance budgeting	Leistungsplanung *(f)*
performance evaluation	Leistungsbeurteilung *(f)*
performance indicator	Leistungsbarometer *(n)*
	Leistungskennzahl *(f)*
performance measurement	Leistungsmessung *(f)*
performance monitoring	Leistungskontrolle *(f)*
performance rating	Leistungsbeurteilung *(f)*
performance review	Beurteilungsgespräch *(n)*
	Leistungsbeurteilung *(f)*
performance standard	Leistungsmaßstab *(m)*
performance: earnings ...	Ertragsleistung *(f)*
performance: job ...	Arbeitsergebnis *(n)*
	Arbeitsleistung *(f)*
performance: monitor ... (to)	Leistung *(f)* kontrollieren
performance: product ...	Produktleistung *(f)*
performance: profit ...	Abschluß *(m)*
	Ergebnis *(n)*
	Unternehmenserfolg *(m)*
performance: share price ...	Richtung *(f)* des Kursniveaus *(n)*
performance: standard ...	Vorgabeleistung *(f)*
period: accounting ...	Abrechnungszeitraum *(m)*
	Rechnungsperiode *(f)*

peripheral equipment	Peripheriegeräte *(npl)*
peripherals	Peripherien *(fpl)*
perpetual inventory	permanente Inventur *(f)*
personal computer (PC)	Personal-Computer *(m)* (PC)
personal growth	persönliche Weiterentwicklung *(f)*
personnel department	Personalabteilung *(f)*
personnel management	Personalleitung *(f)*
	Personalmanagement *(n)*
personnel manager	Personalleiter *(m)*
personnel policy	Personalpolitik *(f)*
personnel rating	Personalbeurteilung *(f)*
personnel specification	Qualifikationsprofil *(n)*
PERT (programme evaluation and review technique)	PERT (Programme Evaluation and Review Technique) *(f)*
	Ereignis-Knotenplan *(m)*
pertinence tree	Zuständigkeitsbaum *(m)*
petty cash	Portokasse *(f)*
petty expenses	kleine Spesen *(pl)*
	kleine Unkosten *(pl)*
phase in (to)	allmählich einführen
	stufenweise einführen
phase out (to)	allmählich abbauen
	auslaufen lassen
	stufenweise einstellen
philosophy: company …	Unternehmensphilosophie *(f)*
physical distribution management	Warenverteilung *(f)*
picket	Streikposten *(m)*
pie chart	Kreisdiagramm *(n)*
piecework	Akkordarbeit *(f)*
piggyback	Huckepackverkehr *(m)*
	kombinierter Verkehr *(m)*
	rollende Landstraße *(f)*
pilot production	Testproduktion *(f)*
	Versuchsproduktion *(f)*
pilot run	Testproduktion *(f)*
	Versuchsproduktion *(f)*
pioneer (to)	Pionierarbeit *(f)* leisten
pioneer product	Pionierprodukt *(n)*

piracy	Produktpiraterie (f)
plan	Plan (m)
plan: action ...	Aktionsplan (m)
	Durchführungsplan (m)
plan: departmental ...	Abteilungsplan (m)
plan: market ...	Absatzplan (m)
	Marktplan (m)
plan: open-...	Großraum-
plan: share of production ...	Produktionsanteilsplan (m)
plan: stock option ...	Aktienoptionsplan (m)
plan: tactical ...	taktischer Plan (m)
planned maintenance	geplante Instandhaltung (f)
	geplante Wartung (f)
planned obsolescence	geplanter Verschleiß (m)
planning	Planung (f)
planning department	Planungsabteilung (f)
planning, programming, budgeting system (PPBS)	Planungs-, Programmierungs- (und) Budgetierungssystem (n)
planning: career ...	Laufbahnplanung (f)
planning: company ...	Unternehmensplanung (f)
planning: contingency ...	Notfallplanung (f)
planning: corporate ...	Unternehmensplanung (f)
planning: distribution ...	Vertriebsplanung (f)
planning: financial ...	Finanzplanung (f)
planning: forward ...	Zukunftsplanung (f)
planning: human resource ... (HRP)	Personalplanung (f)
planning: long-range ...	langfristige Planung (f)
planning: long-term ...	langfristige Planung (f)
planning: management succession ...	Führungsnachfolgeplanung (f)
planning: manpower ...	Personalplanung (f)
planning: market ...	Marktplanung (f)
planning: office ...	Bürogestaltung (f)
planning: operational ...	kurz- bis mittelfristige Planung (f)
planning: organization ...	Organisationsplanung (f)
planning: product ...	Produktplanung (f)
planning: production ...	Produktionsplanung (f)

planning: production ... and control	Produktionsplanung *(f)* und -kontrolle *(f)*
planning: profit ...	Erfolgsplanung *(f)*
	Planung *(f)* des Betriebsergebnisses *(n)*
planning: project ...	Projektplanung *(f)*
planning: sales ...	Absatzplanung *(f)*
planning: short-term ...	kurzfristige Planung *(f)*
planning: staff ...	Personalplanung *(f)*
planning: strategic ...	strategische Planung *(f)*
planning: systems ...	Systemplanung *(f)*
plant bargaining	innerbetriebliche Tarifverhandlungen *(fpl)*
plant capacity	Anlagenkapazität *(f)*
	Betriebskapazität *(f)*
plant hire	Industrieanlagen-Leasing *(n)*
plant layout study	Untersuchung *(f)* der Betriebsanlagen *(fpl)*
plant location	Unternehmensstandort *(m)*
plant maintenance	Betriebsinstandhaltung *(f)*
plant maintenance: total	umfassende Betriebsinstandhaltung *(f)*
plant manager	Betriebsleiter *(m)*
	Werksleiter *(m)*
player: team ...	teamfähiger Manager *(m)*
	Teammitglied *(n)*
	teamorientierter Manager *(m)*
playing: role-...	Rollenspiel *(n)*
ploughback	Gewinneinbehaltung *(f)* zu Investitionszwecken *(mpl)*
PMTS (predetermined motion time system)	System *(n)* vorbestimmter Zeiten *(fpl)*
point of sale (POS)	Verkaufsort *(m)*
point-of-sale advertising	POS-Werbung *(f)*
point-of-sale material	Point-of-sale-Material *(n)*
point: break-even ...	Break-Even-Punkt *(m)*
	Deckungspunkt *(m)*
	Gewinnschwelle *(f)*
	Nutzschwelle *(f)*
point: unique selling ... (USP)	Alleinstellungsanspruch *(m)*
	einer Marke *(f)* oder eines Produkt(e)s *(n)*
points-rating method	Punktbewertung *(f)*
	Punktsystem *(n)*

poison pill	*Vorkehrung (f) zur Abwehr (f) von Firmenübernahmen (fpl)*
policy execution	Durchführung (f) der Unternehmenspolitik (f)
policy formulation	Formulierung (f) der Unternehmenspolitik (f)
policy: business ...	Geschäftspolitik (f)
policy: company ...	Unternehmenspolitik (f)
policy: distribution ...	Vertriebspolitik (f)
policy: dividend ...	Dividendenpolitik (f)
policy: investment ...	Investitionspolitik (f)
policy: personnel ...	Personalpolitik (f)
policy: pricing ...	Preispolitik (f)
policy: promotional ...	Verkaufsförderungspolitik (f)
policy: remittance ...	Überweisungspolitik (f)
policy: sales ...	Absatzgrundsätze (mpl)
	Absatzpolitik (f)
	Verkaufspolitik (f)
policy: selling ...	Verkaufspolitik (f)
policy: wage ...	Lohnpolitik (f)
	Tarifpolitik (f)
pooling arrangements	Poolbildung (f)
	Pooling (n)
poor: cash-...	illiquid
	nicht flüssig
portfolio management	Portfolio-Management (n)
portfolio selection	Portfolio-Auswahl (f)
portfolio: asset ...	Kreditportfolio (n)
	Kreditvolumen (n)
portfolio: balanced ...	ausgeglichenes Portfolio (n)
portfolio: brand ...	Markenpalette (f)
	Markenportfolio (n)
portfolio: business ...	Geschäftsportfolio (n)
portfolio: product ...	Produktpalette (f)
	Produktportfolio (n)
portfolio: stock ...	Aktienbestand (m)
	Aktiendepot (n)
	Aktienportfolio (n)
POS (point of sale)	Verkaufsort (m)
position: competitive ...	Wettbewerbsposition (f)
	Wettbewerbsstellung (f)

position: financial ...	Finanzlage *(f)*
	Finanzstatus *(m)*
positioning	Positionierung *(f)*
	Produktpositionierung *(f)*
positioning: brand ...	Markenpositionierung *(f)*
positive discrimination	*Bevorzugung (f) bei der Personalauslese (f) um der beruflichen Chancengleichheit (f) willen*
	Quotenregelung *(f)*
potential buyer	potentieller Käufer *(m)*
potential: development ...	Entwicklungspotential *(n)*
potential: growth ...	Wachstumspotential *(n)*
potential: management ...	Führungspotential *(n)*
	Management-Potential *(n)*
potential: market ...	Absatzpotential *(n)*
	Marktpotential *(n)*
potential: sales ...	Absatzmöglichkeiten *(fpl)*
	Absatzpotential *(n)*
power: earning ...	Ertragskraft *(f)*
PPBS (planning, programming, budgeting system)	Planungs-, Programmierungs- (und) Budgetierungssystem *(n)*
PR (public relations)	PR (Public Relations *(pl)*)
	Öffentlichkeitsarbeit *(f)*
practices: management ...	Management-Prinzipien *(npl)*
	Verhaltensnormen *(fpl)* im Management *(n)*
practices: restrictive ... *(industrial)*	restriktive Arbeitspraktiken *(fpl)*
practices: restrictive ... *(legal)*	restriktive Geschäftspraktiken *(fpl)*
	Wettbewerbsbeschränkungen *(fpl)*
predator	Unternehmensaufkäufer *(m)*
predetermined motion time system (PMTS)	System *(n)* vorbestimmter Zeiten *(fpl)*
pre-emptive bid	*mögliche Mitbieter (mpl) abschreckendes Übernahmeangebot (n)*
premium	Prämie *(f)*
premium bonus	Prämienlohn *(m)*
present value: net ... ... (NPV)	Barwert *(m)*
	Kapitalwert *(m)*
present value method	Barwertmethode *(f)*
	Methode *(f)* des Gegenwartswertes *(m)*

president	Präsident *(m)*
president: vice-...	Vizepräsident *(m)*
pressure	Druck *(m)*
prestige pricing	*Preisbildung (f), die sich an den Sozialprestigeerwartungen (fpl) der Käufer (mpl) orientiert*
preventive maintenance	vorbeugende Instandhaltung *(f)*
price (to)	bewerten
	Preis *(m)* festsetzen
price-cutting	Preisunterbietung *(f)*
price determination	Preisfestsetzung *(f)*
price differential	Preisgefälle *(n)*
	Preisunterschied *(m)*
price discrimination	Preisdiskriminierung *(f)*
price-earnings ratio (P/E)	Kurs-Gewinn-Verhältnis *(n)*
price escalation	sich gegenseitig verstärkender Preisauftrieb *(m)*
price-fixing	Preisfestsetzung *(f)*
price increase	Preiserhöhung *(f)*
price index	Preisindex *(m)*
price index: consumer	Verbraucherpreisindex *(m)*
price index: retail ... ... (RPI)	Einzelhandelspreisindex *(m)*
price leader	Preisführer *(m)*
price range	Preisskala *(f)*
	Preisspanne *(f)*
price structure	Preisstruktur *(f)*
price: competitive ...	Konkurrenzpreis *(m)*
	konkurrenzfähiger Preis *(m)*
price: differential ...	differenzierter Preis *(m)*
price: market ...	Marktpreis *(m)*
price: resale ... maintenance (RPM)	Preisbindung *(f)* der zweiten Hand *(f)*
price: spot ...	Kassapreis *(m)*
	Lokopreis *(m)*
price: standard ...	Einheitspreis *(m)*
	fester Verrechnungspreis *(m)*
	Standardpreis *(m)*
prices: cut ... (to)	Preise *(mpl)* herabsetzen
	Preise *(mpl)* senken

pricing	Preisfestsetzung *(f)*
	Preisgestaltung *(f)*
pricing policy	Preispolitik *(f)*
pricing strategy	Preisstrategie *(f)*
pricing: differential ...	Differentialpreisfestsetzung *(f)*
	Preisdifferenzierung *(f)*
	unterschiedliche Preisgestaltung *(f)*
pricing: marginal ...	marginale Preisfestsetzung *(f)*
pricing: penetration ...	Penetrationspreispolitik *(f)*
pricing: prestige ...	*Preisbildung (f), die sich an den*
	Sozialprestigeerwartungen (fpl) der Käufer
	(mpl) orientiert
pricing: transfer ...	Festlegung *(f)* der Verrechnungspreise
	(mpl)
primary commodity	Rohstoff *(m)*
print out (to)	ausdrucken
printout	Ausdruck *(m)*
	Druckausgabe *(f)*
prioritize (to)	Prioritäten *(fpl)* setzen
private enterprise	freies Unternehmertum *(n)*
	Privatwirtschaft *(f)*
privatization	Privatisierung *(f)*
privatize (to)	privatisieren
pro rata	anteil(s)mäßig
proactive	initiativ
proactive strategy	initiative Strategie *(f)*
probability theory	Wahrscheinlichkeitstheorie *(f)*
problem analysis	Problemanalyse *(f)*
problem area	Problembereich *(m)*
problem assessment	Problembeurteilung *(f)*
problem solving	Problemlösung *(f)*
procedural	verfahrensrechtlich
procedure	Verfahren *(n)*
procedure: administrative control ...	administratives Kontrollverfahren *(n)*
	verwaltungstechnisches Kontrollverfahren *(n)*
procedure: grievance ...	Beschwerdeverfahren *(n)*
	Schlichtungsverfahren *(n)*
procedures: systems and ...	Systeme *(npl)* und Verfahren *(npl)*

process (to)	abfertigen
	bearbeiten
	verarbeiten
process control	Prozeßkontrolle *(f)*
	Prozeßsteuerung *(f)*
process costing	Kostenrechnung *(f)* für Serienfertigung *(f)*
process equipment layout	Betriebsanlage *(f)* nach Werkstattprinzip *(n)*
process: decision ...	Entscheidungsprozeß *(m)*
process: flow ... chart	Arbeitsablaufbogen *(m)*
process: logistic ...	logistisches Verfahren *(n)*
process: production ...	Produktionsprozeß *(m)*
	Produktionsverfahren *(n)*
processing: automatic data ... (ADP)	automatische Datenverarbeitung *(f)*
processing: batch ...	Stapelverarbeitung *(f)*
processing: central ... unit (CPU)	Zentraleinheit *(f)* (ZE)
processing: data ...	Datenverarbeitung *(f)*
processing: electronic ...	elektronische Verarbeitung *(f)*
processing: electronic data ... (EDP)	elektronische Datenverarbeitung *(f)*
processing: information ...	Informationsverarbeitung *(f)*
processing: word ...	Textverarbeitung *(f)*
processor: word ... (WP)	Textverarbeiter *(m)*
	Textverarbeitungseinrichtung *(f)*
	Wortprozessor *(m)*
procurement	Beschaffung *(f)*
	Einkauf *(m)*
procurement manager	Beschaffungsmanager *(m)*
	Einkaufsmanager *(m)*
product abandonment	Produktaufgabe *(f)*
	Produkteliminierung *(f)*
product advertising	Produktwerbung *(f)*
product analysis	Produktanalyse *(f)*
product area	Produktbereich *(m)*
product conception	Produktkonzeption *(f)*
product costing	Ermittlung *(f)* der Erzeugniskosten *(pl)*
	Produktkostenrechnung *(f)*
product design	Produktgestaltung *(f)*
product development	Produktentwicklung *(f)*

product differentiate (to)	sich deutlich von Konkurrenzprodukten *(npl)* unterscheiden
product differentiation	Produktdifferenzierung *(f)*
product diversification	Produktdiversifizierung *(f)*
	Produktionsbreite *(f)*
product dynamics	Produktdynamik *(f)*
product engineering	Fertigungstechnik *(f)*
product generation	Produkterzeugung *(f)*
product group	Produktgruppe *(f)*
product image	Produktimage *(n)*
product improvement	Produktverbesserung *(f)*
product introduction	Produkteinführung *(f)*
product launch	Produkteinführung *(f)*
product life	wirtschaftliche Lebensdauer *(f)* eines Produkt(e)s *(n)*
product life cycle	Produktlebenszyklus *(m)*
product life expectancy	Lebenserwartung *(f)* eines Produkt(e)s *(n)*
product line	Produktgruppe *(f)*
	Produktkategorie *(f)*
	Produktlinie *(f)*
product management	Produkt-Management *(n)*
product manager	Produkt-Manager *(m)*
product mix	Produkt-Mix *(n)*
	Produktpalette *(f)*
	Produktprogramm *(n)*
product performance	Produktleistung *(f)*
product planning	Produktplanung *(f)*
product portfolio	Produktpalette *(f)*
	Produktportfolio *(n)*
product profile	Produktprofil *(n)*
product profitability	Produktrentabilität *(f)*
product range	Produktpalette *(f)*
	Sortiment *(n)*
product reliability	Produktzuverlässigkeit *(f)*
product research	Produktforschung *(f)*
product strategy	Produktstrategie *(f)*
product testing	Produkterprobung *(f)*
	Produktprüfung *(f)*
product: by-...	Nebenprodukt *(n)*

product: core ...	Hauptprodukt (n)
product: new-... development	Entwicklung (f) neuer Produkte (npl)
product: pioneer ...	Pionierprodukt (n)
product: star ...	Renner (m)
	Verkaufsschlager (m)
production	Herstellung (f)
	Fertigung (f)
	Produktion (f)
production complex	gesamte Produktionsanlagen (fpl)
production control	Fertigungskontrolle (f)
	Produktionskontrolle (f)
production costs	Produktionskosten (pl)
production director	Produktionsleiter (m)
production engineering	Produktionstechnik (f)
production line	Fließband (n)
	Fertigungsstraße (f)
production management	Produktionsmanagement (n)
production manager	Produktionsmanager (m)
production planning	Produktionsplanung (f)
production planning and control	Produktionsplanung (f) und -kontrolle (f)
production process	Produktionsprozeß (m)
	Produktionsverfahren (n)
production run	Produktionsablauf (m)
	Produktionsverlauf (m)
production schedule	Produktionsplan (m)
production scheduling	Arbeitsvorbereitung (f)
	Produktionsplanung (f)
production standard	Produktionsnorm (f)
production target	Produktionsziel (n)
production technique	Fertigungsmethode (f)
	Herstellungsmethode (f)
	Produktionsmethode (f)
production: batch ...	Sortenfertigung (f)
	Sortenproduktion (f)
production: continuous-flow ...	Fließfertigung (f)
	Massenproduktion (f)
production: factors of ...	Produktionsfaktoren (mpl)
production: flow ...	Fließfertigung (f)
production: intensive ...	intensive Produktion (f)

production: line ...	Fließbandproduktion *(f)*
production: mass ...	Massenproduktion *(f)*
production: modular ...	Produktion *(f)* nach dem Baukastenprinzip *(n)*
production: pilot ...	Testproduktion *(f)*
	Versuchsproduktion *(f)*
production: share of ... plan	Produktionsanteilsplan *(m)*
productive maintenance	Produktionswartung *(f)*
	Produktivwartung *(f)*
productivity	Produktivität *(f)*
productivity agreement	Produktivitätsabkommen *(n)*
	Produktivitätsvereinbarung *(f)*
productivity bargaining	Tarifverhandlungen *(fpl)* über
	Produktivitätszulagen *(fpl)*
productivity campaign	Produktivitätskampagne *(f)*
productivity drive	gezielte Bemühungen *(fpl)* um
	Produktivitätssteigerung *(f)*
	Produktivitätskampagne *(f)*
productivity measurement	Produktivitätsmessung *(f)*
professionalization	Erhebung *(f)* zum Beruf *(m)*
	Erlangung *(f)* eines beruflichen Status *(m)*
profile: acquisition ...	Akquisitionsprofil *(n)*
profile: company ...	Unternehmensprofil *(n)*
profile: customer ...	Kundenprofil *(n)*
profile: job ...	Arbeitsplatzbeschreibung *(f)*
	Stellenbeschreibung *(f)*
profile: market ...	Marktprofil *(n)*
profile: product ...	Produktprofil *(n)*
profile: risk ...	Risikoprofil *(n)*
profit	Gewinn *(m)*
	Profit *(m)*
profit centre	Profit-Center *(n)*
profit centre accounting	Profit-Center-Ergebnisrechnung *(f)*
profit-factor analysis	Analyse *(f)* der Gewinnfaktoren *(mpl)*
	Gewinnfaktoranalyse *(f)*
profit goal	Gewinnziel *(n)*
profit impact	Gewinnauswirkung *(f)*
profit implication	Gewinnauswirkung *(f)*
profit improvement	Gewinnverbesserung *(f)*
profit margin	Gewinnspanne *(f)*

profit maximization	Gewinnmaximierung (f)
profit motive	Gewinnmotiv (n)
	Gewinnstreben (n)
profit optimization	Gewinnoptimierung (f)
profit outlook	Gewinnaussichten (fpl)
profit performance	Abschluß (m)
	Ergebnis (n)
	Unternehmenserfolg (m)
profit planning	Erfolgsplanung (f)
	Planung (f) des Betriebsergebnisses (n)
profit projection	Gewinnprojektion (f)
profit-related pay	gewinnabhängige Lohn- und
	Gehaltszahlung (f)
profit-sharing	Erfolgsbeteiligung (f)
	Ergebnisbeteiligung (f)
	Gewinnbeteiligung (f)
profit strategy	Gewinnstrategie (f)
profit target	Gewinnziel (n)
profit-volume ratio (P/V)	Umsatzrentabilität (f)
profit: cost-volume-... analysis	Kosten-/Umsatz-/Gewinnanalyse (f)
profit: distributed ...	verteilter Gewinn (m)
	ausgeschüttete Gewinne (mpl)
profit: gross ...	Bruttogewinn (m)
profit: net ...	Nettogewinn (m)
profit: undistributed ...	einbehaltene Gewinne (mpl)
profitability	Rentabilität (f)
profitability analysis	Rentabilitätsanalyse (f)
profitability: product ...	Produktrentabilität (f)
profits tax	Körperschaftsteuer (f)
program (to)	programmieren
program: computer ...	Computerprogramm (n)
programme (to)	programmieren
programme	Programm (n)
programme budgeting	Aufstellung (f) des Ist-Budgets (n)
	Programmbudgetierung (f)
programme evaluation and review technique (PERT)	Ereignis-Knotenplan (m)
	Programme Evaluation and Review Technique (f) (PERT)
programme package	Programmpaket (n)

programme: development ...	Entwicklungsprogramm *(n)*
programme: investment ...	Investitionsprogramm *(n)*
programme: trading ...	Handelsprogramm *(n)*
programmed instruction	Programmbefehl *(m)*
	Programminstruktion *(f)*
programmed learning	programmierter Lernprozeß *(m)*
	programmiertes Lernen *(n)*
programmed management	Führung *(f)* durch Vorgabe *(f)* von
	Programmen *(npl)*
	programmiertes Management *(n)*
programmer: computer ...	Programmierer *(m)*
programming	Programmierung *(f)*
programming: computer ...	maschinelle Programmierung *(f)*
programming: dynamic ...	dynamische Programmierung *(f)*
programming: linear ...	lineare Programmierung *(f)*
	Linearplanung *(f)*
programming: mathematical ...	mathematische Programmierung *(f)*
programming: non-linear ...	nichtlineare Optimierung *(f)*
	nichtlineare Programmierung *(f)*
programming: parametric ...	parametrische Programmierung *(f)*
programming: planning, ...,	Planungs-, Programmierungs- (und)
budgeting system (PPBS)	Budgetierungssystem *(n)*
programming: scientific ...	wissenschaftliche
	Programmierung *(f)*
progress control	Fortschrittskontrolle *(f)*
progress: work in ...	Halbfabrikate *(npl)*
	unfertige Leistungen *(fpl)*
	unfertige Produkte *(npl)*
progression: salary ... curve	Gehaltsprogressionskurve *(f)*
project analysis	Projektanalyse *(f)*
project assessment	Projektbewertung *(f)*
project management	Projekt-Management *(n)*
project manager	Projektmanager *(m)*
project planning	Projektplanung *(f)*
project: capital ... evaluation	Investitionsrechnungsverfahren *(n)*
project: chunk a ... (to)	ein Projekt *(n)* in seine Einzelteile *(npl)*
	zerlegen
project: integrated ...	integriertes Projekt-Management *(n)*
management (IPM)	

projection	Prognose (f)
	Vorausberechnung (f)
projection: profit ...	Gewinnprojektion (f)
promotion (*personnel*)	Beförderung (f) (*von Mitarbeitern (mpl)*)
promotion: executive ...	Beförderung (f) von Führungskräften (f)
promotion: sales ...	Verkaufsförderung (f)
promotional	fördernd
	Verkaufsförderungs-
	werbend
promotional mix	Absatzförderungsmix (n)
	Verkaufsförderungsmix (n)
promotional policy	Verkaufsförderungspolitik (f)
proposal: value ...	ernstgemeinter Vorschlag (m)
	Kosten-Nutzen-Angebot (n)
proposition: business ...	geschäftlicher Vorschlag (m)
proposition: unique selling ...	Alleinstellungsanspruch (m)
(USP)	einer Marke (f) oder eines
	Produkt(e)s (n)
prospective customer	potentieller Kunde (m)
	voraussichtlicher Kunde (m)
prospects: market ...	Marktaussichten (fpl)
protection: consumer ...	Verbraucherschutz (m)
protection: data ...	Datenschutz (m)
protection: turf ...	*Wahrung (f) des eigenen Ressorts (n)*
psychology: industrial ...	Betriebspsychologie (f)
psychometric testing	psychometrische Messung (f)
	psychometrische Untersuchungsmethodik (f)
public enterprise	öffentliche Wirtschaftsbetriebe (mpl)
	öffentlicher Sektor (m)
public relations (PR)	Öffentlichkeitsarbeit (f)
	Public Relations (pl) (PR)
public utility	öffentlicher Versorgungsbetrieb (m)
public: go ... (to)	an der Börse (f) zugelassen werden
publicly listed company	börsennotierte Gesellschaft (f)
publishing: desktop ...	Desktop-Publishing (n)
purchasing	Einkauf (m)
purchasing manager	Einkaufsleiter (m)
purchasing motivator	Kaufanreiz (m)
	Kaufmotiv (n)

purchasing power	Kaufkraft *(f)*
purchasing power parity	Kaufkraftparität *(f)*

Q

QC (quality control)	Qualitätskontrolle *(f)*
	Qualitätssteuerung *(f)*
quality assessment	Qualitätsbeurteilung *(f)*
	Qualitätsbewertung *(f)*
	Qualitätseinschätzung *(f)*
quality assurance	Qualitätssicherung *(f)*
quality circle	Optimierungs-Team *(n)*
	Qualitätszirkel *(m)*
	Quality Circle *(m)*
quality control (QC)	Qualitätskontrolle *(f)*
	Qualitätssteuerung *(f)*
quality control: total ... ... (TQC)	umfassende Qualitätskontrolle *(f)*
quality management	Qualitätsmanagement *(n)*
quality management: total ... ... (TQM)	Total Quality Management *(n)* (TQM)
quantitative analysis	quantitative Analyse *(f)*
quantity: break-even ...	Break-Even-Umsatz *(m)*
quantity: economic batch ...	wirtschaftliche Fertigproduktmenge *(f)*
quantity: economic manufacturing ...	wirtschaftliche Produktionsmenge *(f)*
quantity: economic order ...	wirtschaftliche Losgröße *(f)*
queuing theory	Warteschlangentheorie *(f)*
quick assets	leicht realisierbare Aktiva *(pl)*
quick fix	provisorische Lösung *(f)*
quota: sales ...	Absatzquote *(f)*
	Verkaufsquote *(f)*
quoted company	börsennotiertes Unternehmen *(n)*
quotient	Quotient *(m)*

R

R & D (research and development)	FE, F & E (Forschung (f) und Entwicklung (f))
raid a company (to)	*Aktien (fpl) einer Unternehmung (f) gezielt und überfallartig aufkaufen*
raider: corporate ...	Corporate Raider (m)
	Raider (m)
raising: capital ...	Kapitalaufnahme (f)
	Kapitalbeschaffung (f)
RAM (random-access memory)	Direktzugriffsspeicher (m)
	Schreiblesespeicher (m)
random access	wahlfreier Zugriff (m)
random-access memory (RAM)	Direktzugriffsspeicher (m)
	Schreiblesespeicher (m)
random observation method	Methode (f) der Arbeitsstichproben (fpl)
random sampling	zufallsgesteuerte Stichprobenauswahl (f)
range: price ...	Preisskala (f)
	Preisspanne (f)
range: product ...	Produktpalette (f)
	Sortiment (n)
ranking	Rangeinteilung (f)
	Rangfolge (f)
	Rangordnung (f)
rat race	ständiger Konkurrenzkampf (m)
	Pöstchenjägerei (f)
rate of return	Rendite (f)
	Verzinsung (f)
rate of return: internal ... ... (IRR)	interner Zinsfuß (m)
rate: bank ...	Darlehenszinssatz (m)
	Diskontsatz (m)
rate: base ...	Eckzins (m) für Ausleihungen (fpl)
rate: forward ...	Devisenterminkurs (m)
rate: going ...	Marktkurs (m)
	Marktpreis (m)
	üblicher Satz (m)
rating: credit ...	Beurteilung (f) der Kreditwürdigkeit (f)
	Bonitätsbeurteilung (f)

rating: market ...	Marktbewertung *(f)*
	Markteinschätzung *(f)*
	Marktstellung *(f)*
rating: merit ...	Leistungsbeurteilung *(f)*
	Personalbeurteilung *(f)*
rating: performance ...	Leistungsbeurteilung *(f)*
rating: personnel ...	Personalbeurteilung *(f)*
rating: points-... method	Punktbewertung *(f)*
	Punktsystem *(n)*
ratio: accounting ...	Betriebskennziffer *(f)*
ratio: administration- production ...	Verhältnis *(n)* von Verwaltung *(f)* zu Produktion *(f)*
ratio: capital-output ...	Kapitalkoeffizient *(m)*
ratio: cash ...	Barliquidität *(f)*
	Kassenliquidität *(f)*
ratio: cover ...	Deckungsverhältnis *(n)*
ratio: current ...	Liquiditätsgrad *(m)*
	Liquiditätskennzahl *(f)*
ratio: debt ...	Verschuldungsgrad *(m)*
	Verschuldungskoeffizient *(m)*
ratio: debt-equity ...	Verhältnis *(n)* von Fremd- zu Eigenkapital *(n)*
	Verschuldungsgrad *(m)*
	Verschuldungskoeffizient *(m)*
ratio: financial ...	finanzielle Kennzahl *(f)*
	Finanzierungskennzahl *(f)*
ratio: gearing ...	Verhältnis *(n)* zwischen Fremd- und Eigenkapital *(n)*
ratio: liquidity ...	Liquiditätsgrad *(m)*
	Liquiditätskennziffer *(f)*
ratio: management ...	betriebswirtschaftliche Kennzahl *(f)*
ratio: price-earnings ... (P/E)	Kurs-Gewinn-Verhältnis *(n)*
ratio: profit-volume ... (P/V)	Umsatzrentabilität *(f)*
rationale	Begründung *(f)*
	Gedankengänge *(mpl)*
	Gründe *(mpl)*
rationalization	Rationalisierung *(f)*
rationalize (to)	rationalisieren
rationing: capital ...	Kapitalrationierung *(f)*
re-image (to)	ein neues Image *(n)* aufbauen

reach a deal (to)	ein Geschäft *(n)* machen
	ein Geschäft *(n)* abschließen
	einen Deal *(m)* machen
reactive	reaktiv
reactive strategy	reaktive Strategie *(f)*
read-only memory (ROM)	Fest(wert)speicher *(m)*
	Nurlesespeicher *(m)*
real income	Realeinkommen *(n)*
	Reallohn *(m)*
real time	Echtzeit *(f)*
	Realzeit *(f)*
realize (to) (*profit*)	(Gewinne *(mpl)*) realisieren
recognition: brand …	Markenwiedererkennung *(f)*
recognition: mutual …	gegenseitige Anerkennung *(f)*
reconfiguration	Rekonfiguration *(f)*
reconstruction: company …	Sanierung *(f)* eines Unternehmens *(n)*
	Umstrukturierung *(f)* einer Unternehmung *(f)*
record: track …	Leistungsnachweise *(mpl)*
	was man vorzuweisen hat
	zurückliegende Unternehmensergebnisse *(npl)*
recovery of expenses	Spesenerstattung *(f)*
recovery: overhead …	Aufteilungsverfahren *(n)* für Gemeinkosten
	(pl)
recruit (to)	anstellen
	anwerben
	rekrutieren
recruitment	Anwerbung *(f)* von Arbeitskräften *(fpl)*
	Einstellung *(f)* von Arbeitskräften *(fpl)*
recycle (to)	wiederverwerten
	recyceln
recycling	Recycling *(n)*
	Wiederverwertung *(f)*
redeploy (to)	anderweitig einsetzen
	umgruppieren
redeployment	Umgruppierung *(f)* der Arbeitskräfte *(fpl)*
reduction: cost …	Kostensenkung *(f)*
	Rationalisierung *(f)*
reduction: variety …	Beschränkung *(f)* des Produktsortiments *(n)*
	Standardisierung *(f)*

redundancy	Entlassung *(f)*
refocusing	Neuorientierung *(f)*
registered trademark	eingetragenes Warenzeichen *(n)*
regression analysis	Regressionsanalyse *(f)*
regression analysis: multiple ...	Mehrfach-Regressionsanalyse *(f)*
... (MRA)	
regulate (to)	regeln
	regulieren
regulation	Regelung *(f)*
	Regulierung *(f)*
	Vorschrift *(f)*
reinvent the wheel (to)	das schon Erfundene *(n)* erfinden
relations: business ...	Geschäftsbeziehungen *(fpl)*
relations: employee ...	Beziehungen *(fpl)* zu Arbeitnehmern *(mpl)*
relations: external ...	Außenbeziehungen *(fpl)*
relations: functional ...	funktionale Beziehungen *(fpl)*
relations: human ...	innerbetriebliche
	Mitarbeiterbeziehungen *(fpl)*
	zwischenmenschliche Beziehungen *(fpl)*
relations: industrial ...	Arbeitgeber-Arbeitnehmer-Beziehungen *(fpl)*
relations: labour ...	Arbeitgeber-Arbeitnehmer-Beziehungen *(fpl)*
relations: line ...	instanzielle Rang- und Weisungsbeziehungen
	(fpl)
relations: public ... (PR)	Öffentlichkeitsarbeit *(f)*
	Public Relations *(pl)* (PR)
reliability	Verläßlichkeit *(f)*
	Vertrauenswürdigkeit *(f)*
	Zuverlässigkeit *(f)*
reliability: product ...	Produktzuverlässigkeit *(f)*
relief: tax ...	Steuervergünstigung *(f)*
remittance policy	Überweisungspolitik *(f)*
remuneration	Vergütung *(f)*
remuneration: executive ...	Vergütung *(f)* der Führungskräfte *(fpl)*
reorganization	Reorganisation *(f)*
replacement costs	Wiederbeschaffungskosten *(pl)*
	Wiederbeschaffungswert *(m)*
representation: analog(ue) ...	Analogdarstellung *(f)*
representation: joint ...	gemeinsame Vertretung *(f)*
representation: worker ...	Vertretung *(f)* der Arbeitnehmer *(mpl)*

representative: trade union ...	Vertrauensfrau *(f)*
	Vertrauensmann *(m)*
requirements: job ...	Stellenanforderungen *(fpl)*
rerun (to)	wiederholen
resale price maintenance (RPM)	Preisbindung *(f)* der zweiten Hand *(f)*
research and development	Forschung *(f)* und Entwicklung *(f)*
(R & D)	(FE, F & E)
research department	Forschungsabteilung *(f)*
research: advertising ...	Werbeforschung *(f)*
research: blue-sky ...	zweckfreie Forschung *(f)*
research: consumer ...	Verbraucherforschung *(f)*
research: desk ...	Schreibtischforschung *(f)*
research: economic ...	Wirtschaftsforschung *(f)*
research: field ...	Feldforschung *(f)*
	Primärforschung *(f)*
research: market ...	Marktforschung *(f)*
research: marketing ...	Marketing-Forschung *(f)*
research: motivational ...	Motivationsforschung *(f)*
research: operations ... (OR)	Operationsforschung *(f)*
	Operations Research *(n)* (OR)
	Unternehmensforschung *(f)*
research: operational ... (OR)	Operationsforschung *(f)*
	Operations Research *(n)* (OR)
	Unternehmensforschung *(f)*
research: product ...	Produktforschung *(f)*
reserve: contingency ...	Reserve *(f)* für unvorhergesehene Ausgaben *(fpl)*
	Rückstellung *(f)* für Eventualverbindlichkeiten *(fpl)*
resistance: consumer ...	Käuferwiderstand *(m)*
	Verbraucherzurückhaltung *(f)*
resource allocation	Bereitstellung *(f)* von Ressourcen *(fpl)*
	Planung *(f)* und Bereitstellung *(f)* von Produktionsmitteln *(npl)*
resource appraisal	Bewertung *(f)* von Ressourcen *(fpl)*
resource management	Betriebsmittelverwaltung *(f)*
	Ressourcenmanagement *(n)*
resourcing: manpower ...	Personalbeschaffung *(f)*
resourcing: staff ...	Personalbeschaffungsplanung *(f)*

response: anticipatory ...	Vorwegnahme *(f)*
response: lag ...	verspätete Reaktion *(f)*
responsibilities: allocation of ...	Zuweisung *(f)* von Aufgabengebieten *(npl)*
	Zuweisung *(f)* von Zuständigkeitsbereichen *(mpl)*
responsibility accounting	Verantwortungsrechnung *(f)*
responsibility centre	betriebliches Verantwortungszentrum *(n)*
responsibility: functional ...	funktionale Verantwortlichkeit *(f)*
responsibility: linear ...	lineare Verantwortung *(f)*
responsive: consumer-...	konsumentennah
	kundennah
restriction: trade ...	Handelsbeschränkung *(f)*
	Handelshemmnis *(n)*
restrictive practices (*industrial*)	restriktive Arbeitspraktiken *(fpl)*
restrictive practices (*legal*)	Wettbewerbsbeschränkungen *(fpl)*
	restriktive Geschäftspraktiken *(fpl)*
restructure (to)	umstrukturieren
restructuring	Umstrukturierung *(f)*
results: payment by ...	Akkordlohnsysten *(n)*
retail price index (RPI)	Einzelhandelspreisindex *(m)*
retained profits	einbehaltene Gewinne *(mpl)*
retire (to)	in den Ruhestand *(m)* treten
	sich pensionieren lassen
retirement	Pensionierung *(f)*
	Versetzung *(f)* in den Ruhestand *(m)*
retirement: early ...	vorzeitige Pensionierung *(f)*
retraining	Umschulung *(f)*
retrieval: data ...	Datenwiedergewinnung *(f)*
retrieval: information ...	Informationsrückgewinnung *(f)*
	Informationswiedergewinnung *(f)*
return	Ertrag *(m)*
	Gewinn *(m)*
	Rendite *(f)*
	Verzinsung *(f)*
return on assets	Anlagenrendite *(f)*
	Verzinsung *(f)* der Aktiva *(pl)*
return on capital	Kapitalrendite *(f)*
return on capital employed (ROCE)	Rendite *(f)* des eingesetzten Kapitals *(n)*

return on equity (ROE)	Eigenkapitalrendite *(f)*
	Eigenkapitalrentabilität *(f)*
return on investment (ROI)	Anlagenrentabilität *(f)*
	Rentabilität *(f)* des Kapitaleinsatzes *(m)*
return on sales	Umsatzrendite *(f)*
	Umsatzrentabilität *(f)*
return: fair ...	angemessener Gewinn *(m)*
	angemessene Rendite *(f)*
return: internal rate of ... (IRR)	interner Zinsfuß *(m)*
return: rate of ...	Rendite *(f)*
	Verzinsung *(f)*
revaluation of assets	Neubewertung *(f)* von Vermögenswerten *(mpl)*
revenue: average ...	Durchschnittseinkünfte *(fpl)*
	Durchschnittseinnahmen *(fpl)*
review (to)	prüfen
	überprüfen
review: financial ...	Finanzüberprüfung *(f)*
	Überprüfung *(f)* der Finanzlage *(f)*
review: performance ...	Beurteilungsgespräch *(n)*
	Leistungsbeurteilung *(f)*
review: salary ...	Gehaltsübersicht *(f)*
revolving credit	revolvierender Kredit *(m)*
	Revolvingkredit *(m)*
rich: cash-...	flüssig
	liquid
rights issue	Bezugsrechtsemission *(f)*
risk analysis	Risikoanalyse *(f)*
risk assessment	Risikobewertung *(f)*
	Risikoeinschätzung *(f)*
risk capital	Risikokapital *(n)*
risk management	Risikomanagement *(n)*
risk profile	Risikoprofil *(n)*
risks: minimize ... (to)	Risiken *(npl)* minimieren
robot	Roboter *(m)*
robotics	Robotertechnik *(f)*
robotize (to)	Roboter *(mpl)* einsetzen
	automatisieren
robust	robust
	widerstandsfähig

ROCE (return on capital employed)	Rendite *(f)* des eingesetzten Kapitals *(n)*
ROE (return on equity)	Eigenkapitalrendite *(f)*
	Eigenkapitalrentabilität *(f)*
ROI (return on investment)	Anlagenrentabilität *(f)*
	Rentabilität *(f)* des Kapitaleinsatzes *(m)*
role-playing	Rollenspiel *(n)*
role set	*Rollenrepertoire (n) eines einzelnen (m)*
roll out (to)	herstellen
ROM (read-only memory)	Fest(wert)speicher *(m)*
	Nurlesespeicher *(f)*
rotation: job ...	Jobrotation *(f)*
	systematischer Stellenwechsel *(m)*
round figures: in	in runden Zahlen *(fpl)*
round off (to)	abrunden
route (to)	leiten
routine	Programm *(n)*
	Programmteil *(m)*
	Routine *(f)*
routine: diagnostic ...	Beseitigung *(f)* von Fehlerquellen *(fpl)*
routing	Festlegung *(f)* der Handelswege *(mpl)*
	Festlegung *(f)* der Route *(f)*
royalty	Tantieme *(f)*
RPI (retail price index)	Einzelhandelspreisindex *(m)*
RPM (resale price maintenance)	Preisbindung *(f)* der zweiten Hand *(f)*
running expenses	laufende Ausgaben *(fpl)*

S

safety management	Sicherheitsmanagement *(n)*
safety stock	eiserner Bestand *(m)*
	mündelsichere Wertpapiere *(npl)*
	Reservebestand *(m)*
safety: industrial ...	Arbeitssicherheit *(f)*
	Betriebssicherheit *(f)*
safety: margin of ...	Sicherheitsmarge *(f)*
salary grade	Gehaltsstufe *(f)*
salary progression curve	Gehaltsprogressionskurve *(f)*
salary review	Gehaltsübersicht *(f)*

salary structure	Gehaltsstruktur *(f)*
sale: impulse ...	Verkauf *(m)* von Impulswaren *(fpl)*
sale: point of ... (POS)	Verkaufsort *(m)*
sale: point-of-... advertising	POS-Werbung *(f)*
sales analysis	Absatzanalyse *(f)*
sales appeal	Verkaufsappeal *(m)*
sales area	Absatzgebiet *(n)*
	Verkaufsgebiet *(n)*
sales budget	Verkaufsbudget *(n)*
sales coverage	Abdeckung *(f)* durch den Verkauf *(m)*
	Marktabdeckung *(f)*
sales department	Verkaufsabteilung *(f)*
sales drive	Verkaufskampagne *(f)*
sales engineer	Verkaufsingenieur *(m)*
	technischer Kaufmann *(m)*
sales estimate	Absatzkalkulation *(f)*
	Absatzprognose *(f)*
sales expansion effort	Bemühungen *(fpl)* um Verkaufssteigerungen *(fpl)*
sales expectations	Absatzerwartungen *(fpl)*
	Verkaufserwartungen *(fpl)*
sales force	Außendienstmitarbeiter *(mpl)*
	Verkaufsaußendienst *(m)*
sales forecast	Absatzprognose *(f)*
	Verkaufsprognose *(f)*
sales goal	Absatzziel *(n)*
sales management	Verkaufsleitung *(f)*
	Verkaufsmanagement *(n)*
sales manager	Verkaufsleiter *(m)*
sales mix	Absatzprogramm *(n)*
sales planning	Absatzplanung *(f)*
sales policy	Absatzgrundsätze *(mpl)*
	Absatzpolitik *(f)*
	Verkaufspolitik *(f)*
sales potential	Absatzmöglichkeiten *(fpl)*
	Absatzpotential *(n)*
sales promotion	Verkaufsförderung *(f)*
sales quota	Absatzquote *(f)*
	Verkaufsquote *(f)*

sales slump	Absatzkrise *(f)*
sales talk	Verkaufsgespräch *(n)*
sales target	Absatzziel *(n)*
	Absatzsoll *(n)*
sales territory	Absatzgebiet *(n)*
	Verkaufsbezirk *(m)*
	Vertriebsgebiet *(n)*
sales test	*Durchführung (f) von Werbetests (mpl) in regionalen Absatzmärkten (mpl)*
sales turnover	Geschäftsumsatz *(m)*
	Warenumsatz *(m)*
sales volume	Absatzvolumen *(n)*
	Umsatzvolumen *(n)*
sales: return on ...	Umsatzrendite *(f)*
	Umsatzrentabilität *(f)*
sampling: activity ...	Arbeitsstichproben *(fpl)*
sampling: random ...	zufallsgesteuerte Stichprobenauswahl *(f)*
sampling: statistical ...	Markt- und Meinungsforschung *(f)*
satisfaction: consumer ...	Verbraucherzufriedenheit *(f)*
satisfaction: job ...	Arbeitszufriedenheit *(f)*
	Zufriedenheit *(f)* am Arbeitsplatz *(m)*
saturation: market ...	Marktsättigung *(f)*
scab	Streikbrecher *(m)*
scale: diseconomy of ...	Größennachteil *(m)*
	Kostenprogression *(f)*
scale: economy of ...	Größenvorteil *(m)*
	Kostendegression *(f)*
scale: sliding ...	gleitende Skala *(f)*
scan: environmental ...	Environmental Scanning *(n)*
scanning	Bildabtastung *(f)*
	Scanning *(n)*
scatter diagram	Punktediagramm *(n)*
	Streubild *(n)*
	Streudiagramm *(n)*
scenario	Szenario *(n)*
scenario: best-case ...	Best-Case-Szenario *(n)*
	optimistischstes Szenario *(n)*

scenario: worst-case ...	pessimistischstes Szenario *(n)*
	Worst-Case-Szenario *(n)*
schedule (to)	ansetzen
	festlegen
	planen
	vorsehen
schedule	Plan *(m)*
schedule: production ...	Produktionsplan *(m)*
schedule: work ...	Zeitplan *(m)*
scheduling	Arbeitsvorbereitung *(f)*
	Termin- und Kapazitätsplanung *(f)*
scheduling: production ...	Arbeitsvorbereitung *(f)*
	Produktionsplanung *(f)*
scheme: bonus ...	Prämienlohnsystem *(n)*
	Prämienregelungsplan *(m)*
scheme: incentive ...	leistungsbezogenes Lohnsystem *(n)*
scheme: suggestion ...	betriebliches Vorschlagswesen *(n)*
science: behavioural ...	Verhaltensforschung *(f)*
science: management ...	Management-Lehre *(f)*
scientific management	wissenschaftliche Unternehmensführung *(f)*
	wissenschaftliches Management *(n)*
scientific progamming	wissenschaftliche Programmierung *(f)*
screen (to)	sieben
	überprüfen
search: executive ...	Suche *(f)* nach Führungskräften *(fpl)*
second guess (to)	hinterher kritisieren
	vorausahnen
	vorhersagen
	zuvorkommen
securities	Wertpapiere *(npl)*
securitization	Substitution *(f)* von Bankkrediten *(mpl)* durch handelbare Wertpapiere *(npl)*
	wertpapiermäßige Unterlegung *(f)* von Kreditforderungen *(fpl)*
securitize (to)	Kreditforderungen *(fpl)* wertpapiermäßig unterlegen
	verbriefen
security leak	Sicherheitslücke *(f)*
security: collateral ...	dingliche Sicherheit *(f)*

security: gilt-edged ...	erstklassige Wertpapiere *(npl)*
security: industrial ...	Betriebssicherheit *(f)*
security: job ...	Arbeitsplatzsicherheit *(f)*
security: unlisted ...	Freiverkehrswerte *(mpl)*
seed money	Finanzierung *(f)* von Produktideen *(fpl)*
	Kapital *(n)* für eine Unternehmensneugründung *(f)*
	Wagniskapital *(n)*
seeking: goal-...	Zielfindung *(f)*
segment (to)	heruntersegmentieren
	segmentieren
segment: market ...	Marktsegment *(n)*
segmentation	Marktsegmentierung *(f)*
	Segmentierung *(f)*
segmentation: market ...	Marktsegmentierung *(f)*
selection: media ...	Medienauswahl *(f)*
	Medienselektion *(f)*
	Medienwahl *(f)*
selection: portfolio ...	Portfolio-Auswahl *(f)*
self-actualization	Eigendynamik *(f)*
self-appraisal	Selbsteinschätzung *(f)*
self-liquidating	sich selbst abdeckend
self-motivation	Selbstmotivierung *(f)*
sell out (to)	ausverkaufen
	das Lager *(n)* räumen
	verkaufen
sell-by date	letztes Verkaufsdatum *(n)*
sell: hard ...	aggressive Verkaufsmethoden *(fpl)*
	aggressive Verkaufstaktik *(f)*
	Hardsell *(m)*
sell: soft ...	Softsell *(m)*
	weiche Verkaufstaktik *(f)*
	zwanglose Warenwerbung *(f)*
sellers' market	Verkäufermarkt *(m)*
selling policy	Verkaufspolitik *(f)*
selling: direct ...	Direktverkauf *(m)*
selling: switch ...	Köderwerbung *(f)*
	Lockmittelwerbung *(f)*

semiconductor	Halbleiter *(m)*
semi-skilled labour	angelernte Arbeiter *(mpl)*
semi-variable costs	sprungfixe Kosten *(pl)*
	Sprungkosten *(pl)*
sensitive: cost-...	kostenempfindlich
sensitive: market-...	marktempfindlich
sensitivity analysis	Sensitivitätsanalyse *(f)*
sensitivity training	Sensitivitätstraining *(n)*
sensitize (to)	empfindlich machen
	sensibilisieren
sequential analysis	Sequenzanalyse *(f)*
	Verlaufsanalyse *(f)*
series: time ...	Zeitreihe *(f)*
service: after-sales ...	Kundenbetreuung *(f)*
	Kundendienst *(m)*
service: customer ...	Kundendienst *(m)*
services: advisory ...	Beratungsdienste *(mpl)*
services: computer ...	Computer-Dienste *(mpl)*
services: computer ... bureau	Computer-Dienststelle *(f)*
services: extension ...	Fortbildungsangebote *(npl)*
services: management ...	Management-Dienste *(mpl)*
set-up costs	Gründungskosten *(pl)*
	Rüstkosten *(pl)*
severance pay	Entlassungsabfindung *(f)*
sexual harassment	sexuelle Belästigung *(f)*
share capital	Aktienkapital *(n)*
share of production plan	Produktionsanteilsplan *(m)*
share price performance	Richtung *(f)* des Kursniveaus *(n)*
share: earnings per ... (EPS)	Gewinn *(m)* je Aktie *(f)*
share: golden ...	*Kapitalanteil (m) mit besonderen Vorrechten (npl)*
share: market ...	Marktanteil *(m)*
shareholding	Aktienbesitz *(m)*
sharing: job-...	Job-Sharing *(n)*
sharing: profit-...	Erfolgsbeteiligung *(f)*
	Ergebnisbeteiligung *(f)*
	Gewinnbeteiligung *(f)*
sharing: time-...	Time-Sharing *(n)*
shelf-life	Haltbarkeit *(f)*

shift: day ...	Tagschicht *(f)*
shift: night ...	Nachtschicht *(f)*
shiftwork	Schichtarbeit *(f)*
shipping	Spedition *(f)*
shop floor	Produktionsstätte *(f)*
	Werkstatt *(f)*
shop steward	gewerkschaftliche Vertrauensfrau *(f)*
	gewerkschaftlicher Vertrauensmann *(m)*
shop: closed ...	gewerkschaftspflichtiger Betrieb *(m)*
shop: open ...	nicht gewerkschaftspflichtiger Betrieb *(m)*
short-range planning	kurzfristige Planung *(f)*
short-term planning	kurzfristige Planung *(f)*
shortfall	Defizit *(n)*
	Fehlbetrag *(m)*
shortlist (to)	in die engere Wahl *(f)* ziehen
shortlist	Auswahlliste *(f)*
	engere Kandidatenliste *(f)*
shut-down	Stillegung *(f)*
significant	bedeutend
	bedeutungsvoll
	wichtig
simplex method	Simplex-Methode *(f)*
simplification: job ...	Stellenvereinfachung *(f)*
simplification: work ...	Arbeitsvereinfachung *(f)*
simulate (to)	simulieren
simulation	Simulation *(f)*
simulation: computer ...	Computer-Simulation *(f)*
single currency	einheitliche Währung *(f)*
single market	Binnenmarkt *(m)*
single market (*of the EC*)	europäischer Binnenmarkt *(m)*
single sourcing	eingleisige Beschaffung *(f)*
sinking fund	Amortisationsfonds *(m)*
	Tilgungsfonds *(m)*
sit-down strike	Sitzstreik *(m)*
skilled labour	Facharbeiter *(mpl)*
	gelernte Arbeiter *(mpl)*
skills analysis	Analyse *(f)* der Fähigkeiten *(fpl)*
	Fähigkeitsanalyse *(f)*

slack	Flaute *(f)*
	Konjunkturflaute *(f)*
sliding scale	gleitende Skala *(f)*
slim down (to)	schrumpfen
slot	Speicherplatz *(m)*
	Steckplatz *(m)*
slump	Konjunkturrückgang *(m)*
	Rezession *(f)*
slump: sales ...	Absatzkrise *(f)*
slush fund	Schmiergeldfonds *(m)*
smart card	Chipkarte *(f)*
social analysis	Sozialdiagnose *(f)*
socio-cultural	soziokulturell
socio-economic	sozioökonomisch
sociometric	soziometrisch
soft landing	*Aufschwungsphase (f) nach einer Periode (f) restriktiver Wirtschaftspolitik (f)*
soft sell	Softsell *(m)*
	weiche Verkaufstaktik *(f)*
	zwanglose Warenwerbung *(f)*
software	Software *(f)*
software application	Softwareanwendung *(f)*
	Softwareanwendungsmöglichkeit *(f)*
software broker	Zwischenhändler *(m)* für Software-Vertrieb *(m)*
sofware company	Softwarefirma *(f)*
software engineer	Software-Engineer *(m)*
software package	Softwarepaket *(n)*
sole agent	Alleinvertreter *(m)*
	Exklusivvertreter *(m)*
solving: problem ...	Problemlösung *(f)*
source and disposition of funds	Mittelherkunft *(f)* und -einsatz *(m)*
sourcing	Beschaffung *(f)*
	Einkaufsmanagement *(n)*
	Sourcing *(n)*
sourcing: dual ...	zweigleisige Beschaffung *(f)*
sourcing: single ...	eingleisige Beschaffung *(f)*
span of control	Kontrollspanne *(f)*
	Leitungsspanne *(f)*

span: time ... of discretion	zulässige Zeitspanne (f) für unterdurchschnittliche Leistung (f)
spare capacity	freie Kapazität (f)
specification: job ...	Stellenanforderungsprofil (n)
	Stellenbeschreibung (f)
specification: personnel ...	Qualifikationsprofil (n)
spellcheck	Rechtschreibprüfung (f)
spill-over effect	*Auswirkung (f) der Werbung (f) auf Konkurrenzprodukte (npl)*
spin-off effect	Nebeneffekt (m)
spirit: entrepreneurial ...	Unternehmergeist (m)
sponsorship	Sponsoring (n)
	Sponsorschaft (f)
spot price	Kassapreis (m)
	Lokopreis (m)
spreadsheet	Matrixbilanz (f)
	Tabellenberechnungsprogramm (n)
	Verteilungsbogen (m)
squeeze: credit ...	Kreditdrosselung (f)
	Kreditrestriktion (f)
staff	Belegschaft (f)
	Mitarbeiter (mpl)
	Personal (n)
staff and line	Stab (m) und Linie (f)
staff appraisal	Personalbeurteilung (f)
staff assistant	Stabsassistent (m)
staff audit	Personalbestandsanalyse (f)
staff commitment	Personaleinsatz (m)
staff cut-back	Arbeitskräfteabbau (m)
staff forecasting	Personalprognose (f)
staff management	Personalleitung (f)
	Personalmanagement (n)
staff manager	Personalchef (m)
staff mobility	Mobilität (f) des Personals (n)
staff organization	Stabsorganisation (f)
staff planning	Personalplanung (f)
staff resourcing	Personalbeschaffungsplanung (f)
staff strategy	Personalpolitik (f)
staff transfer	Versetzung (f) der Mitarbeiter (mpl)

staff turnover	Fluktuation (f)
	Personalwechsel (m)
staff: line and ... organization	Stablinienorganisation (f)
staff: management ...	Führungspersonal (n)
staffing	Personaleinstellung (f)
	Stellenbesetzung (f)
stag	Aktienspekulant (m)
	Konzertzeichner (m)
stagflation	Stagflation (f)
stagger	Staffelung (f)
staggered holidays	gestaffelter Urlaub (m)
stake	Anteil (m)
stand-alone	alleinstehend
	betriebssystemunabhängig
	Einzel-
	Stand-alone-
stand-alone word processor	Einzeltextverarbeiter (m)
	Einzeltextverarbeitungseinrichtung (f)
	Einzelwortprozessor (m)
standard	Maßstab (m)
	Norm (f)
	Standard (m)
standard costing	Plankostenrechnung (f)
	Standardkostenrechnung (f)
standard costs	Sollkosten (pl)
	Standardkosten (pl)
standard deviation	Normalabweichung (f)
	Standardabweichung (f)
standard of living	Lebensstandard (m)
standard performance	Vorgabeleistung (f)
standard price	Einheitspreis (m)
	fester Verrechnungspreis (m)
	Standardpreis (m)
standard time	Normalzeit (f)
	Standardzeit (f)
standard: budget ...	Budgetnorm (f)
standard: cost ...	Kalkulationsnorm (f)
standard: financial ...	Finanznorm (f)
standard: performance ...	Leistungsmaßstab (m)

standard: production ...	Produktionsnorm *(f)*
standardization	Standardisierung *(f)*
standardize (to)	normen
	standardisieren
	vereinheitlichen
star product	Renner *(m)*
	Verkaufsschlager *(m)*
start-up	Unternehmensneugründung *(f)*
start-up costs	Anlaufkosten *(pl)*
	Gründungskosten *(pl)*
	Startkosten *(pl)*
state of the art	Stand *(m)* der Technik *(f)*
statement: financial ...	Bilanz *(f)*
statement: mission ...	Erklärung *(f)* der
	Unternehmensgrundsätze *(mpl)*
statement: vision ...	Erklärung *(f)* der strategischen
	Vision *(f)*
statistical control	statistische Kontrolle *(f)*
statistical sampling	Markt- und Meinungsforschung *(f)*
status report	Bericht *(m)* über den Stand *(m)* eines
	Projekt(e)s *(n)*
	Kreditauskunft *(f)*
stimulus: competitive ...	Wettbewerbsanreiz *(m)*
stock control	Lagerbestandskontrolle *(f)*
stock market	Aktienbörse *(f)*
	Aktienmarkt *(m)*
stock option	Aktienbezugsrecht *(n)*
	Aktienoption *(f)*
stock option plan	Aktienoptionsplan *(m)*
stock portfolio	Aktienbestand *(m)*
	Aktiendepot *(n)*
	Aktienportfolio *(n)*
stock turnover	Lagerumschlag *(m)*
stock valuation	Lagerbewertung *(f)*
stock: blue-chip ...	Aktienspitzenwerte *(mpl)*
	erstklassige Standardwerte *(mpl)*
	erstklassiges Wertpapier *(n)*
stock: buffer ...	Puffervorrat *(m)*
stock: gilt-edged ...	erstklassige Wertpapiere *(npl)*

stock: safety ...	eiserner Bestand *(m)*
	mündelsichere Wertpapiere *(npl)*
	Reservebestand *(m)*
stockbroker	Börsenmakler *(m)*
	Broker *(m)*
	Effektenmakler *(m)*
stockbroking	Effektengeschäft *(n)*
stocktaking	Lageraufnahme *(f)*
	Lagerbestandsaufnahme *(f)*
stocktaking: continuous ...	fortlaufende Inventur *(f)*
	fortlaufende Warenbestandsaufnahme *(f)*
storage	Lagerung *(f)*
	Speicherung *(f)*
storage: computer ...	Datenspeicherung *(f)*
strategic alliance	strategische Allianz *(f)*
strategic business unit	strategische Unternehmenseinheit *(f)*
strategic interdependence	strategische Wechselbeziehung *(f)*
strategic plan	strategischer Plan *(m)*
strategic planning	strategische Planung *(f)*
strategy formulation	Formulierung *(f)* der Unternehmensstrategie *(f)*
strategy implementation	Durchführung *(f)* der Strategie *(f)*
strategy: brand ...	Markenstrategie *(f)*
strategy: business ...	Geschäftsstrategie *(f)*
strategy: competitive ...	Wettbewerbsstrategie *(f)*
strategy: corporate ...	Unternehmensstrategie *(f)*
strategy: defensive ...	defensive Strategie *(f)*
strategy: diversification ...	Diversifikationsstrategie *(f)*
strategy: executive manpower ...	Führungskräftestrategie *(f)*
strategy: expansion ...	Expansionsstrategie *(f)*
	Wachstumsstrategie *(f)*
strategy: financial ...	Finanzstrategie *(f)*
strategy: growth ...	Wachstumsstrategie *(f)*
strategy: marketing ...	Marketingstrategie *(f)*
strategy: negotiation ...	Verhandlungsstrategie *(f)*
strategy: pricing ...	Preisstrategie *(f)*
strategy: proactive ...	initiative Strategie *(f)*
strategy: product ...	Produktstrategie *(f)*
strategy: profit ...	Gewinnstrategie *(f)*

strategy: reactive ...	reaktive Strategie *(f)*
strategy: staff ...	Personalpolitik *(f)*
strategy: survival ...	Überlebensstrategie *(f)*
strategy: user ...	Benutzerstrategie *(f)*
	Verbraucherstrategie *(f)*
stream: business ...	Geschäftsgang *(m)*
	Geschäftsverkehr *(m)*
stream: on ...	in Betrieb *(m)*
streamline (to)	rationalisieren
strengths, weaknesses, opportunities and threats (SWOT) analysis	*strategische Analyse (f) der wichtigsten Erfolgsfaktoren (mpl)*
stress: work ...	Arbeitsstreß *(m)*
strike: official ...	offizieller Streik *(m)*
strike: sit-down ...	Sitzstreik *(m)*
strike: sympathy ...	Sympathiestreik *(m)*
strike: unofficial ...	inoffizieller Streik *(m)*
strike: wildcat ...	wilder Streik *(m)*
stripping: asset-...	Anlagenausschlachtung *(f)*
	Ausschlachtung *(f)* einer Unternehmung *(f)*
structure (to)	gestalten
	strukturieren
structure	Struktur *(f)*
structure : authority ...	Aufteilung *(f)* der Weisungsgewalt *(f)*
structure: capital ...	Kapitalstruktur *(f)*
structure: corporate ...	Unternehmensstruktur *(f)*
structure: cost ...	Kostenstruktur *(f)*
structure: grid ...	Gitterstruktur *(f)*
structure: managerial ...	Führungsstruktur *(f)*
structure: market ...	Marktstruktur *(f)*
structure: organization ...	Organisationsstruktur *(f)*
structure: price ...	Preisstruktur *(f)*
structure: salary ...	Gehaltsstruktur *(f)*
structure: wage ...	Lohnstruktur *(f)*
structured	strukturiert
structuring	Strukturierung *(f)*
structuring: work ...	Arbeitsgestaltung *(f)*
study: case ...	Fallstudie *(f)*
study: feasibility ...	Durchführbarkeitsstudie *(f)*

study: gap ...	Abweichungsanalyse *(f)*
study: market ...	Marktstudie *(f)*
	Marktuntersuchung *(f)*
study: methods ...	Arbeitsmethodenuntersuchung *(f)*
	Bewegungsstudie *(f)*
study: motion ...	Bewegungsstudie *(f)*
study: plant layout ...	Untersuchung *(f)* der Betriebsanlagen *(fpl)*
study: time ...	Zeitstudie *(f)*
study: time and methods ...	Refa-Studie *(f)*
	Zeit- und Bewegungsstudie *(f)*
study: time and motion ...	Refa-Studie *(f)*
	Zeit- und Bewegungsstudie *(f)*
study: work ...	Arbeitsstudie *(f)*
style: house ...	Stil *(m)* des Hauses *(n)*
style: management ...	Führungsstil *(m)*
sub-optimization	Suboptimierung *(f)*
subcontract (to)	einen Unterauftrag *(m)* vergeben
	einen Zulieferungsauftrag *(m)* vergeben
subcontracting	Auswärtsvergabe *(f)*
subliminal advertising	unterschwellige Werbung *(f)*
subsidiarity	Subsidiarität *(f)*
subsidiary company	Tochtergesellschaft *(f)*
succession planning: management	Führungsnachfolgeplanung *(f)*
suggestion scheme	betriebliches Vorschlagswesen *(n)*
summary dismissal	fristlose Entlassung *(f)*
sunrise industry	junge Wachstumsindustrie *(f)*
sunset industry	absterbender Industriezweig *(m)*
supervise (to)	Aufsicht *(f)* führen
	beaufsichtigen
	überwachen
supervision	Aufsicht *(f)*
supervisor	Aufseher *(m)*
supervisory board	Aufsichtsrat *(m)*
supervisory management	Kontrollfunktionen *(fpl)* der Unternehmensleitung *(f)*
	Kontrollfunktionen *(fpl)* des Managements *(n)*
support activity	Stützung *(f)*
survey: attitude ...	Einstellungsuntersuchung *(f)*

survey: market ...	Marktbefragung (f)
	Marktumfrage (f)
survival strategy	Überlebensstrategie (f)
swap	Swap (m)
swap: forward ...	Termin-Swap (m)
switch selling	Köderwerbung (f)
	Lockmittelwerbung (f)
switch trading	Switch-Geschäft (n)
SWOT (strengths, weaknesses, opportunities and threats) analysis	*strategische Analyse (f) der wichtigsten Erfolgsfaktoren (mpl)*
sympathy strike	Sympathiestreik (m)
symposium	Symposion (n)
	Tagung (f)
syndicate	Konsortium (n)
	Syndikat (n)
synergism	Synergieeffekte (mpl)
	Synergismus (m)
synergy	Synergie (f)
	Zusammenwirken (n)
system	System (n)
system-managed company	nach System (n) geführtes Unternehmen (n)
system: business ...	Geschäftsbetrieb (m)
	Organisation (f) eines Unternehmens (n)
system: computerized information ... (COINS)	computerisiertes Informationssystem (n)
system: expert ...	Expertensystem (n)
system: information ...	Informationssystem (n)
system: integrated management ...	integriertes Management-System (n)
system: management ...	Management-System (n)
system: management information ... (MIS)	Management-Informationssystem (n)
system: planning, programming, budgeting ... (PPBS)	Planungs-, Programmierungs- (und) Budgetierungssystem (n)
system: predetermined motion time ... (PMTS)	System (n) vorbestimmter Zeiten (fpl)
system: wage ...	Lohnsystem (n)
systematize (to)	systematisieren

systems analysis	Systemanalyse *(f)*
systems and procedures	Systeme *(npl)* und Verfahren *(npl)*
systems approach	Systemverfahren *(n)*
	Systemvorgehen *(n)*
systems design	Systemgestaltung *(f)*
systems engineer	Systemingenieur *(m)*
systems engineering	Systemplanung *(f)*
systems management	System-Management *(n)*
	Systemverwaltung *(f)*
systems planning	Systemplanung *(f)*
systems theory	Systemtheorie *(f)*
systems: estimating ... costs	Systemkostenvoranschlag *(m)*

T

TA (transactional analysis)	Transaktionsanalyse *(f)*
table: input-output ...	Input-Output-Tabelle *(f)*
tactical plan	taktischer Plan *(m)*
tactical planning	taktische Planung *(f)*
tactics: competitive ...	Wettbewerbstaktik *(f)*
take-home pay	Nettogehalt *(n)*
	Nettolohn *(m)*
take-off	wirtschaftlicher Aufschwung *(m)*
take-over	Übernahme *(f)*
take-over bid (TOB)	Übernahmeangebot *(n)*
talk: sales ...	Verkaufsgespräch *(n)*
talks: pay ...	Lohnverhandlungen *(fpl)*
	Tarifverhandlungen *(fpl)*
tangible assets	materielle Vermögenswerte *(mpl)*
	Sachvermögen *(n)*
target (to)	Ziele *(npl)* identifizieren
	zielen auf
	zu erreichen bemüht sein
target	Ziel *(n)*
target market	Zielmarkt *(m)*
	Zielgruppe *(f)*
target-setting	Zielsetzung *(f)*
target: production ...	Produktionsziel *(n)*

target: profit ...	Gewinnziel (n)
targeting	Zielidentifizierung (f)
	Zielsetzung (f)
tariff barrier	Zollschranke (f)
tariff barrier: non-... ... (NTB)	Zollfreigrenze (f)
task force	Projektgruppe (f)
tax-deductible	steuerlich absetzbar
tax incentive	steuerlicher Anreiz (m)
tax relief	Steuervergünstigung (f)
tax: corporation ...	Körperschaftssteuer (f)
tax: income ...	Einkommensteuer (f)
tax: profits ...	Körperschaftssteuer (f)
tax: value added ... (VAT)	Mehrwertsteuer (f)
taxation relief: double	Steuernachlaß (m) aufgrund
	eines Doppelbesteuerungsabkommens (n)
teaching: computer-assisted ... (CAT)	computerunterstützter Unterricht (m)
team-building	Team-Bildung (f)
team leader	Gruppenleiter (m)
	Teamchef (m)
team player	teamfähiger Manager (m)
	Teammitglied (n)
	teamorientierter Manager (m)
tech: high-...	High-Tech-
	Hochtechnologie (f)
tech: low-...	Low-Tech-
technical manager	technischer Direktor (m)
technique: management ...	Managementtechnik (f)
	Führungstechnik (f)
technique: production ...	Fertigungsmethode (f)
	Herstellungsmethode (f)
	Produktionsmethode (f)
technique: programme evaluation and review ... (PERT)	Ereignis-Knokenplan (m)
	Programme Evaluation and Review Technique (f) (PERT)
technological forecasting	Prognose (f) der technologischen Entwicklung (f)
technology transfer	Technologietransfer (m)
technology: information ...	Informationstechnologie (f)

teleconference	Telekonferenz *(f)*
telemarketing	Telefonmarketing *(n)*
telematics	Telematik *(f)*
telesales	Telefonverkauf *(m)*
	Telefonwerbung *(f)*
teletext	Bildschirmtext *(m)* (Btx)
	Videotext *(m)*
tender (to)	anbieten
	ein Angebot *(n)* machen
	sich an einer Ausschreibung *(f)* beteiligen
tender	Angebot *(n)*
tendering: competitive ...	Mitabgabe *(f)* von Angeboten *(npl)*
terminal	Terminal *(n)*
terminal: computer ...	Datenendgerät *(n)*
	Terminal *(n)*
territory: sales ...	Absatzgebiet *(n)*
	Verkaufsbezirk *(m)*
	Vertriebsgebiet *(n)*
test marketing	Test-Marketing *(n)*
test run	Probelauf *(m)*
test: aptitude ...	Eignungsprüfung *(f)*
	Eignungstest *(m)*
test: market ...	Markttest *(m)*
testing: field ...	Feld-Tests *(mpl)*
	Überprüfung *(f)* im Feld *(n)*
testing: product ...	Produkterprobung *(f)*
	Produktprüfung *(f)*
testing: psychometric ...	psychometrische Messung *(f)*
	psychometrische Untersuchungsmethodik *(f)*
theme: advertising ...	Werbethema *(n)*
theory: administrative ...	Verwaltungstheorie *(f)*
theory: communications ...	Kommunikationstheorie *(f)*
theory: contingency ...	Kontingenztheorie *(f)*
theory: decision ...	Entscheidungstheorie *(f)*
theory: game ...	Spieltheorie *(f)*
theory: information ...	Informationstheorie *(f)*
theory: management ...	Management-Theorie *(f)*
theory: organization ...	Organisationstheorie *(f)*
theory: probability ...	Wahrscheinlichkeitstheorie *(f)*

theory: queuing ...	Warteschlangentheorie *(f)*
theory: systems ...	Systemtheorie *(f)*
think-tank	Think Tank *(m)*
think the unthinkable (to)	sich Unvorstellbares *(n)* vorstellen
	Undenkbares *(n)* denken
thinking: creative ...	kreatives Denken *(n)*
thinking: lateral ...	laterales Denken *(n)*
third party	dritte Person *(f)*
	Dritter *(m)*
throughput	Datendurchlauf *(m)*
	Durchsatz *(m)*
thrust: competitive ...	Wettbewerbsvorstoß *(m)*
time and methods study	Refa-Studie *(f)*
	Zeit- und Bewegungsstudie *(f)*
time and motion study	Refa-Studie *(f)*
	Zeit- und Bewegungsstudie *(f)*
time frame	Zeitraum *(m)*
	Zeitspanne *(f)*
time-lag	Zeitverzögerung *(f)*
time management	Zeitmanagement *(n)*
time series	Zeitreihe *(f)*
time-sharing	Time-Sharing *(n)*
time sheet	Arbeitsblatt *(m)*
	Arbeitszettel *(m)*
	Stundenzettel *(m)*
time span of discretion	zulässige Zeitspanne *(f)* für
	unterdurchschnittliche Leistung *(f)*
time study	Zeitstudie *(f)*
time: down ...	Ausfallzeit *(f)*
time: lead ...	Beschaffungszeit *(f)*
	Lieferzeit *(f)*
	Vorlaufzeit *(f)*
time: predetermined motion ...	System *(n)* vorbestimmter Zeiten *(fpl)*
system (PMTS)	
time: real ...	Echtzeit *(f)*
	Realzeit *(f)*
time: standard ...	Normalzeit *(f)*
	Standardzeit *(f)*
time: turnaround ...	Turnaround-Zeit *(f)*

title: job ...	Stellenbezeichnung *(f)*
	Berufsbezeichnung *(f)*
TOB (take-over bid)	Übernahmeangebot *(n)*
toolbox	Dienstprogramm *(n)*
	Hilfsprogramm *(n)*
top management	Spitzenmanagement *(n)*
	Top-Management *(n)*
top management approach	Verfahrensweise *(n)* des Top-Managements *(n)*
top up (to)	auffüllen
	ergänzen
top-down	Top-down-
total plant maintenance	umfassende Betriebsinstandhaltung *(f)*
total quality control (TQC)	umfassende Qualitätskontrolle *(f)*
total quality management (TQM)	Total Quality Management *(n)*
TQC (total quality control)	umfassende Qualitätskontrolle *(f)*
TQM (total quality management)	TQM (Total Quality Management *(n)*)
track record	Leistungsnachweise *(mpl)*
	was man vorzuweisen hat
	zurückliegende Unternehmensergebnisse *(npl)*
trade association	Berufsverband *(m)*
trade cycle	Konjunkturzyklus *(m)*
trade imbalance	Handelsungleichgewicht *(n)*
trade name	Firmenname *(m)*
	Firmenbezeichnung *(f)*
	Handelsname *(m)*
trade off (to)	eine Sache *(f)* gegen eine andere austauschen
trade-off	Tauschgeschäft *(n)*
trade restriction	Handelsbeschränkung *(f)*
	Handelshemmnis *(n)*
trade union	Gewerkschaft *(f)*
trade union representative	Vertrauensfrau *(f)*
	Vertrauensmann *(m)*
trade: barter ...	Tauschhandel *(m)*
traded option	börsengehandelte Option *(f)*
trademark: registered ...	eingetragenes Warenzeichen *(n)*
trading area	Absatzgebiet *(n)*
	Einkaufsgebiet *(n)*

trading programme	Handelsprogramm *(n)*
trading: insider ...	Insiderhandel *(m)*
trading: patent ...	Patenthandel *(m)*
trading: switch ...	Switch-Geschäft *(n)*
trainee turnover	Fluktuation *(f)* der Nachwuchskräfte *(fpl)*
training	Ausbildung *(f)*
	Schulung *(f)*
	Training *(n)*
training needs	Ausbildungsbedarf *(m)*
training needs analysis	Analyse *(f)* des Ausbildungsbedarfs *(m)*
training officer	Ausbildungsleiter *(m)*
training within industry (TWI)	innerbetriebliche Ausbildung *(f)*
training: analytical ...	analytische Ausbildung *(f)*
	Ausbildung *(f)* im analytischen Denken *(n)*
training: booster ...	zusätzliche Schulung *(f)*
	zusätzliches Training *(n)*
training: computer-based ... (CBT)	computerunterstützte Ausbildung *(f)*
	rechnergestützte Schulung *(f)*
training: executive ...	Ausbildung *(f)* von Führungskräften *(fpl)*
training: group ...	Gruppenausbildung *(f)*
	Gruppentraining *(n)*
training: hands-on ...	praktische Ausbildung *(f)*
training: in-plant ...	innerbetriebliche Schulung *(f)*
training: management ...	Ausbildung *(f)* der Führungskräfte *(fpl)*
	Manager-Ausbildung *(f)*
training: multimedia ...	multimediale Ausbildung *(f)*
training: off-the-job ...	außerbetriebliche Ausbildung *(f)*
training: on-the-job ...	innerbetriebliche Ausbildung *(f)*
training: part-analysis ...	Ausbildung *(f)* in Teilanalysen *(fpl)*
training: sensitivity ...	Sensitivitätstraining *(n)*
training: vocational ...	Berufsausbildung *(f)*
transactional	Transaktions-
transactional analysis (TA)	Transaktionsanalyse *(f)*
transfer pricing	Festlegung *(f)* der Verrechnungspreise *(mpl)*
transfer: technology ...	Technologietransfer *(m)*
transfer: staff ...	Versetzung *(f)* der Mitarbeiter *(mpl)*
transitional	Übergangs-
transportation	Transport *(m)*

tree: decision ...	Entscheidungsbaum *(m)*
tree: family ...	Stammbaum *(m)*
tree: pertinence ...	Zuständigkeitsbaum *(m)*
trend	Trend *(m)*
trend: economic ...	Konjunkturtrend *(m)*
	Konjunkturverlauf *(m)*
	Wirtschaftstendenzen *(fpl)*
trend: exponential ...	exponentieller Trend *(m)*
trend: market ...	Markttendenzen *(fpl)*
	Markttrend *(m)*
trickle-down theory	Theorie *(f)* des von oben nach unten durchsickernden Wohlstands *(m)*
troubleshooter	Krisenmanager *(m)*
	Troubleshooter *(m)*
troubleshooting	Fehlersuche und -behebung *(f)*
turf protection	*Wahrung (f) des eigenen Ressorts (n)*
turn around (to)	abfertigen
	fertigstellen
	rentabel machen
	sanieren
turnaround time	Turnaround-Zeit *(f)*
turnover	Umsatz *(m)*
	Umschlag *(m)*
turnover: asset ...	Verhältnis *(n)* von Umsatz *(m)* zu Anlagen *(fpl)*
turnover: inventory ...	Lagerumschlag *(m)*
turnover: sales ...	Geschäftsumsatz *(m)*
	Warenumsatz *(m)*
turnover: staff ...	Fluktuation *(f)*
	Personalwechsel *(m)*
turnover: stock ...	Lagerumschlag *(m)*
turnover: trainee ...	Fluktuation *(f)* der Nachwuchskräfte *(fpl)*
TWI (training within industry)	innerbetriebliche Ausbildung *(f)*

U

unbundle (to)	*eine mittels Junk Bonds (mpl) übernommene Unternehmung (f) ausschlachten*
unbundling	*Ausschlachtung (f) einer mittels Junk Bonds (mpl) übernommenen Unternehmung (f)*
under licence	in Lizenz *(f)*
undercapacity	unzureichende Kapazität *(f)*
undercapitalized	unterkapitalisiert
undercut (to)	unterbieten
undermanned	unterbesetzt
undermanning	Unterbesetzung *(f)*
	zu kleine Belegschaft *(f)*
underperform (to)	hinter den Erwartungen *(fpl)* zurückbleiben
underprice (to)	zu billig anbieten
	unter Preis *(m)* anbieten
understaffed	personell unterbesetzt
understaffing	Personalknappheit *(f)*
	Personalmangel *(m)*
	personelle Unterbesetzung *(f)*
undistributed profit	einbehaltene Gewinne *(mpl)*
unfair competition	unlauterer Wettbewerb *(m)*
unfair dismissal	sozialwidrige Kündigung *(f)*
unique selling point/proposition (USP)	Alleinstellungsanspruch *(m)* einer Marke *(f)* oder eines Produkt(e)s *(n)*
unit labour costs	Lohnstückkosten *(pl)*
unlisted company	nicht börsennotierte Gesellschaft *(f)*
unlisted security	Freiverkehrswerte *(mpl)*
unofficial action	von einer Gewerkschaft *(f)* nicht genehmigter Streik *(m)*
	wilder Streik *(m)*
unofficial strike	inoffizieller Streik *(m)*
unscramble (to)	auseinanderklauben
	entschlüsseln
	entwirren
unskilled labour	ungelernte Arbeiter *(mpl)*
unstructured	nicht strukturiert
	unstrukturiert

up the line	auf höheren Führungsebenen *(fpl)*
update (to)	à jour halten
	aktualisieren
	auf den neuesten Stand *(m)* bringen
update	Aktualisierung *(f)*
	Fortschreibung *(f)*
	Updating *(n)*
up-market	anspruchsvoll
	hochwertig
upstream	gegen Bandlaufrichtung *(f)*
	gegenläufig
upswing	Aufschwung *(m)*
	Aufwärtstrend *(m)*
	konjunktureller Auftrieb *(m)*
uptime	verfügbare Betriebszeit *(f)*
	Verfügbarkeitsdauer *(f)*
upturn	Aufschwung *(m)*
	Aufwärtstrend *(m)*
	konjunktureller Auftrieb *(m)*
upwardly mobile	karrierebewußt
use-by date	*haltbar bis*
	Mindesthaltbarkeitsdatum *(n)*
user attitude	Verbrauchereinstellung *(f)*
user-friendly	benutzerfreundlich
user strategy	Benutzerstrategie *(f)*
	Verbraucherstrategie *(f)*
user-unfriendly	benutzerfeindlich
USP (unique selling point/	Alleinstellungsanspruch *(m)* einer Marke *(f)*
proposition)	oder eines Produkt(e)s *(n)*
utility: public ...	öffentlicher Versorgungsbetrieb *(m)*
utilization: capacity ...	Kapazitätsauslastung *(f)*

V

VA (value analysis)	Wertanalyse *(f)*
valuation: stock ...	Lagerbewertung *(f)*
value added	Mehrwert *(m)*
	Wertschöpfung *(f)*
value added tax (VAT)	Mehrwertsteuer *(f)*

value analysis (VA)	Wertanalyse *(f)*
value chain	Wertkette *(f)*
value concept	Wertkonzept *(n)*
value engineering	Konzept-Wertanalyse *(f)*
value proposal	ernstgemeinter Vorschlag *(m)*
	Kosten-Nutzen-Angebot *(n)*
value: asset ...	Substanzwert *(m)*
	Vermögenswert *(m)*
value: book ...	Buchwert *(m)*
value: break-up ...	Ausschlachtungswert *(m)*
	Liquidationswert *(m)*
value: market ...	Kurswert *(m)*
	Marktwert *(m)*
value: net present ... (NPV)	Barwert *(m)*
	Kapitalwert *(m)*
value: present ... method	Barwertsmethode *(f)*
	Methode *(f)* des Gegenwartswertes *(m)*
variable costs	variable Kosten *(pl)*
variable costs: semi-... ...	sprungfixe Kosten *(pl)*
	Sprungkosten *(pl)*
variable expenses	variable Kosten *(pl)*
	veränderliche Kosten *(pl)*
variance	Abweichung *(f)*
	Varianz *(f)*
variance analysis	Abweichungsanalyse *(f)*
variance: cost ...	Kostenabweichung *(f)*
variety reduction	Beschränkung *(f)* des Produktsortiments *(n)*
	Standardisierung *(f)*
VAT (value added tax)	Mehrwertsteuer *(f)*
VDU (visual display unit)	Anzeigeeinheit *(f)*
	Bildschirm *(m)*
	Bildschirmgerät *(n)*
	Bildsichtgerät *(n)*
venture capital	Risikokapital *(n)*
	Wagniskapital *(n)*
venture capitalist	Risikokapitalgeber *(m)*
	Wagniskapitalgeber *(m)*
venture management	risikobereite Unternehmensführung *(f)*
	risikobereite Unternehmensleitung *(f)*

venture: joint ...	Gemeinschaftsunternehmen *(n)*
	Joint Venture *(n)*
venture: joint-... company	an einem Joint Venture *(n)* beteiligte
	Gesellschaft *(f)*
	Gemeinschaftsfirma *(f)*
verbal communication	mündliche Kommunikation *(f)*
	verbale Kommunikation *(f)*
verbal communication:	nichtverbale Kommunikation *(f)*
non-... ...	
verify (to)	beglaubigen
	bestätigen
	(über)prüfen
vertical integration	vertikale Integration *(f)*
vested interest	finanzielle Beteiligung *(f)*
	persönliches Interesse *(n)*
viability	Lebensfähigkeit *(f)*
	Realisierbarkeit *(f)*
	Rentabilität *(f)*
viable	lebensfähig
	realisierbar
	rentabel
vice-chairman	stellvertretender Vorsitzender *(m)*
vice-president	Vizepräsident *(m)*
video	Video-
viewdata	Bildschirmtext *(m)* (Btx)
	Btx (Bildschirmtext *(m)*)
virus: computer ...	Computervirus *(n,m)*
vision	Vision *(f)*
	Weitblick *(m)*
vision statement	Erklärung *(f)* der strategischen Vision *(f)*
visual display unit (VDU)	Anzeigeeinheit *(f)*
	Bildschirm *(m)*
	Bildschirmgerät *(n)*
	Bildsichtgerät *(n)*
vocational guidance	Berufsberatung *(f)*
vocational training	Berufsausbildung *(f)*
volume	Volumen *(n)*
	Umsatz *(m)*
volume: cost-...-profit analysis	Kosten-/Umsatz-/Gewinnanalyse *(f)*

volume: profit-... ratio (P/V)	Umsatzrentabilität *(f)*
volume: sales ...	Absatzvolumen *(n)*
	Umsatzvolumen *(n)*

W

wage ceiling	Höchstlohn *(m)*
	Lohnhöchstgrenze *(f)*
wage differential	Lohngefälle *(n)*
wage drift	Lohnauftrieb *(m)*
	Lohndrift *(f)*
wage freeze	Lohnstopp *(m)*
wage level	Lohnhöhe *(f)*
	Lohnniveau *(n)*
wage policy	Lohnpolitik *(f)*
	Tarifpolitik *(f)*
wage structure	Lohnstruktur *(f)*
wage system	Lohnsystem *(n)*
wage: incentive ...	Leistungslohn *(m)*
wage: minimum ...	Mindestlohn *(m)*
walking around: management by	*interventionistische Betriebsführung (f)*
walkout	Streik *(m)*
WAN (wide area network)	Weitbereichsnetz *(n)*
warehousing	Lagerung *(f)*
	Lagerhaltung *(f)*
wastage: natural ...	Fluktuation *(f)*
waste: industrial ...	Industriemüll *(m)*
wasting assets	kurzlebige Vermögenswerte *(mpl)*
weighted average	gewogener Durchschnitt *(m)*
weighting	Gewichtung *(f)*
	Zulage *(f)*
well-packaged	gut gepackt
	gut verpackt
wheeling and dealing	Gemauschel *(n)*
	Geschäftemacherei *(f)*
	Machenschaften *(fpl)*
white-collar (worker)	Büroangestellter *(m)*
	Schreibtischarbeiter *(m)*

white goods	weiße Gebrauchsgüter *(npl)*
white knight	*raiderabwehrender Investor (m)*
whiz-kid	Senkrechtstarter *(m)*
wide area network (WAN)	Weitbereichsnetz *(n)*
wildcat strike	wilder Streik *(m)*
Winchester disk	Winchesterplatte *(f)*
wind down (to)	reduzieren
	zurückschrauben
wind up (to)	auflösen
	liquidieren
winding up	Abwicklung *(f)* eines Geschäfts *(n)*
	Auflösung *(f)* eines Geschäfts *(n)*
	Liquidation *(f)*
window	Fenster *(n)*
	Sichtfenster *(n)*
	Window *(n)*
window-dressing	Bilanzkosmetik *(f)*
	Mache *(f)*
	Schaufensterdekoration *(f)*
window of opportunity	günstige Gelegenheit *(f)*
	günstiger Augenblick *(m)*
word processing	Textverarbeitung *(f)*
word processor (WP)	Textverarbeiter *(m)*
	Textverarbeitungseinrichtung *(f)*
	Wortprozessor *(m)*
word processor: stand-alone	Einzeltextverarbeiter *(m)*
... ...	Einzeltextverarbeitungseinrichtung *(f)*
	Einzelwortprozessor *(m)*
work by contract	Arbeit *(f)* gemäß vertraglicher Vereinbarung *(f)*
work content	Arbeitsinhalt *(m)*
	Stelleninhalt *(m)*
work cycle	Arbeitszyklus *(m)*
work in progress	Halbfabrikate *(npl)*
	unfertige Leistungen *(fpl)*
	unfertige Produkte *(npl)*
workload	Arbeitsbelastung *(f)*
	Arbeitspensum *(n)*

work measurement	(Arbeits-)Zeitermittlung *(f)*
work schedule	Zeitplan *(m)*
work simplification	Arbeitsvereinfachung *(f)*
workstation	Workstation *(f)*
work stress	Arbeitsstreß *(m)*
work structuring	Arbeitsgestaltung *(f)*
work study	Arbeitsstudie *(f)*
work-to-rule	Bummelstreik *(m)*
	Dienst *(m)* nach Vorschrift *(f)*
work: clerical ... measurement (CWM)	Leistungsbeurteilung *(f)* der Büroangestellten *(f/mpl)*
	Leistungsbewertung *(f)* des Büropersonals *(n)*
worker buyout	Mitarbeiter-Buyout *(m,n)*
worker participation	Mitbestimmung *(f)*
worker representation	Vertretung *(f)* der Arbeitnehmer *(mpl)*
working capital	Betriebskapital *(n)*
working hours	Arbeitsstunden *(fpl)*
working hours: flexible	flexible Arbeitszeiten *(fpl)*
	gleitende Arbeitszeit *(f)*
working party	Arbeitsgruppe *(f)*
workplace	Arbeitsplatz *(m)*
	Arbeitsstätte *(f)*
	Arbeitsstelle *(f)*
works committee	Betriebsrat *(m)*
works council	Betriebsrat *(m)*
works manager	Betriebsleiter *(m)*
	Werksleiter *(m)*
world-class	Spitzen-
	Weltklasse *(f)*
worst-case scenario	pessimistischstes Szenario *(n)*
	Worst-Case-Szenario *(n)*
worth: net ...	Eigenkapital *(n)*
	Gesellschaftsvermögen *(n)*
WP (word processor)	Textverarbeiter *(m)*
	Textverarbeitungseinrichtung *(f)*
	Wortprozessor *(m)*
write off (to)	abschreiben

write-off	Abschreibung *(f)*
	als wertlos abzuschreibende Sache *(f)*
	kann man vergessen

Y

yardstick	Maßstab *(m)*
year: base ...	Vergleichsjahr *(n)*
year: financial ...	Geschäftsjahr *(n)*
	Rechnungsjahr *(n)*
year: fiscal ...	Geschäftsjahr *(n)*
	Rechnungsjahr *(n)*
yield	Ertrag *(m)*
	Rendite *(f)*
	Verzinsung *(f)*
yield: average ...	Durchschnittsertrag *(m)*
	Durchschnittsrendite *(f)*
yield: earnings ...	Gewinnrendite *(f)*
yuppie	Yuppie *(m)*

Z

Z chart	Z-Diagramm *(n)*
zero-base budget	Finanzplanung *(f)* von Anfang *(m)* Null *(f)*
zero defects	keine Defekte *(mpl)*
	Nullfehler-
zero-rating	ohne Mehrwertsteuer *(f)*
zero-sum game	*Spiel (n), bei dem sich Gewinne (mpl) und Verluste (mpl) ausgleichen*

DEUTSCH-ENGLISCH

A

abbauen: allmählich ...	phase out (to)
Abbildung	imaging
Abdeckung (f) durch den Verkauf (m)	sales coverage
Abdeckung (f): Markt...	sales coverage
abfertigen	process (to)
	turn around (to)
Abfertigung (f)	dispatching
Abfindungszahlung (f) an einen vorzeitig zum Ausscheiden (n) aus seinem Vertrag gezwungenen Spitzenmanager (m)	golden handshake
Abfindungszahlung (f): Garantie einer beträchtlichen ... im Falle (m) der Entlassung (f)	golden parachute
Abkommen (n): Produktivitäts...	productivity agreement
Ablauf (m): Prüfung (f)	management audit
der ...systeme (npl) einer Unternehmung	operations audit
Ablaufdiagramm (n)	flow chart
Ablaufstufen (fpl): Analyse (f) der kritischen ...	critical path analysis (CPA)
Abrechnungszeitraum (m)	accounting period
abrunden	round off (to)
Absatzanalyse (f)	sales analysis
Absatzerwartungen (fpl)	sales expectations
absatzfähig	marketable
Absatzförderungsmix (n)	promotional mix
Absatzgebiet (n)	sales area
	sales territory
	trading area
Absatzkalkulation (f)	sales estimate
Absatzkanal (m)	distribution channel
Absatzkrise (f)	sales slump
Absatzmöglichkeiten (fpl)	sales potential
Absatzplan (f)	market plan
Absatzplanung (f)	sales planning
Absatzpolitik (f)	sales policy

Absatzpotential *(n)*	market potential
	sales potential
Absatzprognose *(f)*	sales estimate
	sales forecast
Absatzprogramm *(n)*	sales mix
Absatzquote *(f)*	sales quota
Absatzsoll *(n)*	sales target
Absatzvolumen *(n)*	sales volume
Absatzweg *(m)*	distribution channel
Absatzziel *(n)*	sales goal
	sales target
abschätzen	appraise (to)
Abschätzung *(f)*	appraisal
abschließen: ein Geschäft *(n)* ...	reach a deal (to)
Abschluß *(m)*	profit performance
Abschluß *(m)*: **Konzern**...	consolidated accounts
	group accounts
Abschottung (f): interne ... von Abteilungen (fpl) eines Kreditinstitut(e)s (n)	Chinese wall
Abschreckungsmittel *(n)*	disincentive
abschreiben	write off (to)
abschreiben: Verluste *(mpl)* ...	cut one's losses (to)
Abschreibung *(f)*	capital allowance
	write-off
Abschreibungsbetrag *(m)*	depreciation allowance
Abschwung *(m)*	downswing
Abschwung (m): plötzlicher ... nach einer Periode (f) des Wirtschaftswachstums (n)	hard landing
absetzbar: steuerlich ...	tax-deductible
absetzen	market (to)
absichern	hedge (to)
absondern: Teile *(mpl)* ...	hive off (to)
absterbender Industriezweig *(m)*	sunset industry
Abteilung *(f)*: **Betriebs**...	operating division
Abteilung *(f)*: **Buchhaltungs**...	accounting department
	accounts department
Abteilung *(f)*: **Forschungs**...	research department
Abteilung *(f)*: **Personal**...	personnel department
Abteilung *(f)*: **Planungs**...	planning department

Abteilung *(f)*: technische … und Konstruktionsbüro *(n)*	engineering and design department
Abteilung *(f)*: Verkaufs…	sales department
Abteilungsleiter *(m)*	departmental head
	departmental manager
Abteilungsleitung *(f)*	departmental management
Abteilungsplan *(m)*	departmental plan
Abteilungsvorstand *(m)*	departmental head
Abwehr (f): Vorkehrung (f) zur … von Firmenübernahmen (fpl)	poison pill
Abweichung *(f)*	gap
	variance
Abweichung *(f)*: Etats …	budgetary variance
Abweichung *(f)*: Kosten…	cost variance
Abweichung *(f)*: Normal…	standard deviation
Abweichung *(f)*: Standard…	standard deviation
Abweichungsanalyse *(f)*	gap study
	variance analysis
abwickeln	liquidate (to)
Abwicklung *(f)* eines Geschäfts *(n)*	winding up
adaptive Kontrolle *(f)*	adaptive control
administratives Kontrollverfahren *(n)*	administrative control procedure
Agent *(m)*: Werbe…	advertising agent
aggressive Verkaufstaktik *(f)*	hard sell
aggressive Verkaufsmethoden *(fpl)*	hard sell
Akkord *(m)*: Gruppen…	group incentive
Akkordarbeit *(f)*	piecework
Akkordlohnsystem *(n)*	payment by results
Akquisition *(f)*	acquisition
Akquisitionsprofil *(n)*	acquisition profile
Aktie *(f)*: Gewinn *(m)* je …	earnings per share (EPS)
Aktienbesitz *(m)*	shareholding
Aktienbestand *(m)*	stock portfolio
Aktienbezugsrecht *(n)*	stock option
Aktienbörse *(f)*	stock market
Aktiendepot *(n)*	stock portfolio
Aktienkapital *(n)*	share capital
Aktienkapital *(n)*: Verwässerung *(f)* des …s	dilution of equity

Aktienmarkt *(m)*	equity market
	stockmarket
Aktienmehrheit *(f)*	controlling interest
Aktienoption *(f)*	stock option
Aktienoptionsplan *(m)*	stock option plan
Aktienportfolio *(n)*	stock portfolio
Aktienspekulant *(m)*	stag
Aktienspitzenwerte *(npl)*	blue-chip stock
Aktionsplan *(m)*	action plan
Aktiva *(pl)*	assets
Aktiva *(pl)*: leicht realisierbare ...	quick assets
Aktive *(pl)*: Verzinsung *(f)* der ...	return on assets
Aktiva- und Passivamanagement *(n)*	asset liability management
aktivieren	activate (to)
	assetize (to)
aktualisieren	update (to)
Aktualisierung *(f)*	update
Akzeptanz *(f)* durch die Verbraucher *(mpl)*	consumer acceptance
Akzeptanz *(f)*: Marken...	brand acceptance
al pari	at par
Algorithmus *(m)*	algorithm
alleinstehend	stand-alone
Alleinstellungsanspruch *(m)* einer Marke *(f)* oder eines Produkt(e)s *(n)*	unique selling point/ proposition (USP)
Alleinvertreter *(m)*	sole agent
alles offen lassend	open-ended
allgemeines Management *(n)*	general management
Allianz *(f)*: strategische ...	strategic alliance
allmählich abbauen	phase out (to)
allmählich einführen	phase in (to)
als Desktop-Veröffentlichung *(f)* herausbringen	desktop publish (to)
als wertlos abzuschreibende Sache *(f)*	write-off
Amortisation *(f)*	payback
Amortisationsdauer *(f)*	payback period
Amortisationsfonds *(m)*	sinking fund
an der Börse *(f)* zugelassen werden	go public (to)
an einem Joint Venture *(n)* beteiligte Gesellschaft *(f)*	joint-venture company
an Wert *(m)* gewinnen	appreciate (to)

an Wert *(m)* verlieren	depreciate (to)
Analogdarstellung *(f)*	analog(ue) representation
Analogrechner *(m)*	analog computer
Analyse *(f)* der Fähigkeiten *(fpl)*	skills analysis
Analyse *(f)* der Gewinnfaktoren *(mpl)*	profit-factor analysis
Analyse *(f)* der kritischen Ablaufstufen *(fpl)*	critical path analysis (CPA)
Analyse *(f)* des Ausbildungsbedarfs *(m)*	training needs analysis
Analyse *(f)* des Deckungsbeitrag(e)s *(m)*	contribution analysis
Analyse *(f)* des kritischen Pfades *(m)*	critical path analysis (CPA) network analysis
Analyse *(f)*: Absatz...	sales analysis
Analyse *(f)*: Abweichungs...	gap study variance analysis
Analyse *(f)*: Arbeits ...	operations analysis
Analyse *(f)*: Bedarfs...	needs analysis
Analyse *(f)*: Betriebs...	operations analysis
Analyse *(f)*: Break-Even-...	break-even analysis
Analyse *(f)*: Deckungspunkt...	break-even analysis
Analyse *(f)*: Entscheidungs...	decision analysis
Analyse *(f)*: Fähigkeits...	skills analysis
Analyse *(f)*: Finanz...	financial analysis
Analyse *(f)*: funktionale ...	functional analysis
Analyse *(f)*: Gewinnfaktor...	profit-factor analysis
Analyse *(f)*: Gewinnschwellen...	break-even analysis
Analyse *(f)*: Input-Output-...	input-output analysis
Analyse *(f)*: Investitions...	investment analysis
Analyse *(f)*: Konkurrenz...	competitor analysis
Analyse *(f)*: Konzept-Wert...	value engineering
Analyse *(f)*: Kosten-/Umsatz-/Gewinn...	cost, volume, profit analysis
Analyse *(f)*: Kosten-Nutzen-...	cost-benefit analysis (CBA)
Analyse *(f)*: Kosten...	cost analysis
Analyse *(f)*: Marginal...	marginal analysis
Analyse *(f)*: Media-...	media analysis
Analyse *(f)*: Medien...	media analysis
Analyse *(f)*: Mehrfach-Regressions...	multiple regression analysis (MRA)
Analyse *(f)*: morphologische ...	morphological analysis
Analyse *(f)*: Personalbestands...	manpower audit staff audit

Analyse (f): Problem...	problem analysis
Analyse (f): Produkt...	product analysis
Analyse (f): Produktivitäts...	efficiency audit
Analyse (f): Projekt...	project analysis
Analyse (f): quantitative ...	quantitative analysis
Analyse (f): Regressions...	regression analysis
Analyse (f): Rentabilitäts...	profitable analysis
Analyse (f): Risiko...	risk analysis
Analyse (f): Sensitivitäts...	sensitivity analysis
Analyse (f): Sequenz...	sequential analysis
Analyse (f): Stellen...	job analysis
Analyse (f): strategische ... der wichtigsten Erfolgsfaktoren (mpl)	SWOT (strengths, weaknesses opportunities, threats) analysis
Analyse (f): System...	system analysis
Analyse (f): Tiefen...	depth analysis
Analyse (f): Transaktions...	transactional analysis
Analyse (f): Umfeld...	environmental analysis
Analyse (f): Varianz...	variance analysis
Analyse (f): Verlaufs...	sequential analysis
Analyse (f): Wert...	value analysis (VA)
analysieren: Einsatzerfolg (m) ...	debrief (to)
analytisch: Ausbildung (f) im ...en Denken (n)	analytical training
analytische Ausbildung (f)	analytical training
analytische Buchführung (f)	analytic accounting
analytische Buchhaltung (f)	analytic accounting
anbieten	tender (to)
anbieten: unter Preis (m) ...	underprice (to)
anbieten: zu billig ...	underprice (to)
andere Lohnerhöhungen (fpl) mit den eigenen Lohnforderungen (f) übersteigen	leapfrog (to)
anderes (n): etwas ganz ...	a different ball game
Änderung (f): organisatorische ...	organizational change
anderweitig einsetzen	redeploy (to)
Anerkennung (f): gegenseitige ...	mutual recognition
Anfang (m): Finanzplanung von ... Null (f)	zero-base budget
Anforderung (f): Stellen...	job challenge
Anforderung (f): Stellen...sprofil (n)	job specification

Anforderungen *(fpl)*: Stellen...	job requirements
Angebot *(n)*	tender
Angebot *(n)*: ein ... machen	tender (to)
Angebot *(n)*: Fortbildungs...e *(pl)*	extension services
Angebot *(n)*: Lock...	loss-leader
Angebot *(n)*: Lockvogel...	loss-leader
Angebot *(n)*: Übernahme...	takeover bid
Angebote *(npl)*: Mitabgabe von ...n	competitive tendering
angelernte Arbeiter *(mpl)*	semi-skilled labour
angemessene Rendite *(f)*	fair return
angemessener Gewinn *(m)*	fair return
Anhebung *(f)*: Stellen...	job improvement
Anlage *(f)*: Betriebs... nach Werkstattprinzip *(n)*	process equipment layout
Anlage *(f)*: gesamte Produktions...n *(pl)*	production complex
Anlage *(f)*: immaterielle ...werte *(mpl)*	intangible assets
Anlage *(f)*: Verhältnis *(n)* von Umsatz *(m)* zu ...n	asset turnover
Anlagenausschlachtung *(f)*	asset-stripping
Anlagenkapazität *(f)*	plant capacity
Anlagenrendite *(f)*	return on assets
Anlagenrentabilität *(f)*	return on investment (ROI)
Anlagenwirtschaft *(f)*	asset management
Anlagevermögen *(n)*	fixed assets
	invested capital
Anlagewerte *(mpl)*: immaterielle ...	intangible assets
Anlaufkosten *(mpl)*	start-up costs
Anleihekapital *(n)*	loan capital
Anpassungskontrolle *(f)*	adaptive control
Anreiz *(m)*	incentive
Anreiz *(m)*: finanzieller ...	financial incentive
Anreiz (m) für unentbehrhrliche Spitzenmanager (mpl)	golden handcuffs
Anreiz *(m)*: Gruppen...	group incentive
Anreiz *(m)*: steuerlicher ...	tax incentive
Anreiz *(m)*: Wettbewerbs...	competitive stimulus
Anrufbeantworter *(m)*	answerphone
anschließen	interface (to)
ansetzen	schedule (to)
ansetzen: einen zu hohen Preis *(m)* ...	overprice (to)
anspruchsvoll	up-market

anspruchsvoll: weniger ...	down-market
anstellen	recruit (to)
Anstellungsvertrag *(m)* eines Managers *(m)*	management contract
Anteil *(m)*: Markt...	market share
Anteil *(m)*	stake
Anteil *(m)*: Produktions...splan *(m)*	share of production plan
anteil(s)mäßig	*pro rata*
Anwendung *(f)*: Software...	software application
Anwendungsmöglichkeit *(f)*: Software...	software application
anwerben	recruit (to)
Anwerbung *(f)* (von Arbeitskräften *(fpl)*)	recruitment
Anzeigeeinheit *(f)*	visual display unit (VDU)
Anzeigegerät *(n)*	display unit
Appeal *(m)*: Verkaufs...	sales appeal
Arbeitskonflikt *(m)*	labour dispute
Arbeit *(f)*: Akkord...	piecework
Arbeit *(f)*: Ausbildung *(f)* am ...splatz *(m)*	on-the-job training
Arbeit *(f)*: Beziehungen *(fpl)* zu ...nehmern *(mpl)*	employee relations
Arbeit *(f)*: Ermittlung *(f)* von ...sablaufstudien *(fpl)*	methods engineering
Arbeit *(f)*: Erweiterung *(f)* der ...saufgaben *(fpl)*	job enlargement
Arbeit *(f)* gemäß vertraglicher Vereinbarung *(f)*	work by contract
Arbeit *(f)*: Interesse *(n)* an der ...	job interest
Arbeit *(f)*: Öffentlichkeits...	public relations (PR)
Arbeit *(f)*: Pionier... leisten	pioneer (to)
Arbeit *(f)*: restriktive ...spraktiken *(fpl)*	restrictive practices (*industrial*)
Arbeit *(f)*: Schwarz...	moonlighting
Arbeit *(f)*: unmittelbar geleistete ...szeit *(f)*	direct labour
arbeiten	perform (to)
Arbeiter *(m)*	blue collar worker
Arbeiter *(mpl)*: angelernte ...	semi-skilled labour
Arbeiter *(mpl)* Fach...	skilled labour
Arbeiter *(mpl)*: gelernte ...	skilled labour
Arbeiter *(mpl)*: ungelernte ...	unskilled labour
Arbeitgeber-Arbeitnehmer-Beziehungen *(fpl)*	industrial relations
	labour relations
Arbeitnehmer *(mpl)*: Vertretung *(f)* der ...	worker representation
Arbeits-	operational

Arbeitsablaufbogen *(m)*	flow process chart
Arbeitsanalyse *(f)*	operations analysis
Arbeitsbedingungen *(fpl)*	conditions of employment
Arbeitsbedingungen (fpl): mit ... verbundene Motivationsfaktoren (mpl)	hygiene factors
Arbeitsbelastung *(f)*	workload
Arbeitsbereicherung *(f)*	job enrichment
Arbeitsbewertung *(f)*	job evaluation
Arbeitsblatt *(n)*	time sheet
Arbeitscharakteristika *(npl)*	job characteristics
Arbeitsergebnis *(n)*	job performance
Arbeitsgestaltung *(f)*	work structuring
Arbeitsgruppe *(f)*	working party
arbeitshemmender Faktor *(m)*	disincentive
Arbeitsinhalt *(m)*	job content
	work content
arbeitsintensiv	labour-intensive
Arbeitskampfmaßnahmen *(fpl)*	industrial action
Arbeitskonflikt *(m)*	industrial dispute
Arbeitskräfte *(fpl)*	manpower
Arbeitskräfte *(fpl)*: Anwerbung *(f)* von ...n	recruitment
Arbeitskräfte *(fpl)*: Einstellung *(f)* ungelernter ...	dilution of labour
Arbeitskräfte *(fpl)*: Einstellung *(f)* nicht benötigter ...	featherbedding
Arbeitskräfte *(fpl)*: Einstellung *(f)* von ...n	recruitment
Arbeitskräfte *(fpl)*: Umgruppierung *(f)* der ...	redeployment
Arbeitskräfteabbau *(m)*	staff cut-back
Arbeitskräftemobilität *(f)*	labour mobility
Arbeitsleistung *(f)*	job performance
Arbeitsmethodenuntersuchung *(f)*	methods study
Arbeitsmobilität *(f)*	labour mobility
Arbeitsnachweis *(m)*	employment bureau
Arbeitspensum *(n)*	workload
Arbeitsplatz *(m)*	workplace
Arbeitsplatz *(m)*: Zufriedenheit *(f)* am ...	job satisfaction
Arbeitsplatzbeschreibung *(f)*	job profile
Arbeitsplatzgestaltung *(f)*	human engineering
Arbeitsplatzsicherheit *(f)*	job security

Arbeitsplatzsicherheitsvereinbarung *(f)*	job security agreement
Arbeitspraktiken *(fpl):* restriktive ...	restrictive practices (*industrial*)
Arbeitssicherheit *(f)*	industrial safety
Arbeitsstätte *(f)*	workplace
Arbeitsstelle *(f)*	workplace
Arbeitsstichproben *(fpl)*	activity sampling
Arbeitsstichproben *(fpl):* Methode *(f)* der ... *(fpl)*	random observation method
Arbeitsstreß *(m)*	work stress
Arbeitsstudie *(f)*	workstudy
Arbeitsstunden *(fpl)*	working hours
Arbeitsunfall *(m)*	industrial injury
Arbeitsvereinfachung *(f)*	work simplification
Arbeitsvermittlung *(f)*	employment bureau
Arbeitsvorbereitung *(f)*	production scheduling
	scheduling
Arbeitsvorgänge *(mpl)*	operations
Arbeitszeit *(f):* gleitende ...	flexible working hours
Arbeitszeit *(f):* unmittelbar geleistete ...	direct labour
Arbeitszeiten *(fpl):* flexible ...	flexible working hours
Arbeitszettel *(m)*	time sheet
Arbeitszufriedenheit *(f)*	job satisfaction
Arbeitszyklus *(m)*	work cycle
Arbitrage *(f)*	arbitrage
Arbitrageur *(m)*	arbitrageur
Artikel *(m):* Lock...	loss leader
Assessment-Center *(n)*	assessment centre
Assistent *(m):* Direktions...	assistant to manager
Assistent *(m):* Linien...	line assistant
Assistent *(m):* Stabs...	staff assistant
audiovisuelle Unterrichtsmittel *(npl)*	audiovisual aids
auf Armeslänge *(f)*	arm's length
auf Computer *(mpl)* umstellen	computerize (to)
auf den Markt *(m)* bringen	market (to)
auf den neuesten Stand *(m)* bringen	update (to)
auf der Tagesordnung *(f)* stehen	be on the agenda (to)
auf höheren Führungsebenen *(fpl)*	up the line
auf nachgeordneten Führungsebenen *(fpl)*	down the line
auf Pacht- und Leihbasis *(f)*	lease-lend

aufbauen: ein neues Image *(n)*...	re-image (to)
auffüllen	top up (to)
Aufgabe *(f)*: Produkt...	product abandonment
Aufgabe *(f)*: Zuteilung *(f)* von ...n *(pl)*	job assignment
Aufgabe *(f)*: Zuweisung *(f)* von ...ngebieten	allocation of responsibilities
Aufgabenzuteilung *(f)*	job assignment
Aufgliederung *(f)* des Stelleninhalt(e)s *(m)*	operations breakdown
aufhören: rechtzeitig zu spekulieren ...	cut one's losses (to)
aufkaufen: Aktien (fpl) einer Unternehmung (f) gezielt und überfallartig ...	raid a company (to)
aufkaufen: den Markt *(m)* ...	corner the market (to)
Aufkaufgruppe *(f)*	corner
Auflistung *(f)*	listing
auflösen	liquidate (to)
	wind up (to)
Auflösung *(f)*	disintegration
	dissolution
Auflösung *(f)* eines Geschäfts *(n)*	winding up
Aufnahme *(f)*: Kapital...	capital raising
Aufschlag *(m)*	mark-up
Aufschlag *(m)*: Preis...	mark-up
Aufschwung *(m)*	boom
	upswing
	upturn
Aufschwungphase (f) nach einer Periode (f) restriktiver Wirtschaftpolitik (f)	soft landing
Aufseher *(m)*	supervisor
Aufsicht *(f)*	supervision
Aufsicht *(f)* führen	supervise (to)
Aufsichtsrat *(m)*	board of directors
	supervisory board
Aufsichtsratskontrolle *(f)*	board control
Aufsichtsratsmitglied *(n)*	non-executive director
	outside director
Aufsichtsratssitzung *(f)*	board meeting
aufsplittern	compartmentalize (to)
Aufstellung *(f)* des Ist-Budgets *(n)*	programme budgeting
Aufstieg *(m)* der Führungskräfte *(fpl)*	executive advancement
aufteilen: in Sparten *(fpl)* ...	compartmentalize

Aufteilung *(f)* **der Weisungsgewalt** *(f)*	authority structure
Aufteilungsverfahren *(n)* **für Gemeinkosten** *(pl)*	overheads recovery
Auftrag *(m)*: **wirtschaftlicher ...**	economic mission
Auftrieb *(m)*: **konjunktureller ...**	upswing
	upturn
Aufwärtstrend *(m)*	upswing
	upturn
Augenblick *(m)*: **günstiger ...**	window of opportunity
Ausbildung *(f)*	training
Ausbildung *(f)*: **analytische ...**	analytical training
Ausbildung *(f)*: **außerbetriebliche ...**	off-the-job training
Ausbildung *(f)*: **Berufs...**	vocational training
Ausbildung *(f)*: **computerunterstützte ...**	computer-based training (CBT)
Ausbildung *(f)*: **Gruppen...**	group training
Ausbildung *(f)* **der Führungskräfte** *(fpl)*	management training
Ausbildung *(f)* **im analytischen Denken** *(n)*	analytical training
Ausbildung *(f)* **in Teilanalysen** *(fpl)*	part-analysis training
Ausbildung *(f)* **von Führungskräften** *(fpl)*	executive training
Ausbildung *(f)*: **innerbetriebliche ...**	on-the-job training
	training within industry (TWI)
Ausbildung *(f)*: **Manager-...**	management training
Ausbildung *(f)*: **multimediale ...**	multimedia training
Ausbildungsbedarf *(m)*	training needs
Ausbildungsbedarf *(m)*: **Analyse** *(f)* **des ..s**	training needs analysis
Ausbildungsleiter *(m)*	training officer
Ausdruck *(m)*	printout
ausdrucken	print out (to)
auseinanderklauben	unscramble (to)
Ausfallzeit *(f)*	down time
ausführen	implement (to)
Ausgabe *(f)*	issue
Ausgabe *(f)*: **Computer-...**	computer output
Ausgabe *(f)*: **direkte ...n** *(pl)*	direct expenses
Ausgabe *(f)*: **indirekte ...n** *(pl)*	indirect expenses
Ausgabe *(f)*: **laufende Betriebs...**	current expenditure
Ausgabe *(f)*: **laufende ...n**	running expenses
ausgeben	disburse (to)
ausgegebenes Kapital *(n)*	issued capital

ausgeglichenes Portfolio *(n)*	balanced portfolio
ausgeschüttete Gewinne *(mpl)*	distributed profit
Aushilfsarbeiter *(m)*	part-timer
Auslastung *(f)*: **Kapazitäts...**	capacity utilization
Auslastungsfaktor *(m)*	load factor
auslaufen lassen	phase out (to)
auslegen	disburse (to)
Ausleihungen *(fpl)*: **Eckzins** *(m)* **für ...**	base rate
auslöschen: ein Programm *(n)* **unabsichtlich ...**	crash a program (to)
Aussage *(f)*: **Werbe...**	advertising message
ausschlachten: eine mittels Junk Bonds (mpl)	unbundle (to)
übernommene Unternehmung (f) ...	
Ausschlachtung *(f)* **einer Unternehmung** *(f)*	asset-stripping
Ausschlachtung (f) einer mittels Junk	unbundling
Bonds (mpl) übernommenen	
Unternehmung (f)	
Ausschlachtungswert *(m)*	break-up value
ausschlaggebendes Moment *(n)*	name of the game
Ausschreibung *(f)*: **sich an einer ... beteiligen**	tender (to)
Außenbeziehungen *(fpl)*	external relations
Außendienst *(m)*: **Personal** *(n)* **im ...**	front-line employees
Außendienst *(m)*: **Verkaufs...**	sales force
Außendienstmitarbeiter *(mpl)*	sales force
außerbetriebliche Ausbildung *(f)*	off-the-job training
außerhäuslich	out-house
Äußerlichkeiten *(fpl)*	externalities
äußerster Termin *(m)*	latest date
Aussichten *(fpl)*: **Gewinn...**	profit outlook
Aussichten *(fpl)*: **Markt...**	market prospects
Aussperrung *(f)*	lockout
Ausstattung *(f)*: **Kapital...**	gearing
Ausstellung *(f)*	issue
Ausstrahlungseffekt *(m)*	halo effect
Austausch *(m)*: **Lizenz...**	cross-licensing
austauschen: eine Sache *(f)* **gegen eine andere ...**	trade off (to)
ausverkaufen	sell out (to)
Auswahl *(f)*: **Medien...**	media selection
Auswahl *(f)*: **Portfolio-...**	portfolio selection
Auswahlliste *(f)*	shortlist

Auswärtsvergabe *(f)*	outsourcing
Auswirkung *(f)*	impact
***Auswirkung** (f) **der Werbung** (f) **auf Konkurrenzprodukte** (npl)*	spill-over effect
à jour halten	update (to)
auszahlen	buy out (to)
	disburse (to)
Auszahlung *(f)*	disbursement
Automation *(f)*	automation
automatische Datenverarbeitung *(f)*	automatic data processing (ADP)
automatisieren	automate (to)
	robotize (to)
Automatisierung *(f)*	automation
autorisiertes Kapital *(n)*	authorized capital
Autotelefon *(n)*	car phone
Avantgarde *(f)*	leading edge

B

Baisse *(f)*	bear market
Baissespekulant *(m)*	bear
Baissier *(m)*	bear
Balkendiagramm *(n)*	bar chart
Bandlaufrichtung *(f):* gegen ...	upstream
Bandlaufrichtung *(f):* in ...	downstream
Bank *(f):* Clearing...	commercial bank
Bank *(f):* Computer-...	computer bank
Bank *(f):* Daten...	data bank
Bank *(f):* Effekten- und Emissions...	investment bank
Bank *(f):* Emissions...	investment bank
Bank *(f):* Geschäfts...	commercial bank
Bank *(f):* Handels...	merchant bank
Bank *(f):* Investment...	investment bank
Bank *(f):* Merchant...	merchant bank
Bargeld *(n)*	cash
Barliquidität *(f)*	cash ratio
Barmittel *(npl)*	cash

Barwert *(m)*	net present value (NPV)
Barwertsmethode *(f)*	present value method
Bauelement *(n)*: diskretes ...	add-on equipment
Baukasten *(m)*: Produktion *(f)* nach dem ...prinzip *(n)*	modular production
Baulöwe *(m)*	developer
Baum *(m)*: Entscheidungs...	decision tree
Baum *(m)*: Stamm...	family tree
Baum *(m)*: Zuständigkeits...	pertinence tree
Bauträger *(m)*	developer
bearbeiten	process (to)
bearbeiten: vorläufig nicht weiter ...	put on the back burner (to)
Bearbeitung *(f)*: Informations...	information handling
beaufsichtigen	supervise (to)
beauftragen und Instruktionen *(fpl)* geben	brief (to)
Bedarf *(m)*: Ausbildungs...	training needs
Bedarfsanalyse *(f)*	needs analysis
bedeutend	significant
bedeutungsvoll	meaningful
	significant
Bedingung *(f)*: Arbeits...en *(pl)*	conditions of employment
Befehlsweg *(m)*	chain of command
	line of command
Beförderung *(f)*	advancement
Beförderung *(f)* (*von Mitarbeitern (mpl)*)	promotion (*personnel*)
Beförderung *(f)* der Führungskräfte *(fpl)*	executive advancement
Beförderung *(f)* von Führungskräften *(fpl)*	executive promotion
Befragung *(f)*: Markt...	market survey
Befugnis *(f)*: Beschränkung *(f)* der ...se	contraction of authority
Befugnis *(f)*: Leitungs...	line authority
beglaubigen	verify (to)
Begründung *(f)*	rationale
behandeln: unterschiedlich ...	discriminate (to)
Bekanntheit *(f)* einer Marke *(f)*	brand awareness
Bekanntheitsgrad *(m)*	awareness level
belangbar	actionable
Belästigung *(f)*: sexuelle ...	sexual harassment
Belastung *(f)*: Arbeits...	work load
Belegschaft *(f)*	staff

Belegschaft (f): zu große ...	overmanning
Bemühung (f): gezielte ...en (pl) um Produktivitätssteigerung (f)	productivity drive
Bemühungen (fpl) um Verkaufssteigerungen (fpl)	sales expansion effort
benutzerfeindlich	user-unfriendly
benutzerfreundlich	user-friendly
Benutzerstrategie (f)	user strategy
beratend	consultative
Berater (m)	consultant
Berater (m): Unternehmens...	management consultant
Beratung (f): Berufs...	vocational guidance
Beratung (f): gemeinsame ...	joint consultation
Beratung (f): Personal...	employee counselling
Beratungsdienste (mpl)	advisory services
Bereich (m): Problem...	problem area
Bereich (m): Produkt...	product area
Bereich (m): Unternehmens...	operating division
Bereich (m): Wachstums...	growth area
Bereitschaft (f): Kauf... des Konsumenten (m)	consumer acceptance
Bereitstellung (f): Planung (f) und ... von Produktionmitteln (npl))	resource allocation
Bereitstellung (f) von Ressourcen (fpl)	resource allocation
Bericht (m) über den Stand (m) eines Projekt(e)s (n)	status report
Berichtigung (f): Wert...	depreciation allowance
Beruf (m): Erhebung (f) zum ...	professionalization
beruflich: Erlangung (f eines ...en Status (m)	professionalization
berufliche Aufschlüsselung (f)	job breakdown
berufliche Chancengleichheit (f)	equal employment opportunity
Berufsausbildung (f)	vocational training
Berufsberatung (f)	vocational guidance
Berufsberatung (f) von Aufsteigern (mpl) und arbeitslos gewordenen Führungskräften (fpl)	outplacement
Berufsbezeichnung (f)	job title
Berufskennzeichen (npl)	job characteristics
Berufsmerkmale (npl)	job characteristics
Berufsrisiko (n)	occupational hazard
Berufsverband (m)	trade association

Beschaffung *(f)*	procurement
	sourcing
Beschaffung *(f)*: Daten...	data acquisition
Beschaffung *(f)*: eingleisige ...	single sourcing
Beschaffung *(f)*: Kapital...	capital raising
Beschaffung *(f)*: Personal...	manpower resourcing
Beschaffung *(f)*: zweigleisige ...	dual sourcing
Beschaffungsmanager *(m)*	procurement manager
Beschäftigter *(m)*: ganztägig ...	full-timer
Beschäftigung *(f)*: Ganztags...	full-time employment
Beschäftigten-	manning
Beschränkung *(f)*: Budget...	budget constraint
Beschränkung *(f)* der Befugnisse *(fpl)*	contraction of authority
Beschränkung *(f)* des Produktsortiments *(n)*	variety reduction
Beschränkung *(f)*: Wettbewerbs...en *(fpl)*	restrictive practices *(legal)*
Beschreibung *(f)*: Arbeitsplatz...	job profile
Beschreibung *(f)*: Stellen...	job description
	job specification
Beschwerde *(f)*	grievance
Beschwerdeverfahren *(n)*	grievance procedure
beseitigen: einen Engpaß *(m)* ...	debottleneck (to)
beseitigen: Fehler *(mpl)* ...	debug (to)
Beseitigung *(f)* von Fehlerquellen *(fpl)*	diagnostic routine
besprechen: Einsatz *(m)* (anschließend) ...	debrief (to)
besprechen: sich ... mit	consult (to)
Bestand *(m)*: Personal...sanalyse *(f)*	manpower audit
	staff audit
Bestandskontrolle *(f)*	inventory control
bestätigen	verify (to)
Bestätigung (f) von erfolgreicher Übermittlung (f) eines Fernschreibens (n)	answerback code
Best-Case-Szenario *(n)*	best-case scenario
Beteiligung *(f)*	participation
Beteiligung *(f)*: Erfolgs...	profit-sharing
Beteiligung *(f)*: Ergebnis...	profit-sharing
Beteiligung *(f)*: finanzielle ...	financial involvement
	vested interest
Beteiligung *(f)*: Gewinn...	profit-sharing

Beteiligung *(f)*: Mehrheits...	controlling interest
	majority interest
Beteiligung *(f)*: Minderheits...	minority interest
Beteiligung *(f)*: Unternehmensführung *(f)* unter ... nachgeordneter Führungsebenen *(fpl)*	multiple management
Beteiligungsgesellschaft *(f)*	associate company
Betrag *(m)*: Abschreibungs...	depreciation allowance
Betreuer *(m)*: Marken...	brand manager
Betreuung *(f)*: Kunden...	after-sales service
Betrieb *(m)*	establishment
Betrieb *(m)*: Geschäfts...	business system
Betrieb *(m)*: gewerkschaftspflichtiger ...	closed shop
Betrieb *(m)*: in ...	on stream
Betrieb *(m)*: laufende ...sausgaben *(fpl)*	current expenditure
Betrieb *(m)*: laufende ...skosten *(pl)*	current expenditure
Betrieb *(m)*: nicht gewerkschaftspflichtiger ...	open shop
Betrieb *(m)*: Planung *(f)* des ...sergebnisses *(n)*	profit planning
betrieblich	operational
betriebliche Aufgliederung *(f)*	departmentalisation
betriebliches Verantwortungszentrum *(n)*	responsibility centre
betriebliches Vorschlagswesen *(n)*	suggestion scheme
Betriebs-	operational
Betriebs-: laufende ...ausgaben *(fpl)*	current expenditure
Betriebs-: laufende ...kosten *(pl)*	current expenditure
Betriebs-: Untersuchung *(f)* der ...anlagen *(fpl)*	plant layout study
Betriebsabteilung *(f)*	operating division
Betriebsanalyse *(f)*	operations analysis
Betriebsanlage *(f)* nach Werkstattprinzip *(n)*	process equipment layout
Betriebsdynamik *(f)*	industrial dynamics
Betriebsführung *(f)*	business management
Betriebsführung *(f)*: interventionistische ...	management by walking around
Betriebsinstandhaltung *(f)*	plant maintenance
Betriebsinstandhaltung *(f)*: umfassende ...	total plant maintenance
betriebsinterne Revision *(f)*	internal audit
Betriebskapazität *(f)*	plant capacity
Betriebskapital *(n)*	circulating capital
	working capital

Betriebskennziffer *(f)*	accounting ratio
Betriebskosten *(pl)*	operating expenses
Betriebsleiter *(m)*	operations manager
	plant manager
	works manager
Betriebsleitung *(f)*	operating management
	operations management
Betriebsmittelverwaltung *(f)*	resource management
Betriebsökonom *(m)*	business economist
Betriebspsychologie *(f)*	industrial psychology
Betriebsrat *(m)*	works committee
	works council
Betriebsrechnungswesen *(n)*	management accounting
Betriebssicherheit *(f)*	industrial safety
	industrial security
betriebssystemunabhängig	stand-alone
Betriebstechnik *(f)*	industrial engineering
Betriebsunfall *(m)*	industrial injury
Betriebsvergleich *(m)*	inter-firm comparison
Betriebswirt(schaftler) *(m)*	business economist
Betriebswirtschaft *(f)*	business management
betriebswirtschaftliche Kennzahl *(f)*	management ratio
Betriebszeit *(f)*: verfügbare ...	uptime
Betroffene *(m/fpl)*: nur für unmittelbar ...	need-to-know basis
beurteilen	appraise (to)
	assess (to)
	evaluate (to)
Beurteilung *(f)*	appraisal
	assessment
Beurteilung *(f)*: Bonitäts...	credit rating
Beurteilung *(f)* der Kreditwürdigkeit *(f)*	credit rating
Beurteilung *(f)*: Investitions...	capital expenditure appraisal
Beurteilung *(f)*: Leistungs...	merit rating
	performance appraisal
	performance evaluation
	performance rating
	performance review
Beurteilung *(f)*: Leistungs... der Büroangestellten *(f/mpl)*	clerical work measurement (CWM)

Beurteilung *(f)*: Markt...	market appraisal
	market rating
Beurteilung *(f)*: Personal...	merit rating
	personnel rating
	staff appraisal
Beurteilung *(f)*: Problem...	problem assessment
Beurteilung *(f)*: Qualitäts...	quality assessment
Beurteilungsgespräch *(n)*	performance review
Bewegung *(f)*: Zeit- und ...sstudie *(f)*	time and methods study
	time and motion study
Bewegungsökonomie *(f)*	motion economy
Bewegungsstudie *(f)*	methods study
	motion study
Bewegungsstudienabteilung *(f)*	methods study department
bewerten	appraise (to)
	assess (to)
	evaluate (to)
	price (to)
Bewertung *(f)*	appraisal
	assessment
Bewertung *(f)*: Arbeits...	job evaluation
Bewertung *(f)* der Finanzmittel *(npl)*	financial appraisal
Bewertung *(f)*: dynamische ...	dynamic evaluation
Bewertung *(f)*: Finanz...	financial appraisal
Bewertung *(f)*: Investitions...	capital expenditure appraisal
	investment appraisal
Bewertung *(f)*: Leistungs... des Büropersonals *(n)*	clerical work measurement (CWM)
Bewertung *(f)*: Markt...	market rating
Bewertung *(f)*: Nachfrage...	demand assessment
Bewertung *(f)*: Neu... von Vermögenswerten *(mpl)*	revaluation of assets
Bewertung *(f)*: Projekt...	project assessment
Bewertung *(f)*: Prüfung *(f)* und ... der Manager-Leistung *(f)*	management audit
Bewertung *(f)*: Punkt...	points-rating method
Bewertung *(f)*: Qualitäts ...	quality assessment
Bewertung *(f)*: Risiko...	risk assessment
Bewertung *(f)* von Ressourcen *(fpl)*	resource appraisal

bewilligen	appropriate (to)
bewilligte Marketing-Mittel *(npl)*	marketing appropriation
bewilligter Werbeetat *(m)*	advertising appropriation
bewilligtes Werbebudget *(n)*	advertising appropriation
Bewilligung *(f)* **von Haushaltsmitteln** *(npl)*	budget appropriation
Bewußtheitsgrad *(m)*	awareness level
Bewußtsein *(n)*: **Kosten...**	cost awareness
	cost consciousness
Bewußtsein *(n)*: **Marken...**	brand awareness
Bewußtsein *(n)*: **Markt...**	market awareness
Beziehungen *(fpl)*: **Arbeitgeber-Arbeitnehmer-...**	industrial relations
Beziehungen *(fpl)*: **Außen...**	labour relations
Beziehungen *(fpl)*: **funktionale ...**	external relations
Beziehungen *(f)*: **Geschäfts...**	functional relations
Beziehungen *(fpl)*: **innerbetriebliche Mitarbeiter...**	business relations
	human relations
Beziehungen *(fpl)* **zu Arbeitnehmern** *(mpl)*	employee relations
Beziehungen *(fpl)*: **zwischenmenschliche ...**	human relations
Bezirk *(m)*: **Verkaufs...**	sales territory
Bezugsrechtsemission *(f)*	rights issue
Bilanz *(f)*	balance sheet
	financial statement
Bilanzfrisur *(f)*	creative accounting
Bilanzkosmetik *(f)*	window dressing
Bilanzprüfung *(f)*	balance sheet auditing
Bild *(n)*: **Marken...**	brand image
Bild *(n)*: **Streu...**	scatter diagram
Bildabtastung *(f)*	scanning
Bildschirm *(m)*	visual display unit (VDU)
Bildschirmgerät *(n)*	display unit
	visual display unit (VDU)
Bildschirmtext *(m)* **(Btx)**	viewdata
Bildsichtgerät *(n)*	visual display unit (VDU)
Bildung *(f)*: **Kapital...**	capital formation
billig: zu ... anbieten	underprice (to)
Bindung *(f)*: **Kapital...**	capital commitment
Binnenmarkt *(m)*	single market
Binnenmarkt *(m)*: **europäischer ...**	single market (*of the EC*)

BIP (Bruttoinlandsprodukt, *n*)	GDP (gross domestic product)
blank	cash-strapped
Blindbefehl *(m)*	dummy activity
Board *(m)*	board of directors
Board-Mitglied *(n)*	executive director
Bond *(m)*: Junk ...	junk bond
Bonitätsbeurteilung *(f)*	credit rating
Bonus *(m)*	bonus
Bonus *(m)*: Gruppen...	group bonus
Boom *(m)*	boom
Börse *(f)*: an der ... zugelassen werden	go public (to)
börsengehandelte Option *(f)*	traded option
Börsenmakler *(m)*	stockbroker
börsennotierte Gesellschaft *(f)*	publicly listed company
börsennotierte Gesellschaft *(f)*: nicht-...	unlisted company
börsennotiertes Unternehmen *(n)*	quoted company
Börsennotierung *(f)*	listing
Börsenspekulation *(f)*	jobbing
Botschaft *(f)*: Werbe...	advertising message
Brain-Trust *(m)*	brains trust
Brainstorming *(n)*	brainstorming
Break-Even-Analyse *(f)*	break-even analysis
Break-Even-Punkt *(m)*	break-even point
Break-Even-Umsatz *(m)*	break-even quantity
Breite *(f)*: Produktions...	product diversification
Briefkasten *(m)*	mail box
bringen: auf den Markt *(m)* ...	market (to)
bringen: in Einklang *(m)* ...	conciliate (to)
Broker *(m)*	stock broker
Bruchteile *(mpl)*: in ... zerlegen	fractionalize (to)
Bruttogewinn *(m)*	gross profit
Bruttogewinnspanne *(f)*	gross margin (GM)
Bruttoinlandsprodukt *(n)* (BIP)	gross domestic product (GDP)
Bruttosozialprodukt *(n)* (BSP)	gross national product (GNP)
BIP (Bruttoinlandsprodukt *(n)*)	GDP (gross domestic product)
BSP (Bruttosozialprodukt *(n)*)	GNP (gross national product)
Btx (Bildschirmtext *(m)*)	viewdata
Buchführung *(f)*: analytische...	analytic accounting
Buchhalter *(m)*: Haupt...	chief accountant

Buchhaltung *(f)*	accounting
Buchhaltung *(f)*: analytische ...	analytic accounting
Buchhaltungsabteilung *(f)*	accounting department
	accounts department
Buchhaltungsmodell *(n)*	accounting model
Buchprüfer *(m)*	auditor
Buchprüfung *(f)*	audit
Buchwert *(m)*	book value
Budget *(n)*	budget
Budget *(n)*: Aufstellung *(f)* des Ist-...s	programme budgeting
Budget *(n)*: bewilligtes Werbe...	advertising appropriation
Budget *(n)*: elastisches ...	flexible budget
Budget *(n)*: Investitions...	investment budget
Budget *(n)*: Kapital...	capital budget
Budget *(n)*: Kassen...	cash budget
Budget *(n)*: Marketing-...	marketing budget
Budget *(n)*: Verkaufs-...	sales budget
Budget *(n)*: Werbe...	advertising budget
Budgetbeschränkung *(f)*	budget constraint
budgetieren	budget (to)
Budgetierung *(f)*	budgeting
Budgetierung *(f)*: Kapital...	capital budgeting
Budgetierung *(f)*: Planungs-, Programmierungs- und ...ssystem *(n)*	planning, programming, budgeting system (PPBS)
Budgetierung *(f)*: Programm...	programme budgeting
Budgetierungskontrolle *(f)*	budgeting control
Budgetkontrolle *(f)*	budgetary control
	budgeting control
Budgetnorm *(f)*	budget standard
Budgetprognose *(f)*	budget forecasting
Bummelstreik *(m)*	go-slow
	work-to-rule
Bündelung *(f)*	bundling
Büro *(n)*: elektronisches ...	electronic office
Büro *(n)*: Haupt...	head office
Büro *(n)*: technische Abteilung *(f)* und Konstruktions...	engineering and design department
Büroangestellter *(m)*	clerical worker
	white collar worker

Büroangestellte *(f/mpl):* Leistungsbeurteilung *(f)* der …n	clerical work measurement (CWM)
Büroautomation *(f)*	office automation
Bürogestaltung *(f)*	office planning
Büroleitung *(f)*	office management
Büropersonal *(n):* Leistungsbewertung *(f)* des …s	clerical work measurement (CWM)
Buyout *(m,n):* Management-… (MBO)	management buyout (MBO)
Buyout *(m,n):* Mitarbeiter-…	employee buyout worker buyout
Byte *(n)*	byte

C

Cash-flow *(m)*	cash flow
Cash-flow *(m):* diskontierter …	discounted cash flow (DCF)
Cash-flow *(m):* negativer …	negative cash flow
Cash-flow *(m):* Zuwachs *(m)* des …	incremental cash flow
Cash-Management *(n)*	cash management
Chance *(f):* Markt…	market opportunity
Chancengleichheit *(f)*	equal opportunity
Chancengleichheit *(f):* berufliche …	equal employment opportunity
Chancengleichheit (f): Bevorzugung (f) bei der Personalauslese (f) um der beruflichen … willen	positive discrimination
Chef *(m):* Finanz…	financial director
Chefeinkäufer *(m)*	chief buyer
Chemikalien *(fpl):* gefährliche …	hazchem (hazardous chemicals)
Chip *(m)*	chip
Chipkarte *(f)*	smart card
Chose *(f):* eine ganz andere …	a different ball game
Clearingbank *(f)*	commercial bank
Clearinghaus *(n)*	clearing house
Clearingstelle *(f)*	clearing house
Computer *(m)*	computer
Computer *(m):* auf … *(pl)* umstellen	computerize (to)

Computer *(mpl)*: mit ...n vertraut	computer literate
Computer-Ausgabe *(f)*	computer output
Computer-Bank *(f)*	computer bank
Computer-Dienste *(mpl)*	computer services
Computer-Dienststelle *(f)*	computer services bureau
Computer-Eingabe *(f)*	computer input
Computer-Simulation *(f)*	computer simulation
Computer-Wissen *(n)* besitzend	computer literate
Computerberater *(m)*	computer consultant
computergesteuerte Produktion *(f)*	computer-integrated manufacturing (CIM)
computergestütztes Management *(n)*	computerized management
computerintegrierte Fertigung *(f)*	computer-integrated manufacturing (CIM)
computerisieren	computerize (to)
computerisiertes Informationssystem *(n)*	computerized information system (COINS)
Computerprogramm *(n)*	computer program
Computerspezialist *(m)*	computer expert
computerunterstützte Ausbildung *(f)*	computer-based training (CBT)
computerunterstützte Entwicklung *(f)*	computer-aided design (CAD)
computerunterstützte Fertigung *(f)*	computer-aided manufacturing (CAM)
computerunterstützte Konstruktion *(f)*	computer-aided design (CAD)
computerunterstützte Nachrichtenvermittlung *(f)*	bulletin board
computerunterstützter Unterricht *(m)*	computer-assisted teaching (CAT)
computerunterstütztes Lernen *(n)*	computer-aided learning (CAL)
Computervirus *(n,m)*	computer virus
Container *(m)*	container
Container *(m)*: Umstellung *(f)* auf ... *(pl)*	containerization
Containerisierung *(f)*	containerization
Controller *(m)*	comptroller
Corporate Raider *(m)*	corporate raider
Corporate Culture *(f)*	corporate culture
Corporate Image *(n)*	corporate image
Courtage *(f)*	brokerage

Crash *(m)*	crash
Critical Path Method *(f)* (CPM)	critical path method (CPM)
Culture *(f)*: Corporate ...	corporate culture
Cursor *(m)*	cursor

D

Dachgesellschaft *(f)*	holding company
Darlehenszinssatz *(m)*	bank rate
darum geht es	name of the game
Darstellung *(f)*: Analog...	analog(ue) representation
das Lager *(n)* **räumen**	sell out (to)
das schon Erfundene *(n)* **erfinden**	reinvent the wheel (to)
Data Base *(f)*	data base
Datenablaufplan *(m)*	data flow chart
Datenbank *(f)*	data bank
Datenbasis *(f)*	data base
Datenbeschaffung *(f)*	data acquisition
Datendurchlauf *(m)*	throughput
Datenendgerät *(n)*	computer terminal
Datenflußplan *(m)*	data flow chart
Datensammlung *(f)*	data gathering
Datenschutz *(m)*	data protection
Datensichtgerät *(n)*	display unit
Datenverarbeitung *(f)*	data processing
Datenverarbeitung *(f)*: automatische ...	automatic data processing (ADP)
Datenverarbeitung *(f)*: elektronische ...	electronic data processing (EDP)
Datenverarbeitungszentrum *(n)*	computer centre
Datenwiedergewinnung *(f)*	data retrieval
Dauer *(f)*: Amortisations...	payback period
Dauer *(f)*: wirtschaftliche Lebens... eines Produkt(e)s *(n)*	product life
De-Industrialisierung *(f)*	deindustrialization
Deal *(m)*	deal
Deal *(m)*: einen ... machen	reach a deal (to)
Deckungsbeitrag *(m)*: Analyse *(f)* des ...(e)s	contribution analysis

Deckungspunkt *(m)*	break-even point
Deckungspunktanalyse *(f)*	break-even analysis
Deckungsverhältnis *(n)*	cover ratio
Defekte *(mpl)*: **keine ...**	zero defects
defensive Strategie *(f)*	defensive strategy
Defizit *(n)*	shortfall
Defizitfinanzierung *(f)*	deficit financing
Degression *(f)*: **Kosten...**	economy of scale
Delegation *(f)*	delegation
delegieren	delegate (to)
demotivieren	demotivate (to)
Demotivierung *(f)*	demotivation
den Markt *(m)* **aufkaufen**	corner the market (to)
Denken *(n)*: **Ausbildung** *(f)* **im analytischen ...**	analytical training
Denken *(n)*: **kreatives ...**	creative thinking
Denken *(n)*: **laterales ...**	lateral thinking
denken: Undenkbares ...	think the unthinkable (to)
deregulieren	deregulate (to)
Deregulierung *(f)*	deregulation
Desintegration *(f)*	disintegration
Desinvestition *(f)*	disinvestment
Desktop *(m)*	desktop computer
Desktop-Publishing *(n)*	desktop publishing
Desktop-Veröffentlichung *(f)*: **als ...** **herausbringen**	desktop publish (to)
Devisenterminkurs *(m)*	forward exchange rate
	forward rate
dezentralisieren	decentralize (to)
dezentralisiert und partizipativ	bottom-up
dezentralisiertes Management *(n)*	decentralized management
Dezentralisierung *(f)*	decentralization
	departmentalization
Diagramm *(n)*: **Ablauf...**	flow chart
Diagramm *(n)*: **Balken...**	bar chart
Diagramm *(n,)*: **Fluß...**	flow chart
	flow diagram
Diagramm *(n)*: **Kreis...**	pie chart
Diagramm *(n)*: **Punkte...**	scatter diagram
Diagramm *(n)*: **Streu...**	scatter diagram

Diagramm (*n*): Tätigkeits...	activity chart
Diagramm (*n*): Z-...	Z-chart
die Gewinnschwelle (*f*) **erreichen**	break even (to)
die Rentabilitätsschwelle (*f*) **erreichen**	break even (to)
die Talsohle (*f*) **verlassen**	bottom out (to)
Dienst (*m*): Beratungs-...e (*pl*)	advisory services
Dienst (*m*): Computer-...e (*pl*)	computer services
Dienst (*m*): Kunden...	after-sales service
	customer service
Dienst (*m*): Management-...e (*pl*)	management services
Dienst (*m*) **nach Vorschrift** (*f*)	work-to-rule
Dienstprogramm (*n*)	toolbox
Dienststelle (*f*): Computer-...	computer services bureau
Differential (*n*) **des Cash-flow** (*m*)	incremental cash flow
Differentialpreisfestsetzung (*f*)	differential pricing
differenzieren	differentiate (to)
differenzierter Preis (*m*)	differential price
Differenzierung (*f*): Preis...	differential pricing
Differenzierung (*f*): Produkt...	product differentiation
digital	digital
Digital-	digital
digitalisieren	digitize (to)
Digitalrechner (*m*)	digital computer
digitieren	digitize (to)
dingliche Sicherheit (*f*)	collateral security
direkte Ausgaben (*fpl*)	direct expenses
direkte Kosten (*pl*)	direct costs
direktgekoppelt	on line
Direktionsassistent (*m*)	assistant to manager
Direktmarketing (*n*)	direct marketing
Direktor (*m*)	director
Direktor (*m*): General...	chief executive
	general manager
	managing director (MD)
Direktor (*m*): stellvertretender ...	assistant director
	assistant manager
	deputy manager
Direktor (*m*): stellvertretender General...	deputy managing director
Direktverkauf (*m*)	direct selling

Direktversand *(m)*	direct mail
Direktzugriffsspeicher *(m)*	random access memory (RAM)
Diskette *(f)*	floppy disk
Diskettenlaufwerk *(n)*	disk drive
diskontierter Cash-Flow *(m)*	discounted cash flow (DCF)
Diskontsatz *(m)*	bank rate
diskretes Bauelement *(n)*	add-on equipment
diskriminieren	discriminate (to)
Diskriminierung *(f)*	discrimination
Distribution *(f)*	distribution
Distributionskanal *(m)*	distribution channel
Distributionskette *(f)*	chain of distribution
Diversifikation *(f)*	diversification
Diversifikationsstrategie *(f)*	diversification strategy
diversifizieren	diversify (to)
Diversifizierung *(f)*	diversification
Diversifizierung *(f)*: Produkt...	product diversification
Dividende *(f)*	dividend
Dividendenpolitik *(f)*	dividend policy
Doppelbesteuerungsabkommen *(n)*: Steuernachlaß *(m)* aufgrund eines ...s	double taxation relief
dritte Person *(f)*	third party
Dritter *(m)*	third party
Druck *(m)*	pressure
Druck *(m)*: inflationärer ...	inflationary pressure
Druck *(m)*: Inflations...	inflationary pressure
Druckausgabe *(f)*	printout
Dumping *(n)*	dumping
durch Kundenbesuch *(m)* **werben**	canvass (to)
Durchbruch *(m)*	break-through
Durchdringung *(f)*: Markt...	market penetration
durchführbar	feasible
Durchführbarkeitsstudie *(f)*	feasibility study
durchführen	implement (to)
Durchführung *(f)* **der Strategie** *(f)*	strategy implementation
Durchführung *(f)* **der Unternehmenspolitik** *(f)*	policy execution
Durchführung (f) von Werbetests (mpl) in regionalen Absatzmärkten (mpl)	sales test
Durchführungsplan *(m)*	action plan

Durchsatz *(m)*	throughput
Durchschnitt *(m)*	average
	mean
Durchschnitt *(m)*: gewogener ...	weighted average
durchschnittliche Kosten *(pl)*	average cost
Durchschnittseinkünfte *(fpl)*	average revenue
Durchschnittseinnahmen *(fpl)*	average revenue
Durchschnittsertrag *(m)*	average yield
Durchschnittskosten *(pl)*	average cost
Durchschnittsrendite *(f)*	average yield
Dynamik *(f)*: Betriebs...	industrial dynamics
Dynamik *(f)*: Eigen...	self-actualization
Dynamik *(f)*: Gruppen...	group dynamics
	methetics
Dynamik *(f)*: Industrie...	industrial dynamics
Dynamik *(f)*: Markt...	market dynamics
Dynamik *(f)*: Produkt...	Product dynamics
dynamisch	go-getting
dynamisch sein	be a go-getter (to)
dynamische Bewertung *(f)*	dynamic evaluation
dynamische Programmierung *(f)*	dynamic programming
dynamisches Management-Modell *(n)*	dynamic management model
dynamisches Führungsmodell *(n)*	dynamic management model

E

Echtzeit *(f)*	real time
Eckzins *(m)* für Ausleihungen *(fpl)*	base rate
Ecu *(m)* (Europäische Währungseinheit *(f)*)	ECU (European Currency Unit)
Ecu *(m)*: harter ...	hard ecu
EDV-Sachverständiger *(m)*	computer expert
Effekten- und Emissionsbank *(f)*	investment bank
Effektengeschäft *(n)*	stockbroking
Effektenhandel *(m)*	jobbing
Effektenmakler *(m)*	stockbroker
Effizienz *(f)*	efficiency
EG *(f)* (Europäische Gemeinschaft *(f)*)	EC (European Community)
Eigendynamik *(f)*	self-actualization

Eigenfertigung *(f)*: **Wahl** *(f)* **zwischen … und Kauf** *(m)*	make-or-buy decision
Eigenfinanzierung *(f)*	self-financing
Eigenkapital *(n)*	equity
	net worth
Eigenkapital *(n)*: **Verhältnis** *(n)***zwischen … Fremd- und …**	gearing
	gearing ratio
Eigenkapitalrendite *(f)*	return on equity (ROE)
Eigenkapitalrentabilität *(f)*	return on equity (ROE)
Eigentümer-Unternehmer *(m)*	owner-manager
Eignungsprüfung *(f)*	aptitude test
Eignungstest *(m)*	aptitude test
ein Angebot *(n)* **machen**	tender (to)
ein Geschäft *(n)* **abschließen**	reach a deal (to)
ein Geschäft *(n)* **machen**	reach a deal (to)
ein neues Image *(n)* **aufbauen**	re-image (to)
ein Programm *(n)* **unabsichtlich auslöschen**	crash a program (to)
ein Projekt *(n)* **in seine Einzelteile** *(npl)* **zerlegen**	chunk a project (to)
Ein- und Ausfuhren *(fpl)*: **unsichtbare …**	invisibles
einbehaltene Gewinne *(mpl)*	retained profits
	undistributed profit
eine ganz andere Chose *(f)*	a different ball game
eine Sache *(f)* **gegen eine andere austauschen**	trade-off (to)
einen Deal *(m)* **machen**	reach a deal (to)
einen Unterauftrag *(m)* **vergeben**	subcontract (to)
einen zu hohen Preis *(m)* **ansetzen**	overprice (to)
einen zu hohen Preis *(m)* **verlangen**	overprice (to)
einen Zulieferungsauftrag *(m)* **vergeben**	subcontract (to)
einen Engpaß *(m)* **beseitigen**	debottleneck (to)
einfallsreich	enterprising
einfrieren	freeze (to)
einführen: allmählich …	phase in (to)
einführen: neu …	innovate (to)
einführen: stufenweise …	phase in (to)
Einführung *(f)*	launching
Einführung *(f)* **neuer Mitarbeiter** *(mpl)* **in das Unternehmen** *(n)*	induction
Eingabe *(f)*: **Computer-…**	computer input

eingebaut	built-in
eingeplant	built-in
eingeplanter Verschleiß *(m)*	built-in obsolescence
eingesetztes Kapital *(n)*	capital employed
eingesetztes Kapital *(n)*: Rendite *(f)* des eingesetzten ...s	return on capital employed (ROCE)
eingetragenes Warenzeichen *(n)*	registered trademark
eingleisige Beschaffung *(f)*	single sourcing
eingliedern	integrate (to)
einheitliche Währung *(f)*	single currency
Einheitspreis *(m)*	standard price
Einkauf *(m)*	procurement
	purchasing
einkaufen	buy in (to)
Einkäufer *(m)*: Chef...	chief buyer
Einkäufer *(m)*: Zentral...	chief buyer
Einkaufsgebiet *(n)*	trading area
Einkaufsleiter *(m)*	purchasing manager
Einkaufsmanagement *(n)*	sourcing
Einkaufsmanager *(m)*	procurement manager
Einkaufsverhalten *(n)*	buying behaviour
einklagbar	actionable
Einklang *(m)*: in ... bringen	conciliate (to)
Einkommen *(n)*: verfügbares ...	disposable income
Einkommensteuer *(f)*	income tax
Einkommensteuer *(f)*: negative ...	negative income tax
einmalig	one-off
Einsatz *(m)*	deployment
Einsatz *(m)* (anschließend) besprechen	debrief (to)
Einsatz *(m)* des Personals *(n)*	staff commitment
Einsatz *(m)*: Mittelherkunft *(f)* und -...	source and disposition of funds
Einsatz *(m)*: Rentabilität *(f)* des Kapital...es	return on investment (ROI)
Einsatzanalyse *(f)*	debriefing
Einsatzbesprechung *(f)*	debriefing
Einsatzerfolg *(m)* analysieren	debrief (to)
einschätzen	assess (to)
Einschätzung *(f)*	assessment
	estimate
Einschätzung *(f)*: Markt...	market rating

Einschätzung *(f)*: Qualitäts...	quality assessment
Einschätzung *(f)*: Risiko...	risk assessment
Einschätzung *(f)*: Selbst...	self-appraisal
einsetzen	deploy (to)
einsetzen: anderweitig ...	redeploy (to)
einsetzen: Roboter *(mpl)* ...	robotize (to)
Einstandszahlung (f) an einen abgeworbenen Spitzenmanager (m)	golden hello
einstellen	hire (to)
einstellen: stufenweise ...	phase out (to)
Einstellung *(f)* nicht benötigter Arbeitskräfte *(fpl)*	featherbedding
Einstellung *(f)* ungelernter Arbeitskräfte *(fpl)*	dilution of labour
Einstellung *(f)*: Verbraucher...	user attitude
Einstellung *(f)* von Arbeitskräften *(fpl)*	recruitment
Einstellungsuntersuchung *(f)*	attitude survey
Einverständnis *(n)*: heimliches ...	collusion
einweisen	brief (to)
Einweisung *(f)*	briefing
Einzel-	stand-alone
Einzelhandelspreisindex *(m)*	retail price index (RPI)
Einzelteile *(npl)*: ein Projekt *(n)* in seine ... zerlegen	chunk a project (to)
Einzeltextverarbeiter *(m)*	stand-alone word processor
Einzeltextverarbeitungseinrichtung *(f)*	stand-alone word processor
Einzelwortprozessor *(m)*	stand-alone word processor
eiserner Bestand *(m)*	safety stock
elastisches Budget *(n)*	flexible budget
Elastizität *(f)*	elasticity
Electronic Mail *(f)*	electronic mail (e-mail)
elektrische Gebrauchsgüter (npl): holzverkleidete ...	brown goods
elektronische Datenverarbeitung *(f)*	electronic data processing (EDP)
elektronische Kommunikation	electronic communication
Elektronische Post *(f)*	electronic mail (e-mail)
elektronische Verarbeitung *(f)*	electronic processing
elektronischer Zahlungsverkehr (m) in Verbindung (f) mit einem POS-System (n)	electronic funds transfer at point of sale (EFTPOS)

elektronisches Buchführungssystem *(n)*	electronic accounting system
elektronisches Büro *(n)*	electronic office
Eliminierung *(f)*: Produkt...	product abandonment
Emission *(f)*	issue
Emission *(f)*: Bezugsrechts...	rights issue
Emission *(f)*: Finanzierung *(f)* durch die ... von Schuldtiteln *(mpl)*	debt financing
Emissionsbank *(f)*	investment bank
empfindlich machen	sensitize (to)
empirisch	empirical
Engelt *(n)*: gleiches ...	equal pay
enger Zusammenhang *(m)*	correlation
engere Kandidatenliste *(f)*	shortlist
engere Wahl *(f)*: in die ... ziehen	shortlist (to)
Engpaß *(m)*	bottleneck
Engpaß *(m)*: einen ... beseitigen	debottleneck (to)
Entflechtung *(f)*	divestment
entlassen	fire (to)
entlassen	lay off (to)
entlassen: vorübergehend ...	lay off (to)
Entlassung *(f)*	dismissal
	redundancy
Entlassung *(f)*: fristlose ...	summary dismissal
Entlassung *(f)*: (vorübergehende) ...	lay-off
Entlassungsabfindung *(f)*	severance pay
entmutigen	demotivate (to)
Entmutigung *(f)*	demotivation
Entscheidungsanalyse *(f)*	decision analysis
Entscheidungsbaum *(m)*	decision tree
Entscheidungsfindung *(f)*	decision-making
Entscheidungsmodell *(n)*	decision model
Entscheidungsprozeß *(m)*	decision process
Entscheidungstheorie *(f)*	decision theory
entschlüsseln	unscramble (to)
entwerten	depreciate (to)
Entwicklung *(f)* der Organisation *(f)*	organizational development
Entwicklung *(f)*: Forschung *(f)* und ... (FE, F & E)	research and development (R & D)

Entwicklung *(f)*: Management-...	executive development
	management development
Entwicklung *(f)* neuer Produkte *(npl)*	new-product development
Entwicklung *(f)*: persönliche Weiter...	personal growth
Entwicklung *(f)*: Produkt...	product development
Entwicklung *(f)*: Prognose *(f)* der technologischen ...	technological forecasting
Entwicklungspotential *(n)*	development potential
Entwicklungsprogramm *(n)*	development programme
entwirren	unscramble (to)
Entwurf *(m)*	blueprint
Entwurf *(m)*: Stellen...	job design
Environmental Scanning *(n)*	environmental scan
Ereignis-Knotenplan *(m)*	programme evaluation and review technique (PERT)
erfinden: das schon Erfundene *(n)* ...	reinvent the wheel (to)
Erfolg *(m)*: Unternehmens...	profit performance
Erfolg *(m)*: Werbe...	advertising effectiveness
Erfolgsbeteiligung *(f)*	profit-sharing
Erfolgsfaktor *(m)*: wichtigster ...	key success factor
Erfolgsfaktoren *(mpl)*: strategische Analyse *(f)* der wichtigsten ...	SWOT (strengths, weaknesses, opportunities, threats) analysis
Erfolgsplanung *(f)*	profit planning
ergänzen	top up (to)
Ergebnis *(n)*	profit performance
Ergebnis *(n)*: Arbeits...	job performance
Ergebnisbeteiligung *(f)*	profit-sharing
Ergebnisrechnung *(f)*: Profit-Center-...	profit centre accounting
Ergonometrik *(f)*	ergonometrics
Ergonomie *(f)*	human engineering
Ergonomik *(f)*	ergonomics
Erhebung *(f)* zum Beruf *(m)*	professionalization
Erklärung *(f)* der Unternehmensgrundsätze *(mpl)*	mission statement
Erklärung *(f)* der strategischen Vision *(f)*	vision statement
Erkundung *(f)*: Markt...	market exploration
Erlangung *(f)* eines beruflichen Status *(m)*	professionalization
Erlaubnis *(f)*	licence

Ermittlung (f): (Arbeits-)Zeit...	work measurement
Ermittlung (f) der Erzeugniskosten (pl)	product costing
Ermittlung (f) von Arbeitsablaufstudien (fpl)	methods engineering
ernstgemeinter Vorschlag (m)	value proposal
Erprobung (f): Produkt...	product testing
erreichen: die Gewinnschwelle (f) ...	break even (to)
erreichen: die Rentabilitätsschwelle (f) ...	break even (to)
erreichen: zu ... bemüht sein	target (to)
Erschließungsgesellschaft (f)	developer
erstklassige Standardwerte (mpl)	blue-chip stock
erstklassiges Wertpapier (n)	blue-chip stock
erstklassige Wertpapiere (npl)	gilt
	gilt-edged security
	gilt-edged stock
Ertrag (m)	return
	yield
Ertrag (m): Kapital...	capital gain
Ertrag (m): Vermögens...	earnings on assets
Ertragskraft (f)	earning power
Ertragsleistung (f)	earnings performance
Erwartungen (fpl): Absatz...	sales expectations
Erwartungen (fpl): hinter den ... zurückbleiben	underperform (to)
Erwartungen (fpl): mit einer Stelle verbundene ...	job expectations
Erwartungen (fpl): Verkaufs...	sales expectations
Erweiterung (f) der Arbeitsaufgaben (fpl)	job enlargement
Erwerb (m)	acquisition
Erwerbsgesellschaft (f)	business corporation
Erzeugniskosten (pl): Ermittlung (f) der ...	product costing
Erzeugung (f): Produkt...	product generation
etablierter Markt (m)	mature market
Etat (m)	budget
Etat (m): bewilligter Werbe...	advertising appropriaton
Etat (m): Werbe...	advertising budget
etatisieren	budget (to)
Etatsabweichung (f)	budgetary variance
Etatszuweisung (f)	budget allotment
etwas ganz anderes	a different ball game

Euroanleihe *(f)*	Eurobond
Eurobond *(m)*	Eurobond
Eurodollar *(m)*	Eurodollar
Euromarkt *(m)*	Euromarket
Europäische Gemeinschaft *(f)* (EG)	European Community (EC)
Europäische Währungseinheit *(f)* (Ecu *(m)*)	European Currency Unit (ECU)
Europäische Währungsunion *(f)*	European Monetary Union (EMU)
europäischer Binnenmarkt *(m)*	single market (*of the EC*)
Europäisches Währungssystem *(n)* (EWS)	European Monetary System (EMS)
Eurowährung *(f)*	Eurocurrency
Eventualfälle *(mpl)*	contingencies
Eventualverbindlichkeiten *(fpl)*	contingencies
Eventualverbindlichkeiten *(fpl)*: Rückstellung *(f)* für ...	contingency reserve
EWS *(n)* (Europäisches Währungssystem *(n)*)	EMS (European Monetary System)
Exklusivvertreter *(m)*	sole agent
Expansionsstrategie *(f)*	expansion strategy
Expertensystem *(n)*	expert system
exponentielle Glättung *(f)*	exponential smoothing
exponentieller Trend *(m)*	exponential trend
extern	out-house
externalisieren	externalize (to)
exterritorial	offshore

F

Fabrikgemeinkosten *(pl)*	factory overheads
Facharbeiter *(mpl)*	skilled labour
Factoring *(n)*	factoring
Fähigkeit *(f)*	capability
	competency
Fähigkeit *(f)*: Analyse *(f)* der ...en *(pl)*	skills analysis
Fähigkeit *(f)*: Führungs...en *(pl)*	executive competence
	management competence

Fähigkeit *(f)*: Leistungs…	efficiency
Fähigkeitsanalyse *(f)*	skills analysis
faire (zwischenstaatliche) Handelspraktiken *(fpl)*	level playing-field
fairer Wettbewerb *(m)*	fair competition
Faksimile *(n)*	facsimile
Faksimiledruck *(m)*	facsimile
Faktor *(m)*	factor
Faktor *(m)*: Analyse *(f)* der Gewinn…en *(pl)*	profit-factor analysis
Faktor *(m)*: arbeitshemmender …	disincentive
Faktor *(m)*: Auslastungs…	load factor
Faktor *(m)*: Gewinn…analyse *(f)*	profit-factor analysis
Faktor *(m)*: Kosten…	cost factor
Faktor *(m)*: Motivations…	motivator
Fälligkeitstag *(m)*	due date
Fälligkeitstermin *(m)*	due date
Fallstudie *(f)*	case study
Fax *(n)*	fax
faxen	fax (to)
Faxgerät *(n)*	fax machine
Fazilität *(f)*: Kredit…	borrowing facility
Feedback *(n)*	feedback
Fehlbetrag *(m)*	shortfall
Fehler *(mpl)* beseitigen	debug (to)
Fehler *(m)*: Beseitigung *(f)* von …quellen *(fpl)*	diagnostic routine
Fehlersuche und -behebung *(f)*	troubleshooting
Fehlfunktion *(f)*	dysfunction
	malfunction
Feld *(n)*: Überprüfung *(f)* im …	field testing
Feld-Tests *(mpl)*	field testing
Feldforschung *(f)*	field research
Feldzug *(m)*: Werbe…	advertising drive
Fenster *(n)*	window
Fernkopierer *(m)*	fax machine
Fernschreiben (n): Bestätigung (f) von erfolgreicher Übermittlung (f) eines …s	answerback code
Fernstudium *(n)*	distance learning

Fertigproduktmenge *(f)*: wirtschaftliche ...	economic batch quantity
fertigstellen	turn around (to)
Fertigung *(f)*	production
Fertigung *(f)*: computerintegrierte ...	computer-integrated manufacturing (CIM)
Fertigung *(f)*: computerunterstützte ...	computer-aided manufacturing (CAM)
Fertigung *(f)*: Fließ...	continuous-flow production
Fertigung *(f)*: Kostenrechnung *(f)* für Serien...	process costing
Fertigung *(f)*: Sorten...	batch production
Fertigungsgemeinkosten *(pl)*	factory overheads
Fertigungskapazität *(f)*	manufacturing capacity
Fertigungskontrolle *(f)*	manufacturing control
	production control
Fertigungslöhne *(mpl)*	direct labour
Fertigungsmethode *(f)*	production technique
Fertigungssteuerung *(f)*	manufacturing control
Fertigungsstraße *(f)*	production line
Fertigungstechnik *(f)*	product engineering
fester Verrechnungspreis *(m)*	standard price
Fest(wert)speicher *(m)*	read-only memory (ROM)
Festkosten *(pl)*	fixed costs
	fixed expenses
festlegen	schedule (to)
Festlegung *(f)* **der Handelswege** *(mpl)*	routing
Festlegung *(f)* **der Route** *(f)*	routing
Festlegung *(f)* **der Verrechnungspreise** *(mpl)*	transfer pricing
Festplatte *(f)*	hard disk
festsetzen: Preis *(m)* ...	price (to)
Festsetzung *(f)*: Preis...	price determination
	price-fixing
	pricing
festverzinsliche Schuldtitel *(mpl)*	loan stock
feuern	fire (to)
Filiale *(f)*	branch office
Financial Futures *(pl)*	financial futures
Finanz *(f)*: **Bewertung** *(f)* **der ...mittel** *(npl)*	financial appraisal
Finanz *(f)*: **Überprüfung** *(f)* **der ...lage** *(f)*	financial review

Finanz-Controlling *(n)*	financial control
Finanzanalyse *(f)*	financial analysis
Finanzbewertung *(f)*	financial appraisal
Finanzchef *(m)*	financial director
Finanzfutures *(pl)*	financial futures
finanzielle Beteiligung *(f)*	financial involvement
	vested interest
finanzielle Kennzahl *(f)*	financial ratio
finanzieller Anreiz *(m)*	financial incentive
finanzieren	finance (to)
Finanzierung *(f)*	financing
	funding
Finanzierung *(f)* durch die Emission *(f)* von Schuldtiteln *(mpl)*	debt financing
Finanzierung *(f)*: Defizit...	deficit financing
Finanzierung *(f)*: Eigen...	self-financing
Finanzierung *(f)*: Selbst...	self-financing
Finanzierung *(f)* von Verpflichtungen *(fpl)*	debt financing
Finanzierung *(f)* von Produktideen *(fpl)*	seed money
Finanzierungskennzahl *(f)*	financial ratio
Finanzkontrolle *(f)*	financial control
Finanzlage *(f)*	financial position
Finanzmanagement *(n)*	financial management
Finanzmittel *(npl)*: Bewertung *(f)* der ...	financial appraisal
Finanznorm *(f)*	financial standard
Finanzplanung *(f)*	cash budgeting
	financial planning
Finanzplanung *(f)* von Anfang *(m)* Null *(f)*	zero-base budget
Finanzstatus *(m)*	financial position
Finanzstrategie *(f)*	financial strategy
Finanzterminkontrakte *(mpl)*	financial futures
Finanzüberprüfung *(f)*	financial review
Finanzverwaltung *(f)*	financial administration
Finanzvorstand *(m)*	financial director
Findung *(f)*: Entscheidungs...	decision-making
Findung *(f)*: Ziel...	goal-seeking
Firma *(f)*: flexible ...	flexible firm
Firma *(f)*: Software...	software company
Firmenbezeichnung *(f)*	trade name

Firmenkultur *(f)*	organization culture
Firmenname *(m)*	trade name
Firmenübernahmen (fpl): Vorkehrung *(f)* zur Abwehr *(f)* von ...	poison pill
Firmenwert *(m)*	goodwill
Firmenzeichen *(n)*	company logo
Fiskalpolitik *(f)*	fiscal policy
Fixkosten *(pl)*	fixed costs
	fixed expenses
Flaute *(f)*	downturn
	slack
flexible Arbeitszeiten *(fpl)*	flexible working hours
flexible Firma *(f)*	flexible firm
Fließband *(n)*	production line
Fließbandproduktion *(f)*	line production
Fließfertigung *(f)*	continuous-flow production
	flow production
Floppy-Disk *(f)*	floppy disk
Fluchtgelder *(npl)*	hot money
Fluktuation *(f)*	natural wastage
	staff turnover
Fluktuation *(f)* der Nachwuchskräfte *(fpl)*	trainee turnover
Fluktuation *(f):* Personal...	labour turnover
Fluß *(m):* Informations...	information flow
Fluß *(m):* Material...	materials handling
Fluß *(m):* Produktions...	flow line
Flußdiagramm *(n)*	flow chart
	flow diagram
flüssig	cash-rich
flüssig: nicht ...	cash-poor
flüssige Mittel *(npl)*	liquid assets
Fonds *(m):* Amortisations...	sinking fund
Fonds *(m):* Tilgungs...	sinking fund
fördernd	promotional
Förderung *(f)*	advancement
Förderung *(f):* Verkaufs...	sales promotion
Forderungen *(fpl):* aus zweifelhaften ... herrührende Verluste *(mpl)*	bad-debt losses
Forderungen *(fpl):* zweifelhafte ...	bad debts

Formulierung *(f)* der Unternehmenspolitik *(f)*	policy formulation
Formulierung *(f)* der Unternehmensstrategie *(f)*	strategy formulation
Forschung *(f)*: Feld...	field research
Forschung *(f)*: Marketing-...	marketing research
Forschung *(f)*: Markt...	market research
Forschung *(f)*: Motivations...	motivational research
Forschung *(f)*: Operations...	operational research (OR)
	operations research (OR)
Forschung *(f)*: Primär...	field research
Forschung *(f)*: Produkt...	product research
Forschung *(f)*: Schreibtisch...	desk research
Forschung *(f)* und Entwicklung *(f)* (FE, F & E)	research and development (R & D)
Forschung *(f)*: Unternehmens...	operational research (OR)
Forschung *(f)*: Unternehmens...	operations research (OR)
Forschung *(f)*: Verbraucher...	consumer research
Forschung *(f)*: Verhaltens...	behavioural science
Forschung *(f)*: Werbe...	advertising research
Forschung *(f)*: Wirtschafts...	economic research
Forschung *(f)*: zweckfreie ...	blue sky research
Forschungsabteilung *(f)*	research department
Fortbildungsangebote *(npl)*	extension services
fortlaufend	ongoing
fortlaufende Inventur *(f)*	continuous stocktaking
fortlaufende Warenbestandsaufnahme *(f)*	continuous stocktaking
Fortschreibung *(f)*	update
Fortschrittskontrolle *(f)*	progress control
fraktionieren	fractionalize (to)
Franchise *(f)*	franchise
Franchise *(f)*: in ... vergeben	franchise (to)
franchisieren	franchise (to)
Franchising *(n)*	franchising (n)
freiberuflich tätig werden	freelance (to go)
freie Kapazität *(f)*	spare capacity
freies Unternehmertum *(n)*	private enterprise
Freiverkehrswerte *(mpl)*	unlisted security
freiwillige Zuwendung *(f)*	*ex gratia* payment

Fremdkapital *(n)*: Verhältnis *(n)* von Eigen- zu ...	debt-equity ratio leverage
Fremdkapital (n): von ... unterstützte Übernahme (f)	leveraged buyout (LBO)
Fremdkapital (n): von ... unterstütztes Übernahmeangebot (n)	leveraged bid
frisieren	fiddle (to)
frisieren: Zahlen *(fpl)* ...	massage the figures (to)
Frist *(f)*	deadline
Frist *(f)*: Kapitalrückfluß...	payback period
fristlose Entlassung *(f)*	summary dismissal
führen	manage (to)
Führer *(m)*: Markt...	market leader
Führer *(m)*: Preis...	price leader
Führung *(f)*	leadership
Führung *(f)*: Betriebs...	business management
Führung *(f)* durch Zielvereinbarung *(f)*	management by objectives (MBO)
Führung *(f)* durch Vorgabe *(f)* von Programmen *(npl)*	programmed management
Führung *(f)*: dynamisches ...smodell	dynamic management model
Führung *(f)*: kooperativer ...sstil *(m)*	participative management
Führung *(f)*: Personal...	manpower management
Führung *(f)*: Unternehmens...	business management management
Führung *(f)*: Unternehmens... unter Beteiligung *(f)* nachgeordneter Führungsebenen *(fpl)*	multiple management
Führung *(f)*: Verhaltensgitter *(n)*, aus dem ...sstile *(mpl)* abgeleitet werden	managerial grid
Führungs-	managerial
Führungsebenen *(fpl)*: auf höheren ...	up the line
Führungsebenen *(fpl)*: auf nachgeordneten ...	down the line
Führungsebenen *(fpl)*: Unternehmensführung *(f)* unter Beteiligung *(f)* nachgeordneter ...	multiple management
Führungsfähigkeiten *(fpl)*	executive competence management competence
Führungsfunktion *(f)*	managerial function
Führungskontrolle *(f)*	managerial control

Führungskraft *(f)*	executive
	manager
Führungskräfte *(fpl)*: Aufstieg *(m)* der ...	executive advancement
Führungskräfte *(fpl)*: Ausbildung *(f)* der ...	management training
Führungskräfte *(fpl)*: Ausbildung *(f)* von ...n	executive training
Führungskräfte *(fpl)*: Beförderung *(f)* der ...	executive advancement
Führungskräfte *(fpl)*: Suche *(f)* nach ...n	executive search
Führungskräftestrategie *(f)*	executive manpower strategy
Führungsmodell *(n)*: dynamisches ...	dynamic management model
Führungsnachfolgeplanung *(f)*	management succession planning
Führungspersonal *(n)*	management staff
Führungspotential *(n)*	management potential
Führungsqualitäten *(fpl)*	leadership
Führungsspiel *(n)*	management game
Führungsstil *(m)*	managerial style
Führungsstruktur *(f)*	managerial structure
Führungsteam *(n)*	management team
Führungstechnik *(f)*	management technique
Full-Service-Leasing *(n)*	contract hire
Funktion *(f)*	function
Funktion *(f)*: Führungs...	managerial function
funktional	functional
funktionale Analyse *(f)*	functional analysis
funktionale Aufteilung *(f)*	functional layout
funktionale Beziehungen *(fpl)*	functional relations
funktionale Kostenrechnung *(f)*	functional costing
funktionale Methode *(f)*	functional approach
funktionale Organisation *(f)*	functional organization
funktionale Verantwortlichkeit *(f)*	functional responsibility
funktionales Management *(n)*	functional management
funktionell	functional
funktionieren	perform (to)
Funktionsstörung *(f)*	dysfunction
	malfunction
Funktionstaste *(f)*	function key
für den Massenmarkt *(m)*	down-market
Fusion *(f)*	amalgamation
	merger

Fusionen *(fpl)* und Übernahmen *(fpl)*	mergers and acquisitions (M & A)
fusionieren	amalgamate (to)
fusionieren	merge (to)

G

ganztägig Beschäftigter *(m)*	full-timer
Ganztagsbeschäftigung *(f)*	full-time employment
Garantie (f) einer beträchtlichen Abfindungszahlung (f) im Falle (m) der Entlassung (f)	golden parachute
Gastland *(n)*	host country
Gateway *(n)*	gateway
Gattungs-	generic
Gebiet *(n)*: Absatz...	sales area
	sales territory
	trading area
Gebiet *(n)*: Einkaufs...	trading area
Gebiet *(n)*: Verkaufs...	sales area
Gebiet *(n)*: Vertriebs...	sales territory
Gebiet *(n)*: Wachstums...	growth area
Gebiet *(n)*: Zuweisung *(f)* von Aufgaben...en *(pl)*	allocation of responsibilities
Gebietsleiter *(m)*	area manager
Gebräuche *(mpl)*: Sitten *(fpl)* und ...	custom and practice
Gebrauchsgüter *(npl)*	(consumer) durables
Gebrauchsgüter (npl): holzverkleidete elektrische ...	brown goods
Gebrauchsgüter *(npl)*: weiße ...	white goods
Gebühr *(f)*: Makler...	brokerage
	brokerage fees
Gedankengänge *(mpl)*	rationale
gedeckt: ungenügend ...	overextended
gefährliche Chemikalien *(fpl)*	hazchem (hazardous chemicals)
Gefahrstoffe *(mpl)*	hazchem (hazardous chemicals)
Gefälle *(n)*: Lohn...	wage differential
Gefälle *(n)*: Preis...	price differential
gegen Bandlaufrichtung *(f)*	upstream

Gegengeschäfte *(npl)*	countertrade
gegenläufig	upstream
gegenseitige Anerkennung *(f)*	mutual recognition
Gegenwartswert *(m)*: **Methode** *(f)* **des ...es**	present value method
Gehalt *(n)*: **Lohn- und ...summe** *(f)*	payroll
Gehalt *(n)*: **Vergütung** *(f)* **neben ... oder Lohn** *(m)*	fringe benefits
Gehaltsliste *(f)*	payroll
Gehaltsprogressionskurve *(f)*	salary progression curve
Gehaltsstopp *(m)*: **Lohn- und ...**	pay pause
Gehaltsstruktur *(f)*	salary structure
Gehaltsstufe *(f)*	salary grade
Gehaltsübersicht *(f)*	salary review
Geld *(n)*	cash
Geld *(n)*: **heißes ...**	hot money
Geldmenge *(f)*	money supply
Geldpolitik *(f)*	monetary policy
Geldwäsche *(f)*	laundering
Gelegenheit *(f)*: **günstige ...**	window of opportunity
gelernte Arbeiter *(mpl)*	skilled labour
Gemauschel *(n)*	wheeling and dealing
Gemeinkosten *(pl)*	overheads
Gemeinkosten *(pl)*: **Aufteilungsverfahren** *(n)* **für ...**	overheads recovery
Gemeinkosten *(pl)*: **Fabrik...**	factory overheads
Gemeinkosten *(pl)*: **Fertigungs...**	factory overheads
Gemeinkosten *(pl)*: **Verwaltungs...**	administrative overheads
Gemeinkostenlöhne *(mpl)*	indirect labour
gemeinnützig	non-profit-making
gemeinsame Beratung *(f)*	joint consultation
gemeinsame Problembewältigung *(f)*	brainstorming
gemeinsame Sprache *(f)*	common language
gemeinsame Verhandlung *(f)*	joint negotiation
gemeinsame Vertretung *(f)*	joint representation
gemeinsame Währung *(f)*	common currency
Gemeinsamer Markt *(m)*	Common Market
Gemeinschaft *(f)*: **Europäische ... (EG)**	European Community (EC)
Gemeinschafts-	collaborative
Gemeinschaftsfirma *(f)*	joint-venture company

Gemeinschaftsunternehmen *(n)*	joint venture
Genehmigung *(f)*	licence
Generaldirektor *(m)*	general manager
	managing director (MD)
	chief executive
Generaldirektor *(m)*: stellvertretender ...	deputy managing director
genereller Lohnanstieg *(m)*	across-the-board increase
genereller Preisanstieg *(m)*	across-the-board increase
generisch	generic
Gentleman's Agreement *(n)*	gentleman's agreement
Gentlemen's Agreement *(npl)*	gentleman's agreement
gepackt: gut ...	well-packaged
geplante Instandhaltung *(f)*	planned maintenance
geplante Wartung *(f)*	planned maintenance
geplanter Verschleiß *(m)*	planned obsolescence
Gerichtsbarkeit *(f)*	jurisdiction
gesamte Unternehmensziele *(npl)*	overall company objectives
gesamte Produktionsanlagen *(fpl)*	production complex
Geschäft *(n)*	deal
Geschäft *(n)*: Abwicklung *(f)* eines ...s	winding-up
Geschäft *(n)*: Auflösung *(f)* eines ...s	winding-up
Geschäft *(n)*: Effekten...	stockbroking
Geschäft *(n)*: ein ... abschließen	reach a deal (to)
Geschäft *(n)*: ein ... machen	reach a deal (to)
Geschäft *(n)*: Kopplungs...	package deal
Geschäft *(n)*: Tausch...	trade-off
Geschäfte *(npl)*	operations
Geschäftemacherei *(f)*	wheeling and dealing
geschäftlicher Vorschlag *(m)*	business proposition
Geschäftsabschluß *(m)*: konsolidierter ...	consolidated accounts
Geschäftsbank *(f)*	commercial bank
Geschäftsbetrieb *(m)*	business system
Geschäftsbeziehungen *(fpl)*	business relations
Geschäftsführer *(m)*	managing director (MD)
Geschäftsgang *(m)*	business stream
Geschäftsjahr *(n)*	financial year
	fiscal year
Geschäftslage *(f)*	business outlook
Geschäftspolitik *(f)*	business policy

Geschäftsportfolio (n)	business portfolio
Geschäftspraktiken (fpl): restriktive ...	restrictive practices (legal)
Geschäftsprognose (f)	business forecasting
Geschäftsrückgang (m)	downturn
Geschäftsstrategie (f)	business strategy
Geschäftstätigkeit (f)	operations
Geschäftsumsatz (m)	sales turnover
Geschäftsunternehmen (n)	business corporation
Geschäftsverkehr (m)	business stream
geschlossene Schleife (f)	closed loop
geschlossener Kreislauf (m)	closed loop
Gesellschaft (f): an einem Joint Venture (n) beteiligte ... (f)	joint-venture company
Gesellschaft (f): Beteiligungs...	associate company
Gesellschaft (f): börsennotierte ...	publicly listed company
Gesellschaft (f): Dach...	holding company
Gesellschaft (f): Erschließungs...	developer
Gesellschaft (f): Erwerbs ...	business corporation
Gesellschaft (f): Holding...	holding company
Gesellschaft (f): Kapital...	business corporation
Gesellschaft (f): Konzern...	affiliate company
Gesellschaft (f): Mutter...	parent company
Gesellschaft (f): nicht börsennotierte ...	unlisted company
Gesellschaft (f): Offene Handels...	partnership
Gesellschaft (f): Personen...	partnership
Gesellschaft (f): Schwester...	affiliate company
Gesellschaft (f): Tochter...	subsidiary company
Gesellschaft (f): verbundene ...	affiliate company
Gesellschafter (m)	partner
Gesellschaftsvermögen (n)	net worth
Gespräch (m): Beurteilungs...	performance review
Gespräch (n): Verkaufs...	sales talk
gestaffelter Urlaub (m)	staggered holidays
gestalten	structure (to)
Gestaltung (f): Arbeits...	work structuring
Gestaltung (f): Büro...	office planning
Gestaltung (f): Produkt...	product design
Gestaltung (f): System...	systems design
Gewerkschaft (f)	trade union

Gewerkschaft *(f)*: von einer ... nicht genehmigter Streik *(m)*	unofficial action
gewerkschaftliche Vertrauensfrau *(f)*	shop steward
gewerkschaftlicher Vertrauensmann *(m)*	shop steward
gewerkschaftspflichtiger Betrieb *(m)*	closed shop
Gewichtung *(f)*	weighting
Gewinn *(m)*	pay off
	profit
	return
Gewinn *(m)*: Analyse *(f)* der ...faktoren *(mpl)*	profit-factor analysis
Gewinn *(m)*: angemessener ...	fair return
Gewinn *(m)*: Brutto...	gross profit
Gewinn *(m)*: Brutto...spanne	gross margin (GM)
Gewinn *(m)* je Aktie *(f)*	earnings per share (EPS)
	per share earnings
Gewinn *(m)*: Kapital ...	capital gain
Gewinn *(m)*: Kosten-/Umsatz-/...analyse	cost, volume, profit analysis
Gewinn *(m)*: Kurs-... -Verhältnis *(n)*	price-earnings ratio (P/E)
Gewinn *(m)*: Netto...	net profit
Gewinn *(m)*: Rein...	net margin
gewinnabhängige Lohn- und Gehaltszahlung *(f)*	profit-related pay
Gewinnaussichten *(fpl)*	profit outlook
Gewinnauswirkung *(f)*	profit impact
	profit implication
Gewinnbeteiligung *(f)*	profit-sharing
Gewinne *(mpl)* realisieren	realize (*profit*) (to)
Gewinne *(mpl)*: ausgeschüttete ...	distributed profit
Gewinne *(mpl)*: einbehaltene ...	retained profits
Gewinneinbehaltung *(f)* zu Investitionszwecken *(mpl)*	ploughback
gewinnen: an Wert *(m)* ...	appreciate (to)
Gewinnfaktoranalyse *(f)*	profit-factor analysis
Gewinnmaximierung *(f)*	profit maximization
Gewinnmotiv *(n)*	profit motive
Gewinnoptimierung *(f)*	profit optimization
Gewinnprojektion *(f)*	profit projection
Gewinnrendite *(f)*	earnings yield

Gewinnschwelle *(f)*	break-even point
Gewinnschwelle *(f)*: die … erreichen	break even (to)
Gewinnschwellenanalyse *(f)*	break-even analysis
Gewinnspanne *(f)*	profit margin
Gewinnspanne *(f)*: Brutto…	gross margin
Gewinnspanne *(f)*: Netto…	net margin
Gewinnspannen *(fpl)* **halten**	hold margins (to)
Gewinnstrategie *(f)*	profit strategy
Gewinnstreben *(n)*	profit motive
Gewinnverbesserung *(f)*	profit improvement
Gewinnziel *(n)*	profit goal
	profit target
Gewinnzuschlag *(m)*	mark-up
gewogener Durchschnitt *(m)*	weighted average
gezielte Bemühungen *(fpl)* **um Produktivitätssteigerung** *(f)*	productivity drive
Gitterstruktur *(f)*	grid structure
Glättung *(f)*: exponentielle …	exponential smoothing
Gleichberechtigung *(f)*	equality
gleicher Lohn *(m)*	equal pay
gleiches Entgelt *(n)*	equal pay
Gleichheit *(f)*	equality
gleitende Arbeitszeit *(f)*	flexible working hours
gleitende Skala *(f)*	sliding scale
Gleitzeit *(f)*	flexitime
Global Image *(n)*	global image
globalisieren	globalize (to)
Globalisierung *(f)*	globalization
Globalmarketing *(n)*	global marketing
Golden Handshake *(m)*	golden handshake
Goodwill *(m)*	goodwill
Grad *(m)*: Liquiditäts…	liquidity ratio
Grafik *(f)*	graphics
Gratifikation *(f)*	bonus
	ex gratia payment
grauer Markt *(m)*	grey market
Grenzkosten *(pl)*	marginal costs
Grenzkostenrechnung *(f)*	direct costing
	marginal costing

grobe Schätzung *(f)*	guesstimate
Großcomputer *(m)*	mainframe
Größennachteil *(m)*	diseconomy of scale
Größenvorteil *(m)*	economy of scale
Großraum-	open-plan
Großrechner *(m)*	mainframe
Gründe *(mpl)*	rationale
Grundsätze *(mpl)*: Absatz...	sales policy
Grundsätze *(mpl)*: korporative	corporatism
Gründung *(f)*: Unternehmens...	flotation
Gründungskosten *(pl)*	set-up costs
	start-up costs
Gruppe *(f)*: Arbeits...	working party
Gruppe *(f)*: Aufkauf ...	corner
Gruppe *(f)*: Produkt...	product group
	product line
Gruppe *(f)*: Projekt...	task force
Gruppenakkord *(m)*	group incentive
Gruppenanreiz *(m)*	group incentive
Gruppenausbildung *(f)*	group training
Gruppenbonus *(m)*	group bonus
Gruppendynamik *(f)*	group dynamics
	methectics
Gruppenleiter *(m)*	team leader
Gruppentraining *(n)*	group training
günstige Gelegenheit *(f)*	window of opportunity
günstiger Augenblick *(m)*	window of opportunity
gut gepackt	well-packaged
gut verpackt	well-packaged
Güter *(npl)*: Industrie...	industrial goods
Güter *(npl)*: Investitions...	capital goods
Güter *(npl)*: Kapital...	capital goods
Güter *(npl)*: Konsum...	consumer goods
Güter *(npl)*: Verbrauchs...	consumer goods
Güter *(npl)*: Wirtschafts...	capital assets

H

Hacker *(m)*	hacker
Hacker-Delikt *(n)*	hacking
Hacker-Tätigkeit *(f)*	hacking
Halbfabrikate *(npl)*	work in progress
Halbleiter *(m)*	semiconductor
Halbtagsbeschäftigung *(f)*	part-time employment
Halbtagskraft *(f)*	part-timer
haltbar bis	use-by date
Haltbarkeit *(f)*	shelf life
halten: à jour ...	update (to)
Hand *(f)*: von ...	hands-on
Handarbeiter *(m)*	blue-collar (worker)
Handel *(m)*: Festlegung *(f)* der ...swege *(mpl)*	routing
Handel *(m)*: Offene ...sgesellschaft *(f)*	partnership
Handel *(m)*: Patent...	patent trading
Handel *(m)*: Tausch ...	barter trade
	counter trade
handelbare Wertpapiere *(npl)*: Substitution *(f)* von Bankkrediten *(mpl)* durch ...	securitization
Handelsartikel *(m)*	commodity
Handelsbank *(f)*	merchant bank
Handelsbeschränkung *(f)*	trade restriction
Handelshemmnis *(n)*	trade restriction
Handelsname *(m)*	trade name
Handelspraktiken *(fpl)*: faire (zwischenstaatliche) ...	level playing-field
Handelsprogramm *(n)*	trading programme
Handelsungleichgewicht *(n)*	trade imbalance
Handelsware *(f)*	commodity
Händler *(m)*	dealer
Händler *(m)*: Zwischen... für Software-Vertrieb *(m)*	software broker
Hardcopy *(f)*	hard copy
Harddisk *(m)*	hard disk
Hardkopie *(f)*	hard copy
Hardsell *(m)*	hard sell

Hardware *(f)*	hardware
harmonisieren	harmonize (to)
Harmonisierung *(f)*	harmonization
harter Ecu *(m)*	hard ecu
Häufigkeitsverteilung *(f)*	frequency distribution
Hauptbuchhalter *(m)*	chief accountant
Hauptbüro *(n)*	head office
Hauptprodukt *(n)*	core product
Haus *(n)*: Stil *(m)* des ...es	house style
Haushalt *(m)*	budget
Haushaltsmittel *(npl)*: Bewilligung *(f)* von ...n	budget appropriation
Haushaltsplan *(m)*: im ... unterbringen	budget (to)
Haushaltsvoranschlag *(m)*	budget forecast
Hausse *(f)*	boom
	bull market
Haussespekulant *(m)*	bull
Haussier *(m)*	bull
Headhunter *(m)*	head-hunter
Hebelwirkung *(f)*	leverage
Hedgegeschäft *(npl)*	hedging operation
Hedgegeschäfte *(npl)*	hedging
Hedging *(n)*	hedging
	hedging operation
heimliches Einverständnis *(n)*	collusion
heißes Geld *(n)*	hot money
herabsetzen: Preise *(mpl)* ...	cut prices (to)
hergestellt: nach Maß *(n)* ...	customized
Herkunft *(f)*: Mittel... und -einsatz *(m)*	source and disposition of funds
herstellen	roll out (to)
Herstellung *(f)*	production
Herstellungsmethode *(f)*	production technique
heruntersegmentieren	segment (to)
Heuristik *(f)*	heuristics
High Potential *(n)*	high-flier
High-Tech-	high-tech
Highflyer *(m)*	high-flier
Highflyer (m): Berufsweg (m) eines ...s	fast-track
Hilfsoperationen *(fpl)*	ancillary operations
Hilfsprogramm *(n)*	toolbox

hinter den Erwartungen *(fpl)* zurückbleiben	underperform (to)
hinterher kritisieren	second guess (to)
Hire-and-fire-Mentalität *(f)*	hiring and firing
Hire-and-fire-Praxis *(f)*	hiring and firing
Hochkonjunktur *(f)*	boom
Höchstlohn *(m)*	wage ceiling
Hochtalent *(n)*	high-flier
Hochtechnologie *(f)*	high-tech
hochwertig	upmarket
Holdinggesellschaft *(f)*	holding company
holzverkleidete elektrische Gebrauchsgüter (npl)	brown goods
Hörensagen *(n)*: vom ...	grapevine
horizontale Integration *(f)*	horizontal integration
Huckepackverkehr *(m)*	piggyback

I

Ideen *(fpl)* erzeugen	generate ideas (to)
illiquid	cash-poor
im Haushaltsplan *(m)* unterbringen	budget (to)
im Wert *(m)* steigen	appreciate (to)
Image *(n)*: Corporate ...	corporate image
Image *(n)*: ein neues ... aufbauen	re-image (to)
Image *(n)*: Global ...	global image
Image *(n)*: Marken...	brand image
Image *(n)*: Produkt...	product image
Image *(n)*: Unternehmens...	corporate image
immaterielle Anlagewerte *(mpl)*	intangible assets
Impulsgüter *(npl)*	impulse goods
Impulskaufen *(n)*	impulse buying
Impulswaren *(fpl)*	impulse goods
Impulswaren *(fpl)*: Verkauf *(m)* von ...	impulse sale
in Bandlaufrichtung *(f)*	downstream
in Betrieb *(m)*	on stream
in Bruchteile *(mpl)* zerlegen	fractionalize (to)
in den Ruhestand *(m)* treten	retire (to)
in die engere Wahl *(f)* ziehen	shortlist (to)
in Einklang *(m)* bringen	conciliate (to)

in Franchise *(f)* vergeben	franchise (to)
in Lizenz *(f)*	under licence
in Sparten *(fpl)* aufteilen	compartmentalize (to)
Index *(m)*: Wachstums...	growth index
Indexzahl *(f)*	index number
Indexziffer *(f)*	index number
indirekt prozeßgekoppelt	offline
indirekte Ausgaben *(fpl)*	indirect expenses
indirekte Kosten *(pl)*	indirect costs
Industrie *(f)*: Wachstums...	growth industry
Industrieanlagen-Leasing *(n)*	plant hire
Industriedynamik *(f)*	industrial dynamics
Industriegüter *(npl)*	industrial goods
Industriemüll *(m)*	industrial waste
Industriespionage *(f)*	industrial espionage
Industriezweig *(m)*: absterbender ...	sunset industry
Inflation *(f)*: Nachfrage...	demand-pull inflation
Inflation *(f)*: nachfrageinduzierte ...	demand-pull inflation
inflationärer Druck *(m)*	inflationary pressure
Inflationsdruck *(m)*	inflationary pressure
Informatik *(f)*	informatics
Information *(f)*: Management-...en *(pl)*	management information
Information *(f)*: Management-...ssystem *(n)*	management information system (MIS)
Information *(f)*: Markt...en *(pl)*	market intelligence
Information *(f)*: Wirtschafts...	economic intelligence
Informationen *(fpl)*: Kontroll...	control information
Informationsbearbeitung *(f)*	information handling
Informationsbesprechung *(f)*	briefing
Informationsfluß *(m)*	information flow
Informationsnetz *(n)*	information network
Informationsrückgewinnung *(f)*	information retrieval
Informationssystem *(n)*	information system
Informationstechnologie *(f)*	IT (information technology) information technology
Informationstheorie *(f)*	information theory
Informationsverarbeitung *(f)*	information processing
Informationswiedergewinnung *(f)*	information retrieval
informelle Organisation *(f)*	informal organization

Infrastruktur *(f)*	infrastructure
ingenieur- und arbeitswissenschaftliche Organisationsgestaltung *(f)*	industrial engineering
Inhalt *(m)***: Arbeits...**	job content
	work content
Inhalt *(m)***: Aufgliederung** *(f)* **des Stellen...(e)s**	operations breakdown
Inhouse-	in-house
Inhouse-Netz *(n)*	local area network (LAN)
initiativ	proactive
initiative Strategie *(f)*	proactive strategy
initiativfreudig	go-getting
initiativfreudig sein	be a go-getter (to)
Inkremental-	incremental
Inkrementalanalyse *(f)*	incremental analysis
inkrementell	incremental
inkrementelle Analyse *(f)*	incremental analysis
Innenrevision *(f)*	internal audit
innerbetriebliche Ausbildung *(f)*	on-the-job training
	training within industry (TWI)
innerbetriebliche Mitarbeiterbeziehungen *(fpl)*	human relations
innerbetriebliche Schulung *(f)*	in-plant training
innerbetriebliche Tarifverhandlungen *(fpl)*	plant bargaining
Innovationsführerschaft *(f)*	cutting edge
Innovationsmanagement *(n)*	change management (management of change)
innovativ	innovative
innovatorisch	innovative
innovieren	innovate (to)
inoffizieller Streik *(m)*	unofficial strike
Input *(m)*	input
Input-Output-Analyse *(f)*	input-output analysis
Input-Output-Tabelle *(f)*	input-output table
Insidergeschäfte *(npl)*	insider dealing
Insiderhandel *(m)*	insider trading
Instandhaltung *(f)***: Betriebs...**	plant maintenance
Instandhaltung *(f)***: geplante ...**	planned maintenance
Instandhaltung *(f)***: vorbeugende ...**	preventive maintenance

Instanzenweg *(m)*	chain of command
	line of command
instanzielle Rang- und	line relations
Weisungsbeziehungen *(fpl)*	
instanzielle Zuständigkeit (f)	line responsibility
instruieren	brief (to)
Instruktionen *(fpl)*: beauftragen und ... geben	brief (to)
Integration *(f)*	integration
Integration *(f)*: horizontale ...	horizontal integration
Integration *(f)*: vertikale ...	vertical integration
integrieren	integrate (to)
integriertes Management-System *(n)*	integrated management system
integriertes Projekt-Management *(n)*	integrated project management (IPM)
Intelligenz *(f)*: künstliche ...	artificial intelligence
intensiv: arbeits...	labour-intensive
intensiv: kapital...	capital-intensive
intensive Produktion *(f)*	intensive production
interaktiv	interactive
Interesse *(n)* an der Arbeit *(f)*	job interest
Interesse *(n)* an der Stelle *(f)*	job interest
Interesse *(n)*: persönliches ...	vested interest
Interface *(n)*	interface
intern	in-company
	in-house
internalisieren	internalize (to)
internationalisieren	internationalize (to)
interner Zinsfuß *(m)*	internal rate of return (IRR)
interventionistische Betriebsführung *(f)*	management by walking around
Interview *(n)*: Tiefen...	depth interview
	in-depth interview
intuitive Unternehmensführung *(f)*	intuitive management
Inventur *(f)*: fortlaufende ...	continuous stocktaking
Inventur *(f)*: permanente ...	perpetual inventory
Investitionsanalyse *(f)*	investment analysis
Investitionsaufwand *(m)*	capex (capital expenditure)
Investitionsausgaben *(fpl)*	capex (capital expenditure)
Investitionsbeurteilung *(f)*	capital expenditure appraisal

Investitionsbewertung *(f)*	capital expenditure appraisal
	investment appraisal
Investitionsbudget *(n)*	investment budget
Investitionsgüter *(npl)*	capital goods
	investment goods
Investitionsgüter-Leasing *(n)*	equipment leasing
Investitionskriterien *(npl)*	investment criteria
Investitionspapiere *(npl)*: Markt *(m)* für ...	financial market
Investitionspolitik *(f)*	investment policy
Investitionsprogramm *(n)*	investment programme
Investitionsrechnungsverfahren *(n)*	capital project evaluation
Investmentbank *(f)*	investment bank
Investor (m): raiderabwehrender ...	white knight
Ist: Aufstellung *(f)* des ...-Budgets *(n)*	programme budgeting
Ist: Soll-/ ...-Vergleich *(m)*	performance against objectives
Iteration *(f)*	iterative process
iterativ	iterative
iterativer Prozeß *(m)*	iterative process
iteratives Verfahren *(n)*	iterative process

J

jagen: Nachwuchskräfte *(fpl)*...	headhunt (to)
Jit- (Just-in-time-)	JIT (just in time)
Job-Sharing *(n)*	job sharing
Jobrotation *(f)*	job rotation
Joint Venture *(n)*	joint venture
Joint Venture *(n)*: an einem ... beteiligte Gesellschaften *(fpl)*	joint-venture company
junge Wachstumsindustrie *(f)*	sunrise industry
Junk Bonds (mpl): eine mittels ... ... übernommene Unternehmung (f) ausschlachten	unbundle (to)
Junk Bond *(m)*	junk bond
Just-in-time- (Jit-)	just in time (JIT)
Just-in-time-System *(n)* (Jit-)	just in time (JIT)

K

Kalkulation *(f)*	costing
Kalkulation *(f)*: Absatz...	sales estimate
Kalkulationsnorm *(f)*	cost standard
Kampagne *(f)*: Produktivitäts...	productivity campaign
	productivity drive
Kampagne *(f)*: Verkaufs...	sales drive
Kampagne *(f)*: Werbe...	advertising campaign
Kanal *(m)*: Absatz...	distribution channel
Kanal *(m)*: Distributions...	distribution channel
Kandidatenliste *(f)*: engere ...	shortlist
kann man vergessen	write-off
Kapazität *(f)*: Anlagen...	plant capacity
Kapazität *(f)*: Betriebs...	plant capacity
Kapazität *(f)*: Fertigungs...	manufacturing capacity
Kapazität *(f)*: freie ...	spare capacity
Kapazität *(f)*: Produktions...	manufacturing capacity
Kapazität *(f)*: Termin- und ...splanung *(f)*	scheduling
Kapazität *(f)*: Über...	excess capacity
	overcapacity
Kapazität *(f)*: ungenutzte ...	idle capacity
Kapazität *(f)*: unzureichende ...	undercapacity
Kapazitätsauslastung *(f)*	capacity utilization
Kapazitätsausnützung *(f)*: volle ...	full capacity
Kapital *(n)*: Aktien...	share capital
Kapital *(n)*: Anleihe...	loan capital
Kapital *(n)*: ausgegebenes ...	issued capital
Kapital *(n)*: autorisiertes ...	authorized capital
Kapital *(n)*: Betriebs...	circulating capital
	working capital
Kapital *(n)*: Eigen...	equity
	net worth
Kapital *(n)*: Eigen...rendite *(f)*	return on equity (ROE)
Kapital *(n)*: Eigen...rentabilität *(f)*	return on equity (ROE)
Kapital *(n)*: eingesetztes ...	capital employed
Kapital *(n)* für eine Unternehmensneugründung *(f)*	seed money

Kapital *(n)*: Rendite des eingesetzten …s	return on capital employed (ROCE)
Kapital *(n)*: Rentabilität *(f)* des …einsatzes *(m)*	return on investment (ROI)
Kapital *(n)*: Risiko…	risk capital
	venture capital
Kapital *(n)*: Verwaltung *(f)* von …anlagen *(fpl)*	investment management
Kapital *(n)*: Wagnis …	seed money
	venture capital
***Kapitalanteil** (m)* **mit besonderen Vorrechten** *(npl)*	golden share
Kapitalaufnahme *(f)*	capital raising
Kapitalausstattung *(f)*	gearing
Kapitalbeschaffung *(f)*	capital raising
Kapitalbildung *(f)*	capital formation
Kapitalbindung *(f)*	capital commitment
Kapitalbudget *(n)*	capital budget
Kapitalbudgetierung *(f)*	capital budgeting
Kapitaleinsatz *(m)*: **Rentabilität** *(f)* des …es	return on investment (ROI)
Kapitalertrag *(m)*	capital gain
Kapitalgesellschaft *(f)*	business corporation
Kapitalgewinn *(m)*	capital gain
Kapitalgüter *(npl)*	capital goods
	investment goods
kapitalintensiv	capital intensive
kapitalisieren	capitalize (to)
kapitalisiert: über…	overcapitalized
kapitalisiert: unter…	undercapitalized
Kapitalisierung *(f)*	capitalization
Kapitalkoeffizient *(m)*	capital-output ratio
Kapitalrationierung *(f)*	capital rationing
Kapitalrendite *(f)*	return on capital
Kapitalrückfluß *(m)*	pay back
Kapitalrückflußfrist *(f)*	payback period
Kapitalströme *(mpl)*	funds flow
Kapitalstruktur *(f)*	capital structure
Kapitalverlust *(m)*	capital loss
Kapitalvermögen *(n)*	capital assets

Kapitalverwässerung *(f)*	dilution of equity
Kapitalwert *(m)*	net present value (NPV)
Kapitalwertsteigerung *(f)*	capital appreciation
karrierebewußt	upwardly mobile
Kartell *(n)*	cartel
Kassageschäft *(n)*	cash deal
Kassahandel *(m)*	cash deal
Kassapreis *(m)*	spot price
Kassenbudget *(n)*	cash budget
Kassenhaltung *(f)*	cash management
Kassenliquidität *(f)*	cash ratio
Kassenplan *(m)*	cash budget
Kassenprognose *(f)*	cash forecasting
Kategorie *(f)*: Produkt...	product line
Kauf *(m)*	acquisition
Kauf *(m)*: Wahl *(f)* zwischen Eigenfertigung *(f)* und ...	make-or-buy decision
Kaufanreiz *(m)*	purchasing motivator
Kaufbereitschaft *(f)* des Konsumenten *(m)*	consumer acceptance
Käufermarkt *(m)*	buyers' market
Käuferwiderstand *(m)*	consumer resistance
Kauffaktor *(m)*: wichtigster ...	key buying factor
Kaufkraft *(f)*	purchasing power
Kaufkraftparität *(f)*	purchasing power parity
Kaufmotiv *(n)*	purchasing motivator
Kaufverhalten *(n)*	buying behaviour
keine Defekte *(mpl)*	zero defects
Kennzahl *(f)*: betriebswirtschaftliche ...	management ratio
Kennzahl *(f)*: finanzielle ...	financial ratio
Kennzahl *(f)*: Finanzierungs...	financial ratio
Kennzahl *(f)*: Liquiditäts...	current ratio
Kennziffer *(f)*	index number
Kennziffer *(f)*: Betriebs...	accounting ratio
Kennziffer *(f)*: Liquiditäts...	liquidity ratio
Kette *(f)*: Distributions...	chain of distribution
Kette *(f)*: Produktions...	chain of production
Kette *(f)*: Wert...	value chain
Kettenproduktion (f)	chain production

klagbar	actionable
Klassifizierung (f): Stellen...	job classification
kleine Spesen (pl)	petty expenses
kleine Unkosten (pl)	petty expenses
Knotenplan (m): Ereignis...	programme evaluation and review technique (PERT)
Knowhow (n)	know-how
Köderwerbung (f)	switch selling
Koeffizient (m): Kapital...	capital-output ratio
Kollusion (f)	collusion
kombinierter Verkehr (m)	piggyback
Kommunikation (f): elektronische ...	electronic communication
Kommunikation (f): mündliche ...	verbal communication
Kommunikation (f): nichtverbale ...	non-verbal communication
Kommunikation (f): verbale ...	verbal communication
Kommunikationsmedien (npl)	media
Kommunikationsnetz (n)	communications network
Kommunikationstheorie (f)	communications theory
Kommunikationswege (mpl)	channels of communication
kompatibel	compatible
Kompetenz (f)	capability
	competency
Kompetenz (f): Leitungs...	line authority
Konglomerat (n)	conglomerate
Konjunkturabschwächung (f)	downturn
Konjunkturabschwung (m)	downswing
Konjunkturaussichten (fpl)	business outlook
konjunktureller Auftrieb (m)	upswing
	upturn
Konjunkturflaute (f)	slack
Konjunkturrückgang (m)	slump
Konjunkturtrend (m)	economic trend
Konjunkturverlauf (m)	economic trend
Konjunkturvoraussage (f)	business forecasting
Konjunkturzyklus (m)	business cycle
	trade cycle
Konkurrenz (f)	(the) competition
Konkurrenzanalyse (f)	competitor analysis
konkurrenzfähig	competitive

konkurrenzfähiger Preis *(m)*	competitive price
Konkurrenzfähigkeit *(f)*	competitiveness
Konkurrenzkampf *(m):* ständiger ...	rat race
Konkurrenzpreis *(m)*	competitive price
Konkurrenzprodukte *(npl):* sich deutlich von ...n unterscheiden	product differentiate (to)
Konsens *(m)*	consensus
konsolidierter Geschäftsabschluß *(m)*	consolidated accounts
Konsolidierung *(f)*	consolidation
Konsortium *(n)*	consortium
	syndicate
Konstruktion *(f):* computerunterstützte ...	computer-aided design (CAD)
Konstruktion *(f):* technische Abteilung *(f)* und ...sbüro *(n)*	engineering and design department
Konstruktionstechnik *(f)*	design engineering
konsultativ	consultative
konsultieren	consult (to)
Konsument *(m):* Kaufbereitschaft *(f)* des ...en	consumer acceptance
konsumentennah	consumer-responsive
Konsumentenverhalten *(n)*	consumer behaviour
Konsumgüter *(npl)*	consumer goods
Konsumgüter *(npl):* kurzlebige ...	convenience goods
	non-durable goods
Konsumorientierung *(f)*	consumer orientation
Kontingenztheorie *(f)*	contingency theory
Kontroll: administratives ...verfahren *(n)*	administrative control procedure
Kontroll: verwaltungstechnisches ...verfahren *(n)*	administrative control procedure
Kontrolle *(f)*	control
Kontrolle *(f):* adaptive ...	adaptive control
Kontrolle *(f):* Anpassungs...	adaptive control
Kontrolle *(f):* Aufsichtsrats...	board control
Kontrolle *(f):* Bestands...	inventory control
Kontrolle *(f):* Budget...	budgetary control
Kontrolle *(f):* Budgetierungs...	budgeting control
Kontrolle *(f):* Fertigungs...	manufacturing control
	production control
Kontrolle *(f):* Finanz...	financial control

Kontrolle *(f)*: Forschritts...	progress control
Kontrolle *(f)*: Führungs...	managerial control
Kontrolle *(f)*: Kosten...	cost control
Kontrolle *(f)*: Kredit...	credit control
Kontrolle *(f)*: Lager...	inventory control
Kontrolle *(f)*: Leistungs...	performance monitoring
Kontrolle *(f)*: numerische ...	numerical control
Kontrolle *(f)*: Produktions...	production control
Kontrolle *(f)*: Produktionsplanung *(f)* und -...	production planning and control
Kontrolle *(f)*: Prozeß...	process control
Kontrolle *(f)*: Qualitäts...	quality control (QC)
Kontrolle *(f)*: Stapel...	batch control
Kontrolle *(f)*: statistische ...	statistical control
Kontrolle *(f)*: umfassende Qualitäts...	total quality control (TQC)
Kontrolle *(f)*: Verwaltungsrats...	board control
Kontrolleur *(m)*	controller
Kontrollfunktionen *(fpl)* der Unternehmensleitung *(f)*	supervisory management
Kontrollfunktionen *(fpl)* des Managements *(n)*	supervisory management
kontrollieren	monitor (to)
kontrollieren: Leistung *(f)* ...	monitor performance (to)
kontrollierte Kosten *(pl)*	managed costs
Kontrollinformationen *(fpl)*	control information
Kontrollspanne *(f)*	span of control
konzentrieren: sich ... auf	focus (to)
Konzept *(n)*: Wert...	value concept
Konzept-Wertanalyse *(f)*	value engineering
Konzeption *(f)*: Produkt...	product conception
Konzernabschluß *(m)*	consolidated accounts
	group accounts
Konzernentflechtung *(f)*	demerger
Konzerngesellschaft *(f)*	affiliate company
Konzernrechnung *(f)*	consolidated accounts
Konzertzeichner *(m)*	stag
Konzession *(f)*	franchise
Konzessionsbetrieb *(m)*	franchise
kooperativer Führungsstil *(m)*	participative management
Koordination *(f)*	coordination

Kopfjäger *(m)*	head-hunter
koppeln	interface (to)
Kopplung *(f)*: **Rück...**	feedback
Kopplungsgeschäft *(n)*	package deal
Körperschaftssteuer *(f)*	corporation tax
	profits tax
Körpersprache *(f)*	body language
korporative Grundsätze *(mpl)*	corporatism
Korrelation *(f)*	correlation
korrelieren	correlate (to)
Kosten *(pl)*: **Anlauf...**	start-up costs
Kosten *(pl)*: **Betriebs...**	operating expenses
Kosten *(pl)*: **direkte ...**	direct costs
Kosten *(pl)*: **durchschnittliche ...**	average costs
Kosten *(pl)*: **Durchschnitts...**	average costs
Kosten *(pl)*: **Ermittlung** *(f)* **der Erzeugnis...**	product costing
Kosten *(pl)*: **Fest...**	fixed costs
	fixed expenses
Kosten *(pl)*: **Fix...**	fixed costs
	fixed expenses
Kosten *(pl)*: **Gemein...**	overheads
Kosten *(pl)*: **Grenz...**	marginal costs
Kosten *(pl)*: **Grenz...rechnung** *(f)*	direct costing
Kosten *(pl)*: **Gründungs...**	set-up costs
	start-up costs
Kosten *(pl)*: **indirekte ...**	indirect costs
Kosten *(pl)*: **kontrollierte ...**	managed costs
Kosten *(pl)*: **laufende Betriebs...**	current expenditure
Kosten *(pl)*: **Opportunitäts...**	opportunity costs
Kosten *(pl)*: **Plan...rechnung** *(f)*	standard costing
Kosten *(pl)*: **Produktions...**	cost of production
	production costs
Kosten *(pl)*: **Proportional...rechnung** *(f)*	direct costing
Kosten *(pl)*: **Rüst...**	set-up costs
Kosten *(pl)*: **Soll...**	standard costs
Kosten *(pl)*: **Sprung...**	semi-variable costs
Kosten *(pl)*: **sprungfixe ...**	semi-variable costs
Kosten *(pl)*: **Standard ...**	standard costs
Kosten *(pl)*: **Standard...rechnung** *(f)*	standard costing

Kosten *(pl)*: Stillegungs...	closing-down costs
Kosten *(pl)*: System...voranschlag *(m)*	estimating systems costs
Kosten *(pl)*: variable ...	variable costs
	variable expenses
Kosten *(pl)*: veränderliche ...	variable expenses
Kosten *(pl)*: Verteilung *(f)* von ... auf ...stellen *(fpl)*	allocation of costs
	cost allocation
Kosten *(pl)*: Verwaltungs...	administrative expenses
Kosten *(pl)*: Verwaltungsgemein...	administrative overheads
Kosten *(pl)*: Wiederbeschaffungs...	replacement costs
Kosten- und Leistungsrechnung *(f)*	management accounting
Kosten-/Umsatz-/Gewinnanalyse *(f)*	cost-volume-profit analysis
Kosten-Nutzen-Analyse *(f)*	cost-benefit analysis (CBA)
Kosten-Nutzen-Angebot *(n)*	value proposal
Kostenabweichung *(f)*	cost variance
Kostenanalyse *(f)*	cost analysis
Kostenaufgliederung *(f)*	assignment of expenditure
Kostenaufschlüsselung *(f)*	assignment of expenditure
Kostenaufteilung *(f)*	assignment of expenditure
Kostenaufteilungsverfahren *(n)*	absorption costing
Kostenbewußtsein *(n)*	cost awareness
	cost consciousness
Kostendegression *(f)*	economy of scale
kosteneffizient	cost-efficient
kostenempfindlich	cost-sensitive
Kostenfaktor *(m)*	cost factor
kostengünstig	cost-effective
Kosteninflation *(f)*	cost-push inflation
Kostenkontrolle *(f)*	cost control
kostenminimal	least-cost
Kostenprogression *(f)*	diseconomy of scale
Kostenrechnung *(f)*	cost accounting
	costing
Kostenrechnung *(f)*: funktionale ...	functional costing
Kostenrechnung *(f)* für Serienfertigung *(f)*	process costing
Kostenrechnung *(f)*: Grenz...	direct costing
	marginal costing
Kostenrechnung *(f)*: Plan...	standard costing
Kostenrechnung *(f)*: Produkt...	product costing

Kostenrechnung *(f)*: Proportional...	direct costing
Kostenrechnung *(f)*: Standard...	standard costing
Kostenrechnungsart *(f)*	accounting model
Kostensenkung *(f)*	cost reduction
Kostenstelle *(f)*	cost centre
Kostenstruktur *(f)*	cost structure
Kostenübernahme *(f)*	absorption
Kostenumlage *(f)*	allocation of costs
	cost allocation
	cost apportionment
kostenwirksam	cost-effective
Kostenwirksamkeit *(f)*	cost-effectiveness
Kostenzurechnung *(f)*	cost apportionment
Kraft *(f)*: Führungs...	executive
	manager
Kraft *(f)*: Ertrags...	earning power
Kräfte *(fpl)*: Arbeits ...	manpower
Kräfte *(fpl)*: Fluktuation *(f)* der Nachwuchs...	trainee turnover
Kräfte *(fpl)*: Markt...	market forces
Krankfeiern *(n)*	absenteeism
kreatives Denken *(n)*	creative thinking
kreatives Marketing *(n)*	creative marketing
Kredit *(m)*: Beurteilung *(f)* der ...würdigkeit *(f)*	credit rating
Kreditauskunft *(f)*	status report
Kreditdrosselung *(f)*	credit squeeze
Kreditfazilität *(f)*	borrowing facility
Kreditforderungen *(fpl)* wertpapiermäßig unterlegen	securitize (to)
Kreditforderungen *(fpl)*: wertpapiermäßige Unterlegung *(f)* von ...	securitization
Kreditkontrolle *(f)*	credit control
Kreditmanagement *(n)*	credit management
Kreditportfolio *(n)*	asset portfolio
Kreditrestriktion *(f)*	credit squeeze
Kreditvolumen *(n)*	asset portfolio
Kreditwürdigkeit *(f)*: Beurteilung *(f)* der ...	credit rating
Kreisdiagramm *(n)*	pie chart

Kreislauf *(m)*: geschlossener ...	closed loop
Krisenmanagement *(n)*	crisis management
Krisenmanager *(m)*	troubleshooter
Kriterien *(npl)*: Investitions...	investment criteria
kritisch: Analyse *(f)* der ...en Ablaufstufen *(fpl)*	critical path analysis (CPA)
kritisch: Analyse *(f)* des ...en Pfades *(m)*	critical path analysis (CPA)
	network analysis
kritisch: Methode *(f)* des ...en Pfades *(m)*	critical path method (CPM)
kritische Masse *(f)*	critical mass
kritisieren: hinterher ...	second guess (to)
Kultur *(f)*	culture
Kunde *(m)*: durch ...nbesuch *(m)* werben	canvass (to)
Kundenbetreuung *(f)*	after-sales service
Kundendienst *(m)*	after-sales service
	customer service
kundennah	consumer-responsive
Kundenorientierung *(f)*	customer orientation
Kundenprofil *(n)*	customer profile
Kundenwerbung *(f)* durch Sonderangebote *(npl)*	leader merchandising
Kündigung *(f)*: sozialwidrige ...	unfair dismissal
Kundschaft *(f)*: Unterrichtung *(f)* der ...	customer orientation
künstliche Intelligenz *(f)*	artificial intelligence
Kurs-Gewinn-Verhältnis *(n)*	price-earnings ratio (P/E)
Kursniveau *(n)*: Richtung *(f)* des ...s	share price performance
Kursor *(m)*	cursor
Kurswert *(m)*	market value
Kurve *(f)*: Gehaltsprogressions...	salary progression curve
Kurve *(f)*: Lern...	learning curve
kurz- bis mittelfristige Planung *(f)*	operational planning
Kurzarbeiter *(m)*	part-timer
kurzfristige Planung *(f)*	short-range planning
	short-term planning
kurzfristige Verbindlichkeiten *(fpl)*	current liabilities
kurzlebige Konsumgüter *(npl)*	convenience goods
	non-durable goods
kurzlebige Vermögenswerte *(mpl)*	wasting assets
Kybernetik *(f)*	cybernetics

L

Lager *(n)*: das ... räumen	sell out (to)
Lageraufnahme *(f)*	stocktaking
Lagerbestandsaufnahme *(f)*	stocktaking
Lagerbestandskontrolle *(f)*	stock control
Lagerbewertung *(f)*	stock valuation
Lagerhaltung *(f)*	inventory management
	warehousing
Lagerkontrolle *(f)*	inventory control
Lagerumschlag *(m)*	inventory turnover
	stock turnover
Lagerung *(f)*	storage
	warehousing
LAN *(n)* (Inhouse-Netz *(n)*)	LAN (local area network)
langfristige Planung *(f)*	long-range planning
	long-term planning
langlebige Verbrauchsgüter *(npl)*	(consumer) durables
Laptop *(m)*	laptop computer
Laserdrucker *(m)*	laser printer
laterales Denken *(n)*	lateral thinking
Laufbahnplanung *(f)*	career planning
laufend	ongoing
laufende Ausgaben *(fpl)*	running expenses
laufende Betriebsausgaben *(pl)*	current expenditure
laufende Betriebskosten *(pl)*	current expenditure
leasen	lease (to)
Leasing *(n)*	leasing
Leasing *(n)*: Industrieanlagen- ...	plant hire
Leasing *(n)*: Investitionsgüter-...	equipment leasing
Leben *(n)*: wirtschaftliche ...sdauer *(f)* eines Produkt(e)s *(n)*	product life
Lebenserwartung *(f)* eines Produkt(e)s *(n)*	product life expectancy
lebensfähig	viable
Lebensfähigkeit *(f)*	viability
Lebenshaltungskosten *(pl)*	cost of living
Lebensstandard *(m)*	standard of living
Lebensstil *(m)*	lifestyle

Lebenszyklus *(m)* *(eines Produkt(e)s (n))*	life cycle *(of a product)*
Lehre *(f)*: **Management-...**	management science
leicht realisierbare Aktiva *(pl)*	quick assets
leisten	perform (to)
Leistung *(f)*: **Arbeits...**	job performance
Leistung *(f)*: **Ertrags...**	earnings performance
Leistung *(f)* **kontrollieren**	monitor performance (to)
Leistung *(f)*: **Kosten- und ...srechnung** *(f)*	management accounting
Leistung *(f)*: **Produkt...**	product performance
Leistung *(f)*: **Prüfung** *(f)* **und Bewertung** *(f)* **der Manager-...**	management audit
Leistung *(f)*: **Sozial...en** *(pl)*	fringe benefits
Leistung *(f)*: **unfertige ...en** *(pl)*	work in progress
Leistung *(f)*: **Vorgabe...**	standard performance
Leistung *(f)*: **zulässige Zeitspanne** *(f)* **für unterdurchschnittliche ...**	time span of discretion
Leistungsbarometer *(n)*	performance indicator
Leistungsbeurteilung *(f)*	merit rating
	performance appraisal
	performance evaluation
	performance rating
	performance review
	merit rating
Leistungsbeurteilung *(f)* **der Büroangestellten** *(f/mpl)*	clerical work measurement (CWM)
Leistungsbewertung *(f)* **des Büropersonals** *(n)*	clerical work measurement (CWM)
leistungsbezogenes Lohnsystem *(n)*	incentive scheme
leistungsfähig	efficient
Leistungsfähigkeit *(f)*	efficiency
Leistungskennzahl *(f)*	performance indicator
Leistungskontrolle *(f)*	performance monitoring
Leistungslohn *(m)*	incentive wage
Leistungsmaßstab *(m)*	performance standard
Leistungsmessung *(f)*	performance measurement
Leistungsnachweise *(mpl)*	track record
Leistungsplanung *(f)*	performance budgeting
leiten	route (to)

Leiter *(m)*: Abteilungs...	departmental head
	departmental manager
Leiter *(m)*: Ausbildungs...	training officer
Leiter *(m)*: Betriebs...	operations manager
	plant manager
	works manager
Leiter *(m)*: Einkaufs...	purchasing manager
Leiter *(m)*: Gebiets...	area manager
Leiter *(m)*: Halb...	semiconductor
Leiter *(m)*: Marketing-...	marketing manager
Leiter *(m)*: Personal...	personnel manager
Leiter *(m)*: Verkaufs...	sales manager
Leiter *(m)*: Vertriebs...	distribution manager
Leiter *(m)*: Werbe...	advertising manager
Leiter *(m)*: Werks...	plant manager
	works manager
Leitung *(f)*: Abteilungs...	departmental management
Leitung *(f)*: Betriebs...	operating management
	operations management
Leitung *(f)*: Büro...	office management
Leitung *(f)*: Kontrollfunktionen *(fpl)* der Unternehmens...	supervisory management
Leitung *(f)*: Manager *(m)* der unteren ...	first-line manager
Leitung *(f)*: Organogramm *(n)* der Unternehmens...	management chart
Leitung *(f)*: Personal...	personnel management
Leitung *(f)*: risikobereite Unternehmens...	venture management
Leitung *(f)*: Sparten...	divisional management
Leitung *(f)*: Unternehmens...	management
Leitung *(f)*: Verkaufs...	sales management
Leitung *(f)*: wirksame Unternehmens...	managerial effectiveness
Leitungsbefugnis *(f)*	line authority
Leitungskompetenz *(f)*	line authority
Leitungsspanne *(f)*	span of control
Lernen *(n)*: computerunterstütztes ...	computer-aided learning (CAL)
Lernen *(n)*: programmiertes ...	programmed learning
Lernkurve *(f)*	learning curve
Lernprozeß *(m)*: programmierter ...	programmed learning

letzter Tag *(m)*	latest date
letztes Verkaufsdatum *(n)*	sell-by date
Liberalisierung *(f)*	liberalization
Lieferzeit *(f)*	delivery time
	lead time
Lifestyle *(m)*	lifestyle
lineare Programmierung *(f)*	linear programming
lineare Verantwortung *(f)*	linear responsibility
Linearplanung *(f)*	linear programming
Linie *(f)*: **Produkt...**	product line
Linie *(f)* **und Stab** *(m)*	line and staff
Linienassistent *(m)*	line assistant
Linienmanagement *(n)*	line management
Linienmanager *(m)*	line executive
	line manager
Linienorganisation *(f)*	line organization
liquid	cash-rich
Liquidation *(f)*	dissolution
	liquidation
	winding up
Liquidationswert *(m)*	break-up value
liquide Mittel *(npl)*	liquid assets
liquidieren	liquidate (to)
	wind up (to)
Liquidierung *(f)*	liquidation
Liquidität *(f)*: **Bar...**	cash ratio
Liquidität *(f)*: **Kassen...**	cash ratio
Liquiditätsgrad *(m)*	current ratio
	liquidity ratio
Liquiditätskennzahl *(f)*	current ratio
Liquiditätskennziffer *(f)*	liquidity ratio
Liquiditätsplan *(m)*	cash budget
Liquiditätsplanung *(f)*	cash budgeting
Liquiditätsprognose *(f)*	cash forecasting
Liquiditätsschwierigkeiten *(fpl)*: **sich in ...** **befindend**	cash-strapped
Liquiditätssteuerung *(f)*	cash management
Liquiditätsvorschau *(f)*	cash forecasting
Lizenz *(f)*	licence

Lizenz *(f)***: in ...**	under licence
Lizenzaustausch *(m)*	cross-licensing
Lockangebot *(n)*	loss-leader
Lockartikel *(m)*	loss-leader
Lockmittelwerbung *(f)*	switch selling
Lockvogelangebot *(n)*	loss-leader
Logistik *(f)*	logistics
logistisch	logistical
logistisches Verfahren *(n)*	logistic process
Logo *(n)*	logo
Lohn *(m)***: Akkord...system** *(n)*	payment by results
Lohn *(m)***: gleicher ...**	equal pay
Lohn *(m)***: Höchst...**	wage ceiling
Lohn *(m)***: leistungsbezogenes ...system** *(n)*	incentive scheme
Lohn *(m)***: Prämien...**	premium bonus
Lohn *(m)***: Prämien...system** *(n)*	bonus scheme
Lohn *(m)***: Vergütung** *(f)* **neben Gehalt** *(n)* **oder ...**	fringe benefits
Lohn- und Gehaltsstopp *(m)*	pay pause
Lohn- und Gehaltssumme *(f)*	payroll
Lohn- und Gehaltszahlung *(f)***: gewinnabhängige ...**	profit-related pay
Lohnanstieg *(m)***: genereller ...**	across-the-board increase
Lohnauftrieb *(m)*	wage drift
Lohndifferenzen *(fpl)*	earnings differential
Lohndrift *(f)*	wage drift
Löhne *(mpl)***: Fertigungs...**	direct labour
Löhne *(mpl)***: Gemeinkosten...**	indirect labour
Lohngefälle *(n)*	wage differential
Lohnhöchstgrenze *(f)*	wage ceiling
Lohnhöhe *(f)*	wage level
Lohnliste *(f)*	payroll
Lohnniveau *(n)*	wage level
Lohnpause *(f)*	pay pause
Lohnpolitik *(f)*	wage policy
Lohnsteuerabzug *(m)*	pay-as-you-earn (PAYE)
	pay-as-you-go
Lohnstopp *(m)*	wage freeze
Lohnstruktur *(f)*	wage structure

Lohnstückkosten *(pl)*	unit labour costs
Lohnsystem *(n)*	wage system
Lohnunterschiede *(mpl)*	earnings differential
Lohnverhandlungen *(fpl)*	pay talks
Lokalisierung *(f)*	localization
Lokopreis *(m)*	spot price
Lösung *(f)*: Problem...	problem solving
Low-Tech-	low-tech

M

machbar	feasible
Mache *(f)*	window dressing
Machenschaften *(fpl)*	wheeling and dealing
machtlos machen	marginalize (to)
Magnetplatte *(f)*	disk
Mail-order *(f)*	mail order
Mailbox *(f)*	mailbox
Mailing *(n)*	mailing
Mainframe-System *(n)*	mainframe
Makler *(m)*	broker
Makler *(m)*: Effekten...	stockbroker
Maklergebühr *(f)*	brokerage
	brokerage fees
Maklerprovision *(f)*	brokerage
Makroeinrichtung *(f)*	macro
Management-Buyout *(m,n)* (MBO)	management buyout (MBO)
Management *(n)*	business management
	management
Management *(n)*: allgemeines ...	general management
Management *(n)* by Exception (MbE, *n*)	management by exception
Management *(n)* by Objectives (MbO, *n*)	management by objectives (MBO)
Management *(n)*: Cash-...	cash management
Management *(n)*: computergestütztes ...	computerized management
Management *(n)* des geordneten Wandels *(m)*	change management (management of change)
Management *(n)*: dezentralisiertes ...	decentralized management
Management *(n)*: dynamisches ...-Modell *(n)*	dynamic management model

Management *(n)*: Einkaufs...	sourcing
Management *(n)*: Finanz...	financial management
Management *(n)*: funktionales ...	functional management
Management *(n)*: Innovations ...	change management (management of change)
Management *(n)*: integriertes Projekt-...	integrated project management (IPM)
Management *(n)*: Kontrollfunktionen *(fpl)* des ...s	supervisory management
Management *(n)*: Kredit...	credit management
Management *(n)*: Krisen...	crisis management
Management *(n)*: Linien...	line management
Management *(n)*: Middle-...	middle management
Management *(n)*: mittleres ...	middle management
Management *(n)*: Personal...	human resource management (HRM)
	personnel management
	staff management
Management *(n)*: Portfolio- ...	portfolio management
Management *(n)*: Produkt-...	product management
Management *(n)*: Produktions...	production management
Management *(n)*: programmiertes ...	programmed management
Management *(n)*: Projekt-...	project management
Management *(n)*: Ressourcen...	resource management
Management *(n)*: Spitzen...	top management
Management *(n)*: System-...	systems management
Management *(n)*: Top- ...	top management
Management *(n)*: Total Quality ... (TQM)	total quality management (TQM)
Management *(n)*: Verhaltensnormen *(fpl)* im ...	management practices
Management *(n)*: Verkaufs...	sales management
Management *(n)*: wirksames ...	effective management
	managerial effectiveness
Management *(n)*: wissenschaftliches ...	scientific management
Management-	managerial
Management-Beratung *(f)*	management consultancy
Management-Dienste *(mpl)*	management services
Management-Entwicklung *(f)*	executive development
	management development

Management-Informationen *(fpl)*	management information
Management-Informationssystem *(n)*	management information system (MIS)
Management-Lehre *(f)*	management science
Management-Potential *(n)*	management potential
Management-Prinzipien *(npl)*	management practices
Management-System *(n)*	management system
Management-Theorie *(f)*	management theory
Managementtechnik *(f)*	management technique
managen	manage (to)
Manager *(m)*	executive
	manager
Manager *(m)*: Anstellungsvertrag *(m)* eines ...s	management contract
Manager *(m)* der unteren Leitung *(f)*	first-line manager
Manager *(m)*: Beschaffungs...	procurement manager
Manager *(m)*: Einkaufs...	procurement manager
Manager *(m)*: Linien...	line executive
	line manager
Manager *(m)*: Marken...	brand manager
Manager *(m)*: Produkt-...	product manager
Manager *(m)*: Produktions...	production manager
Manager *(m)*: Prüfung *(f)* und Bewertung *(f)* der ...-Leistung	management audit
Manager *(m)*: teamfähiger ...	team player
Manager *(m)*: teamorientierter ...	team player
Manager *(m)*: Werbe...	advertising manager
Manager-	managerial
Manager-Ausbildung *(f)*	management training
Mandatsverflechtung *(f)*	interlocking directorate
manuell	hands-on
Marginalanalyse *(f)*	marginal analysis
marginale Preisfestsetzung *(f)*	marginal pricing
Marke *(f)*	brand
Marke *(f)*: Bekanntheit *(f)* einer ...	brand awareness
Markenakzeptanz *(f)*	brand acceptance
Markenbetreuer *(m)*	brand manager
Markenbewußtsein *(n)*	brand awareness
Markenbild *(n)*	brand image

Markenimage *(n)*	brand image
Markenmanager *(m)*	brand manager
Markenname *(m)*	brand name
Markenpalette *(f)*	brand portfolio
Markenportfolio *(n)*	brand portfolio
Markenpositionierung *(f)*	brand positioning
Markenprofil *(n)*	brand image
Markenstrategie *(f)*	brand strategy
Markentreue *(f)*	brand loyalty
Markenwiedererkennung *(f)*	brand recognition
Marketing *(n)*	marketing
Marketing *(n)*: bewilligte ...-Mittel	marketing appropriation
Marketing *(n)*: Global ...	global marketing
Marketing *(n)*: kreatives ...	creative marketing
Marketing *(n)*: Test...	test marketing
Marketingabteilung *(f)*	marketing department
Marketing-Budget *(n)*	marketing budget
Marketing-Forschung *(f)*	marketing research
Marketing-Leiter *(m)*	marketing manager
Marketing-Mittel *(npl)*: bewilligte ...	marketing appropriation
Marketing-Mix *(n)*	marketing mix
Marketingstrategie *(f)*	marketing strategy
Markt *(m)*: auf den ... bringen	market (to)
Markt *(m)*: Binnen...	single market
Markt *(m)*: den ... aufkaufen	corner the market (to)
Markt *(m)*: etablierter ...	mature market
Markt *(m)* für Investitionspapiere *(npl)*	financial market
Markt *(m)*: Gemeinsamer ...	Common Market
Markt *(m)*: grauer ...	grey market
Markt *(m)*: Käufer...	buyers' market
Markt *(m)*: Neben...	fringe market
Markt *(m)*: Rand...	fringe market
Markt *(m)*: Verkäufer...	sellers' market
Markt- und Meinungsforschung *(f)*	statistical sampling
Marktabdeckung *(f)*	sales coverage
Marktanteil *(m)*	market share
Marktaussichten *(f)*	market prospects
marktbar	marketable

Marktbefragung *(f)*	market survey
Marktbeurteilung *(f)*	market appraisal
Marktbewertung *(f)*	market rating
Marktbewußtsein *(n)*	market awareness
Marktchance *(f)*	market opportunity
Marktdurchdringung *(f)*	market penetration
Marktdynamik *(f)*	market dynamics
Markteinschätzung *(f)*	market rating
marktempfindlich	market-sensitive
Markterkundung *(f)*	market exploration
marktfähig	marketable
Marktforschung *(f)*	market research
Marktführer *(m)*	market leader
marktgängig	marketable
Marktinformationen *(fpl)*	market intelligence
Marktkenntnisse *(fpl)*	market awareness
Marktkräfte *(fpl)*	market forces
Marktkurs *(m)*	going rate
Marketleitung *(f)*	market management
Marktlücke *(f)*	gap
	niche
Marktmacher *(m)*	market maker
Marktnische *(f)*	niche
Marktplan *(m)*	market plan
Marktplanung *(f)*	market planning
Marktpotential *(n)*	market potential
Marktpreis *(m)*	going rate
	market price
Marktprofil *(n)*	market profile
Marktprognose *(f)*	market forecast
Marktsättigung *(f)*	market saturation
Marktsegment *(n)*	market segment
Marktsegmentierung *(f)*	market segmentation
	segmentation
Marktstellung *(f)*	market rating
Marktstruktur *(f)*	market structure
Marktstudie *(f)*	market study
Markttendenzen *(fpl)*	market trend
Markttest *(m)*	market test

Markttrend *(m)*	market thrust
	market trend
Marktumfrage *(f)*	market survey
Marktuntersuchung *(f)*	market study
Marktwert *(m)*	market value
Maß *(n)*: nach ... hergestellt	customized
maschinelle Programmierung *(f)*	computer programming
Maschinenbau *(m)*	engineering
Maschinensprache *(f)*	computer language
	machine language
maßgefertigt	custom-made
Masse *(f)*: kritische ...	critical mass
Massenmarkt *(m)*: für den ...	down-market
Massenproduktion *(f)*	continuous-flow production
	mass production
Maßstab *(m)*	benchmark
	standard
	yardstick
Materialfluß *(m)*	materials handling
Materialtransport *(m)*	materials handling
materielle Vermögenswerte *(mpl)*	tangible assets
mathematische Programmierung *(f)*	mathematical programming
Matrix-Organisation *(f)*	matrix organization
	matrix management
Matrixbilanz *(f)*	spreadsheet
Maus *(f)*	mouse
maximieren	maximize (to)
Maximierung *(f)*: Gewinn...	profit maximization
MBO *(m,n)* (Management-Buyout *(m,n)*)	MBO (management buyout)
MbO *(n)* (Management *(n)* by Objectives)	MBO (management by objectives)
Media-Analyse *(f)*	media analysis
Medien *(npl)*	media
Medien *(npl)*: Kommunikations...	media
Medien *(npl)*: Werbe...	advertising media
Medienanalyse *(f)*	media analysis
Medienauswahl *(f)*	media selection
Medienselektion *(f)*	media selection
Medienwahl *(f)*	media selection

Mehrfach-Regressionsanalyse *(f)*	multiple regression analysis (MRA)
mehrfacher Zugang *(m)*	multi-access
Mehrheitsanteil *(m)*	controlling interest
Mehrheitsbeteiligung *(f)*	controlling interest
	majority interest
Mehrwert *(m)*	added value
Mehrwertsteuer *(f)*	value added tax (VAT)
Mehrwertsteuer *(f)*: ohne ...	zero-rating
Meinungsforschung *(f)*: Markt- und ...	statistical sampling
Meinungumfrage *(f)*	opinion survey
Meister *(m)*	foreman
Menge *(f)*: Geld...	money supply
Menge *(f)*: wirtschaftliche Fertigprodukt...	economic batch quantity
Menge *(f)*: wirtschaftliche Produktions...	economic manufacturing quantity
Merchandising *(n)*	merchandising
Merchant Bank *(f)*	merchant bank
Mergers und Acquisitions *(pl)*	mergers and acquisitions (M & A)
Messung *(f)*: Leistungs...	performance measurement
Messung *(f)*: Produktivitäts...	productivity measurement
Messung *(f)*: psychometrische ...	psychometric testing
Methode *(f)*: aggressive Verkaufs...n *(pl)*	hard sell
Methode *(f)*: Barwerts...	present value method
Methode *(f)* der Arbeitsstichproben *(fpl)*	random observation method
Methode *(f)* des Gegenwartswertes *(m)*	present value method
Methode *(f)* des kritischen Pfades	critical path method (CPM)
Methode *(f)*: Fertigungs...	production technique
Methode *(f)*: funktionale ...	functional approach
Methode *(f)*: Herstellungs...	production technique
Methode *(f)*: Organisation *(f)* und ...n *(pl)*	organization and methods (O & M)
Methode *(f)*: Simplex-...	simplex method
Middle-Management *(n)*	middle management
mieten oder kaufen	lease or buy (to)
mieten	lease (to)
Mikrochip *(m)*	microchip
Mikrocomputer *(m)*	micro

Minderheitsbeteiligung *(f)*	minority interest
Mindestanteil *(m)*: Regeln *(fpl)* zur Bestimmung *(f)* vom ... einheimischer Komponenten *(fpl)*	local content rules
Mindesthaltbarkeitsdatum *(n)*	use-by date
Mindestlohn *(m)*	minimum wage
Minimalkosten-	least-cost
minimieren: Risiken *(npl)* ...	minimize risks (to)
Mischkonzern *(m)*	conglomerate
mit Computern *(mpl)* vertraut	computer literate
mit einem Netz *(n)* verbinden	network (to)
mit einer Stelle *(f)* verbundene Erwartungen *(fpl)*	job expectations
Mitabgabe *(f)* von Angeboten *(npl)*	competitive tendering
Mitarbeiter *(mpl)*	staff
Mitarbeiter-Buyout *(m,n)*	employee buyout
	worker buyout
Mitarbeiter *(mpl)*: Außendienst...	sales force
Mitarbeiter *(mpl)*: Beförderung *(f)* von ...n	promotion *(personnel)*
Mitarbeiter *(mpl)*: Einführung *(f)* neuer ... in das Unternehmen	induction
Mitarbeiter *(mpl)*: innerbetriebliche ...beziehungen *(fpl)*	human relations
Mitarbeiter (m): talentloser, nicht aufstrebender ...	low-flier
Mitarbeiter *(mpl)*: Versetzung *(f)* der ...	staff transfer
Mitbestimmung *(f)*	co-determination
	industrial democracy
	worker participation
Mitbestimmung *(f)* entziehen	marginalize (to)
Mitbieter (mpl): mögliche ... abschreckendes Übernahmeangebot (n)	pre-emptive bid
Mitglied *(n)*: Aufsichtsrats...	non-executive director
	outside director
Mitglied *(n)*: Board...	executive director
Mitglied *(n)* des Verwaltungsrat(e)s *(m)*	non-executive director
	outside director
Mitglied *(m)*: Team...	team player

Mitglied *(n)*: Vorstands...	executive director
Mittel *(npl)*: bewilligte Marketing-...	marketing appropriation
Mittel *(npl)*: flüssige ...	liquid assets
Mittel *(npl)*: liquide ...	liquid assets
Mittelherkunft *(f)* und -einsatz *(m)*	source and disposition of funds
Mittelwert *(m)*	mean
Mittler *(m)*: Werbe...	advertising agent
mittleres Management *(n)*	middle management
Mitwirkung *(f)*	participation
Mix *(n)*: Absatzförderungs...	promotional mix
Mix *(n)*: Marketing-...	marketing mix
Mix *(n)*: Produkt-...	product mix
Mix *(n)*: Verkaufsförderungs...	promotional mix
Mobilfunk *(m)*	mobile phone
Mobilität *(f)*: Arbeits...	labour mobility
Mobilität *(f)*: Arbeitskräfte...	labour mobility
Mobilität *(f)* des Personals *(n)*	staff mobility
Mobiltelefon *(n)*: zellulares ...	cellphone
Mode *(f)*	mode
Modell *(n)*	model
Modell *(n)*: Buchhaltungs...	accounting model
Modell *(n)*: dynamisches Führungs...	dynamic management model
Modell *(n)*: dynamisches Management-...	dynamic management model
Modell *(n)*: Entscheidungs...	decision model
Modell *(n)*: Unternehmens...	company model
	corporate model
Modem *(n)*	modem
Modularität *(f)*	modularity
Modus *(m)*	mode
Möglichkeiten *(fpl)*: Absatz...	sales potential
Monetarismus *(m)*	monetarism
Monopol *(n)*	corner
monopolisieren	corner (to)
Montagebahn *(f)*	assembly line
Montageband *(n)*	assembly line
morphologische Analyse *(f)*	morphological analysis
Motiv *(n)*: Gewinn...	profit motive
Motivation *(f)*	motivation
Motivations-	motivational

Motivationsfaktoren (mpl): mit Arbeitsbedingungen (fpl) verbundene ...	hygiene factors
Motivationsfaktor *(m)*	motivator
Motivationsforschung *(f)*	motivational research
motivieren	motivate (to)
Motivierung *(f)*: Selbst...	self-motivation
Müll *(m)*: Industrie...	industrial waste
multimediale Ausbildung *(f)*	multimedia training
mündelsichere Wertpapiere *(npl)*	safety stock
mündliche Kommunikation *(f)*	verbal communication
Muttergesellschaft *(f)*	parent company

N

nach Führungskräften *(fpl)* suchen	head-hunt (to)
nach Maß *(n)* hergestellt	customized
nach System *(n)* geführtes Management *(n)*	system-managed company
Nachfassen *(n)*	follow-up
Nachfolgeplanung *(f)*: Führungs...	management succession planning
Nachfragebewertung *(f)*	demand assessment
nachfrageinduzierte Inflation *(f)*	demand-pull inflation
Nachfrageinflation *(f)*	demand-pull inflation
Nachfrageprognose *(f)*	demand forecasting
Nachfrageprognostizierung *(f)*	demand forecasting
nachgehen	follow up (to)
nachgeordnete Führungsebenen *(fpl)*: auf ...n ...	down the line
nachgeordnete Führungsebenen *(fpl)*: Unternehmensführung *(f)* unter Beteiligung *(f)* ...r ...	multiple management
Nachprüfer *(m)*	controller
Nachrichtenvermittlung *(f)*: computerunterstützte ...	bulletin board
Nachtschicht *(f)*	night shift
Nachweise *(mpl)*: Leistungs...	track record
Nachwuchs *(m)*: Fluktuation *(f)* der ...kräfte *(fpl)*	trainee turnover
Nachwuchskräfte *(fpl)* jagen	head-hunt (to)

Name *(m)*: Marken...	brand name
Nahtstelle *(f)*	interface
Nebeneffekt *(m)*	spin-off effect
Nebenmarkt *(m)*	fringe market
Nebenoperationen *(fpl)*	ancillary operations
Nebenprodukt *(n)*	by-product
negative Einkommensteuer *(f)*	negative income tax
negativer Cash-flow *(m)*	negative cash flow
Nennwert *(m)*	par
Nennwert *(m)*: über dem ...	above par
Nennwert *(m)*: unter dem ...	below par
Nennwert *(m)*: zum ...	at par
Nettogehalt *(n)*	take-home pay
Nettogewinn *(m)*	net profit
Nettogewinnspanne *(f)*	net margin
Nettolohn *(m)*	take-home pay
Nettoumlaufvermögen *(n)*	net current assets
Nettovermögen *(n)*	net assets
Netz *(n)*: Informations...	information network
Netz *(n)*: Inhouse-...	local area network (LAN)
Netz *(n)*: Kommunikations...	communications network
Netz *(n)*: mit einem ... verbinden	network (to)
Netz *(n)*: Vertriebs...	distribution network
Netzkoppler *(m)*	gateway
Netzplantechnik *(f)*	network analysis
Netzwerkbetrieb *(m)*	networking
neu einführen	innovate (to)
Neubewertung *(f)* von Vermögenswerten *(mpl)*	revaluation of assets
Neuorientierung *(f)*	refocusing
Neuprägung (f): modische sprachliche ...	buzz-word
nicht börsennotierte Gesellschaft *(f)*	unlisted company
nicht flüssig	cash-poor
nicht gewerkschaftspflichtiger Betrieb *(m)*	open shop
nicht strukturiert	unstructured
nicht vorrätig	out of stock
nichtlineare Optimierung *(f)*	non-linear programming
nichtlineare Programmierung *(f)*	non-linear programming
nichtverbale Kommunikation *(f)*	non-verbal communication
Niederlassung *(f)*	branch office

Norm *(f)*	standard
Norm *(f)*: Budget...	budget standard
Norm *(f)*: Finanz...	financial standard
Norm *(f)*: Kalkulations...	cost standard
Norm *(f)*: Produktions...	production standard
Normalabweichung *(f)*	standard deviation
Normalzeit *(f)*	standard time
normen	standardize (to)
Notfallplanung *(f)*	contingency planning
Null *(f)*: Finanzplanung *(f)* von Anfang *(m)* ...	zero-base budget
Nullfehler-	zero defects
numerische Kontrolle *(f)*	numerical control
nur für unmittelbar Betroffene *(f/mpl)*	need-to-know basis
Nurlesespeicher *(m)*	read only memory (ROM)
Nutzen *(m)*: Kosten-...-Analyse *(f)*	cost-benefit analysis (CBA)
Nutzen *(m)*: Kosten-...Angebot *(n)*	value proposal
Nutzschwelle *(f)*	break-even point
Nutzungsdauer *(f)*: wirtschaftliche ...	economic life

O

oben: Theorie *(f)* des von ... nach unten durchsickernden Wohlstands *(m)*	trickle-down theory
oben: von unten nach ...	bottom-up
offen	open ended
offen: alles ... lassend	open-ended
Offene Handelsgesellschaft *(f)*	partnership
öffentliche Wirtschaftsbetriebe *(mpl)*	public enterprise
öffentlicher Sektor *(m)*	public enterprise
öffentlicher Versorgungsbetrieb *(m)*	public utility
Öffentlichkeitsarbeit *(f)*	public relations (PR)
offizieller Streik *(m)*	official strike
Offline-	off line
Offshore-	offshore
Offshore-Investmentfonds *(m)*	offshore investment
ohne Mehrwertsteuer *(f)*	zero-rating
Ökonom *(m)*: Betriebs...	business economist

ökonometrisch	econometric
Ökonomie (f): Bewegungs...	motion economy
Online-	on line
Operation (f): Hilfs...en	ancillary operations
Operation (f): Neben...en (pl)	ancillary operations
OR (Operations Research (n))	OR (operational research, operations research)
Operations Research (n) (OR)	operational research (OR)
	operations research (OR)
Operationsforschung (f)	operational research (OR)
	operations research (OR)
Opportunitätskosten (pl)	opportunity costs
optimieren	optimize (to)
Optimierung (f): Gewinn...	profit optimization
Optimierung (f): nichtlineare ...	non-linear programming
Optimierung (f): Sub...	sub-optimization
Optimierungs-Team (n)	quality circle
optimistischstes Szenario (n)	best-case scenario
Option (f): Aktien...	stock option
Option (f): Aktien...plan (m)	stock option plan
Option (f): börsengehandelte ...	traded option
Organisation (f) eines Unternehmens (n)	business system
Organisation (f): Entwicklung (f) der ...	organizational development
Organisation (f): funktionale ...	functional organization
Organisation (f): informelle ...	informal organization
Organisation (f): ingenieur- und arbeitswissenschaftliche ...sgestaltung (f)	industrial engineering
Organisation (f): Linien...	line organization
Organisation (f): Matrix-...	matrix management
	matrix organization
Organisation (f): Stabs...	staff organization
Organisation (f) und Methoden (fpl)	organization and methods (O & M)
Organisation (f): Verhalten (n) in der ...	organizational behaviour
Organisationskultur (f)	organization culture
Organisationsplan (m)	organization chart
Organisationsplanung (f)	organization planning
Organisationsstruktur (f)	organization structure
Organisationstheorie (f)	organization theory

organisatorische Änderung *(f)*	organizational change
organisatorische Entwicklung *(f)*	organizational development
organisatorische Wirksamkeit *(f)*	organizational effectiveness
organisatorischer Aufbau *(m)*	organizational development
organisches Wachstum *(n)*	organic growth
Organogramm *(n)*	organogram
	organization chart
Organogramm *(n)* der Unternehmensleitung *(f)*	management chart
Organogramm *(n)* der Unternehmensführung *(f)*	management chart
Orientierung *(f)*: Konsum...	consumer orientation
Orientierung *(f)*: Kunden...	customer orientation
Outplacement *(n)*	outplacement
Output *(m)*	output
Output *(m)*: Input-...-Analyse	input-output analysis
Output *(m)*: Input-...-Tabelle	input-output table

P

Pacht- und Leihbasis *(f)*: auf ...	lease-lend
Pacht- und Leihvertrag *(m)*	lease-lend
Paket *(n)*: Programm...	programme package
Palette *(f)*: Marken...	brand portfolio
Palette *(f)*: Produkt...	product mix
Pallettierung *(f)*	palletization
Panel *(n)*: Verbraucher...	consumers' panel
Parallelanleihe *(f)*	parallel loan
Paralleleinfuhr *(f)*	parallel import
Parallelimport *(m)*	parallel import
Parallelkredit *(m)*	parallel loan
Parallelwährung *(f)*	parallel currency
Parameter *(m)*	parameter
parametrische Programmierung *(f)*	parametric programming
Pari *(m)*	par
pari: al ...	at par
pari: über ...	above par
pari: unter ...	below par

Parität *(f)*	equality
Parität *(f)*: Kaufkraft...	purchasing power parity
partizipativ: dezentralisiert und ...	bottom-up
Partner *(m)*	partner
Partnerschaft *(f)*	partnership
passend	compatible
passend: zueinander ...	compatible
Passivamanagement *(n)*: Aktiva- und ...	asset liability management
Patenthandel *(m)*	patent trading
Pauschalbetrag *(m)*	lump sum
Pauschalsumme *(f)*	lump sum
PC *(m)* (Personal-Computer *(m)*)	PC (personal computer)
Penetrationspreispolitik *(f)*	penetration pricing
pensionieren: sich ... lassen	retire (to)
Pensionierung *(f)*	retirement
Pensionierung *(f)*: vorzeitige ...	early retirement
Pensum *(n)*: Arbeits...	workload
Periode *(f)*: Rechnungs...	accounting period
periphere Einheiten *(fpl)*	peripherals
Peripheriegeräte *(npl)*	peripheral equipment
Peripherien *(fpl)*	peripherals
permanente Inventur *(f)*	perpetual inventory
Personal *(n)*	human resources
	manpower
	staff
Personal *(n)*: Einsatz *(m)* des ...s	staff commitment
Personal *(n)*: Führungs...	management staff
Personal *(n)* im Außendienst *(m)*	front-line employees
Personal *(n)*: Leistungsbewertung *(f)* des Büro...s	clerical work measurement (CWM)
Personal *(n)*: Mobilität *(f)* des ...s	staff mobility
Personal-	manning
	manpower
Personal-Computer *(m)* (PC)	personal computer (PC)
Personalabbau *(m)*	demanning
Personalabteilung *(f)*	personnel department
Personalberatung *(f)*	employee counselling
Personalbeschaffung *(f)*	manpower resourcing

Personalbeschaffungsplanung *(f)*	staff resourcing
Personalbestandsanalyse *(f)*	manpower audit
	staff audit
Personalbeurteilung *(f)*	merit rating
	personnel rating
	staff appraisal
Personalchef *(m)*	staff manager
Personaleinsatz *(m)*	staff commitment
Personaleinstellung *(f)*	staffing
Personalentwicklung *(f)*	human resource development (HRD)
Personalfluktuation *(f)*	labour turnover
Personalführung *(f)*	manpower management
Personalknappheit *(f)*	understaffing
Personalleiter *(m)*	personnel manager
Personalleitung *(f)*	personnel management
	staff management
Personalmanagement *(n)*	human resource management (HRM)
	personnel management
	staff management
Personalmangel *(m)*	understaffing
Personalplanung *(f)*	human resource planning (HRP)
	manpower planning
	staff planning
Personalpolitik *(f)*	personnel policy
	staff strategy
Personalprognose *(f)*	manpower forecast
	manpower forecasting
	staff forecasting
Personalwechsel *(m)*	staff turnover
personell überbesetzt	overstaffed
personell unterbesetzt	understaffed
personelle Überbesetzung *(f)*	overstaffing
personelle Unterbesetzung *(f)*	understaffing
Personengesellschaft *(f)*	partnership
persönliche Weiterentwicklung *(f)*	personal growth
persönliches Interesse *(n)*	vested interest

PERT (Programme Evaluation and Review Technique *(f)*	PERT (programme evaluation and review technique)
pessimistischstes Szenario *(n)*	worst-case scenario
Pfad *(m)*: **Analyse** *(f)* **des kritischen ...es**	network analysis
Pfad *(m)*: **Tabelle** *(f)* **des kritischen ...es**	milestone chart
Philosophie *(f)*: **Unternehmens...**	company philosophy
Pionierarbeit *(f)* **leisten**	pioneer (to)
Pionierprodukt *(n)*	pioneer product
Plan *(m)*	blueprint
	plan
	schedule
Plan *(m)*: **Absatz...**	market plan
Plan *(m)*: **Abteilungs...**	departmental plan
Plan *(m)*: **Aktienoptions...**	stock option plan
Plan *(m)*: **Aktions...**	action plan
Plan *(m)*: **Durchführungs...**	action plan
Plan *(m)*: **Kassen...**	cash budget
Plan *(m)*: **Liquiditäts...**	cash budget
Plan *(m)*: **Markt...**	market plan
Plan *(m)*: **Organisations...**	organization chart
Plan *(m)*: **Prämienregelungs...**	bonus scheme
Plan *(m)*: **Produktions...**	production schedule
Plan *(m)*: **Produktionsanteils...**	share of production plan
Plan *(m)*: **taktischer ...**	tactical plan
planen	schedule (to)
Plankostenrechnung *(f)*	standard costing
Planspiel *(n)*	business game
	management game
Planung *(f)*	planning
Planung *(f)*: **Absatz...**	sales planning
Planung *(f)* **des Betriebsergebnisses** *(n)*	profit planning
Planung *(f)*: **Erfolgs...**	profit planning
Planung *(f)*: **Finanz...**	cash budgeting
	financial planning
Planung *(f)*: **kurz- bis mittelfristige ...**	operational planning
Planung *(f)*: **kurzfristige ...**	short-range planning
	short-term planning
Planung *(f)*: **langfristige ...**	long-range planning
	long-term planning

Planung *(f)*: Laufbahn...	career planning
Planung *(f)*: Leistungs...	performance budgeting
Planung *(f)*: Liquiditäts...	cash budgeting
Planung *(f)*: Markt...	market planning
Planung *(f)*: Notfall...	contingency planning
Planung *(f)*: Organisations...	organization planning
Planung *(f)*: Personal...	manpower planning
Planung *(f)*: Produkt...	product planning
Planung *(f)*: Produktions...	output budgeting
	production planning
	production scheduling
Planung *(f)*: Produktions... und -kontrolle	production planning and control
Planung *(f)*: Projekt...	project planning
Planung *(f)*: strategische ...	strategic planning
Planung *(f)*: System...	systems engineering
	systems planning
Planung *(f)*: Termin- und Kapazitäts...	scheduling
Planung *(f)* und Bereitstellung *(f)* von Produktionsmitteln *(npl)*	resource allocation
Planung *(f)*: Unternehmens...	company planning
	corporate planning
Planung *(f)*: Vertriebs...	distribution planning
Planung *(f)*: Zukunfts...	forward planning
Planungs-, Programmierungs- (und) Budgetierungssystem *(n)*	planning, programming, budgeting system (PPBS)
Planungsabteilung *(f)*	planning department
Platte *(f)*	disk
Plattenlaufwerk *(n)*	disk drive
pleite	cash-strapped
Point-of-sale-Material *(n)*	point-of-sale material
Politik *(f)*: Absatz...	sales policy
Politik *(f)*: Dividenden...	dividend policy
Politik *(f)*: Durchführung *(f)* der Unternehmens...	policy execution
Politik *(f)*: Fiskal...	fiscal policy
Politik *(f)*: Formulierung *(f)* der Unternehmens...	policy formulation
Politik *(f)*: Geld...	monetary policy

Politik *(f)*: Geschäfts...	business policy
Politik *(f)*: Investitions...	investment policy
Politik *(f)*: Personal...	personnel policy
Politik *(f)*: Preis...	pricing policy
Politik *(f)*: Unternehmens...	company policy
	corporate policy
Politik *(f)*: Verkaufs...	sales policy
	selling policy
Politik *(f)*: Verkaufsförderungs...	promotional policy
Politik *(f)*: Vertriebs...	distribution policy
Poolbildung *(f)*	pooling arrangements
Pooling *(n)*	pooling arrangements
Portfolio *(n)*: Aktien...	stock portfolio
Portfolio *(n)*: ausgeglichenes ...	balanced portfolio
Portfolio *(n)*: Geschäfts...	business portfolio
Portfolio *(n)*: Kredit...	asset portfolio
Portfolio *(n)*: Marken...	brand portfolio
Portfolio *(n)*: Wertpapier...	investment mix
Portfolio-Auswahl *(f)*	portfolio selection
Portfolio-Management *(n)*	portfolio management
Portokasse *(f)*	petty cash
POS-System *(n)*: elektronischer Zahlungsverkehr *(m)* in Verbindung mit einem ...	electronic funds transfer at point of sale (EFTPOS)
POS-Werbung *(f)*	point-of-sale advertising
Positionierung *(f)*	positioning
Positionierung *(f)*: Marken...	brand positioning
Positionierung *(f)*: Produkt...	positioning
Post *(f)*: Elektronische ...	electronic mail (e-mail)
Postbestellung *(f)*	mail order
Postversand *(m)*	mail order
Potential *(n)*: Absatz...	market potential
	sales potential
Potential *(n)*: Entwicklungs...	development potential
Potential *(n)*: Führungs...	management potential
Potential *(n)*: High ...	high-flier
Potential *(n)*: Management-...	management potential
Potential *(n)*: Markt...	market potential
Potential *(n)*: Wachstums...	growth potential

potentieller Käufer *(m)*	potential buyer
potentieller Kunde *(m)*	prospective customer
PR (Public Relations *(pl))*	public relations (PR)
praktische Ausbildung *(f)*	hands-on training
Prämie *(f)*	premium
Prämienlohn *(m)*	premium bonus
Prämienlohnsystem *(n)*	bonus scheme
Prämienregelungsplan *(m)*	bonus scheme
Präsident *(m)*	president
Preis *(m)*: **differenzierter ...**	differential price
Preis *(m)*: **einen zu hohen ... ansetzen**	overprice (to)
Preis *(m)*: **einen zu hohen ... verlangen**	overprice (to)
Preis *(m)*: **Einheits...**	standard price
Preis *(m)*: **Festlegung** *(f)* **der Verrechnungs...e** *(pl)*	transfer pricing
Preis *(m)* **festsetzen**	price (to)
Preis *(m)*: **Kassa...**	spot price
Preis *(m)*: **Konkurrenz...**	competitive price
Preis *(m)*: **konkurrenzfähiger ...**	competitive price
Preis *(m)*: **Loko...**	spot price
Preis *(m)*: **Markt...**	market price
Preis *(m)*: **sich gegenseitig verstärkender ...auftrieb** *(m)*	price escalation
Preis *(m)*: **unter ... anbieten**	underprice (to)
Preisanstieg *(m)*: **genereller ...**	across-the-board increase
Preisaufschlag *(m)*	mark-up
Preisbildung *(f), die sich an den Sozialprestigeerwartungen (fpl) der Kaüfer (mpl) orientiert*	prestige pricing
Preisbindung *(f)* **der zweiten Hand** *(f)*	resale price maintenance (RPM)
Preisdifferenzierung *(f)*	differential pricing
Preisdiskriminierung *(f)*	price discrimination
Preise *(mpl)* **herabsetzen**	cut prices (to)
Preise *(mpl)* **senken**	cut prices (to)
Preiserhöhung *(f)*	price increase
Preisfestsetzung *(f)*	price determination
	price-fixing
	pricing

Preisführer *(m)*	price leader
Preisgefälle *(n)*	price differential
Preisgestaltung *(f)*	pricing
Preisindex *(m)*	price index
Preispolitik *(f)*	pricing policy
Preisskala *(f)*	price range
Preisspanne *(f)*	price range
Preisstrategie *(f)*	pricing strategy
Preisstruktur *(f)*	price structure
Preisunterbietung *(f)*	price-cutting
Preisunterschied *(m)*	price differential
Primärforschung *(f)*	field research
Prinzipien *(npl)*: Management-...	management practices
Prioritäten *(fpl)* setzen	prioritize (to)
privatisieren	privatize (to)
Privatisierung *(f)*	privatization
Privatwirtschaft *(f)*	private enterprise
Probelauf *(m)*	test run
Problem *(n)*: gemeinsame ...bewältigung *(f)*	brainstorming
Problemanalyse *(f)*	problem analysis
Problembereich *(m)*	problem area
Problembeurteilung *(f)*	problem assessment
Problemlösung *(f)*	problem solving
Produkt *(n)*: Entwicklung *(f)* neuer ...e *(pl)*	new-product development
Produkt *(n)*: Haupt...	core product
Produkt *(n)*: Lebenserwartung *(f)* eines ...(e)s	product life expectancy
Produkt *(n)*: Lebenszyklus *(m)* eines ...(e)s	life cycle of a product
Produkt *(n)*: Neben...	by-product
Produkt *(n)*: Pionier...	pioneer product
Produkt *(n)*: unfertige ...e *(pl)*	work in progress
Produkt *(n)*: verlustbringendes ...	loss-maker
Produkt *(n)*: wirtschaftliche Fertig...menge *(f)*	economic batch quantity
Produkt *(n)*: wirtschaftliche Lebensdauer *(f)* eines ...(e)s	product life (expectancy)
Produkterzeugung *(f)*	product generation
Produkt-Management *(n)*	product management
Produkt-Manager *(m)*	product manager
Produkt-Mix *(n)*	product mix
Produktanalyse *(f)*	product analysis

Produktaufgabe *(f)*	product abandonment
Produktbereich *(m)*	product area
Produktdifferenzierung *(f)*	product differentiation
Produktdynamik *(f)*	product dynamics
Produkteinführung *(f)*	new-product launching
	product introduction
	product launch
Produkteliminierung *(f)*	product abandonment
Produktentwicklung *(f)*	product development
Produkterprobung *(f)*	product testing
Produkterzeugung *(f)*	product generation
Produktforschung *(f)*	product research
Produktgestaltung *(f)*	product design
Produktgruppe *(f)*	product group
	product line
Produktideen *(fpl)*: Finanzierung *(f)* von ...	seed money
Produktimage *(n)*	product image
Produktion *(f)*	output
	production
Produktion *(f)*: computergesteuerte ...	computer-integrated manufacturing (CIM)
Produktion *(f)*: Fließband...	line production
Produktion *(f)*: gesamte ...sanlagen *(fpl)*	production complex
Produktion *(f)*: intensive ...	intensive production
Produktion *(f)*: Ketten...	chain production
Produktion *(f)*: Massen...	continuous-flow production
	mass production
Produktion *(f)* nach dem Baukastenprinzip *(n)*	modular production
Produktion *(f)*: Planung *(f)* und Bereitstellung *(f)* von ...smitteln *(npl)*	resource allocation
Produktion *(f)*: Serien...	batch production
Produktion *(f)*: Sorten...	batch production
Produktion *(f)*: Test...	pilot production
	pilot run
Produktion *(f)*: Verhältnis *(n)* von Verwaltung *(f)* zu ...	administration-production ratio
Produktion *(f)*: Versuchs...	pilot production
	pilot run

Produktion *(f):* wirtschaftliche ...smenge *(f)*	economic manufacturing quantity
Produktionsablauf *(m)*	production run
Produktionsanlagen *(fpl):* gesamte ...	production complex
Produktionsbreite *(f)*	product diversification
Produktionsfaktoren *(mpl)*	factors of production
Produktionsfluß *(m)*	flow line
Produktionsgang *(m)*	chain of production
Produktionskapazität *(f)*	manufacturing capacity
Produktionskette *(f)*	chain of production
Produktionskontrolle *(f)*	production control
Produktionskosten *(pl)*	cost of production
	production costs
Produktionsleiter *(m)*	production director
Produktionsmanagement *(n)*	production management
Produktionsmanager *(m)*	production manager
Produktionsmethode *(f)*	production technique
Produktionsmittel *(npl):* Planung *(f)* und Bereitstellung *(f)* von ...n	resource allocation
Produktionsnorm *(f)*	production standard
Produktionsplan *(f)*	production schedule
Produktionsplanung *(f)*	output budgeting
	production planning
	production scheduling
Produktionsplanung *(f)* und -kontrolle *(f)*	production planning and control
Produktionsprozeß *(m)*	production process
Produktionsstätte *(f)*	shop floor
Produktionstechnik *(f)*	production engineering
Produktionsverfahren *(n)*	production process
Produktionsverlauf *(m)*	production run
Produktionswartung *(f)*	productive maintenance
Produktionsziel *(n)*	production target
Produktivität *(f)*	productivity
Produktivität *(f):* Tarifverhandlungen *(fpl)* über ...szulagen *(fpl)*	productivity bargaining
Produktivitätsabkommen *(n)*	productivity agreement
Produktivitätsanalyse *(f)*	efficiency audit

Produktivitätskampagne *(f)*	productivity campaign
	productivity drive
Produktivitätsmessung *(f)*	productivity measurement
Produktivitätssteigerung *(f)*: gezielte Bemühungen *(fpl)* um ...	productivity drive
Produktivitätsvereinbarung *(f)*	productivity agreement
Produktivwartung *(f)*	productive maintenance
Produktkategorie *(f)*	product line
Produktkonzeption *(f)*	product conception
Produktkostenrechnung *(f)*	product costing
Produktlebenszyklus *(m)*	product life cycle
Produktleistung *(f)*	product performance
Produktlinie *(f)*	product line
Produkt-Management *(n)*	product management
Produktpalette *(f)*	product mix
	product portfolio
	product range
Produktpiratierie *(f)*	piracy
Produktplanung *(f)*	product planning
Produktportfolio *(n)*	product portfolio
Produktpositionierung *(f)*	positioning
Produktprofil *(n)*	product profile
Produktprüfung *(f)*	product testing
Produktprogramm *(n)*	product mix
Produktrentabilität *(f)*	product profitability
Produktsortiment *(n)*: Beschränkung *(f)* des ...s	variety reduction
Produktstrategie *(f)*	product strategy
Produktverbesserung *(f)*	product improvement
Produktivwartung *(f)*	productive maintenance
Produktwerbung *(f)*	product advertising
Produktzuverlässigkeit *(f)*	product reliability
Profil *(n)*: Akquisitions...	acquisition profile
Profil *(n)*: Kunden...	customer profile
Profil *(n)*: Marken...	brand image
Profil *(n)*: Markt...	market profile
Profil *(n)*: Produkt...	product profile
Profil *(n)*: Qualifikations...	personnel specification
Profil *(n)*: Risiko...	risk profile
Profil *(n)*: Stellenanforderungs...	job specification

Profil *(n)*: Unternehmens...	company profile
Profit *(m)*	profit
Profit-Center *(n)*	profit centre
Profit-Center-Ergebnisrechnung *(f)*	profit centre accounting
Prognose *(f)*	forecast
	forecasting
	projection
Prognose *(f)*: Absatz...	sales estimate
	sales forecast
Prognose *(f)*: Budget...	budget forecasting
Prognose *(f)* der technologischen Entwicklung *(f)*	technological forecasting
Prognose *(f)*: Geschäfts...	business forecasting
Prognose *(f)*: Kassen...	cash forecasting
Prognose *(f)*: Liquiditäts...	cash forecasting
Prognose *(f)*: Markt...	market forecast
Prognose *(f)*: Nachfrage...	demand forecasting
Prognose *(f)*: Personal...	manpower forecasting
Prognose *(f)*: Verkaufs...	sales forecast
Prognostizierung *(f)*	forecasting
Prognostizierung *(f)*: Nachfrage...	demand forecasting
Programme Evaluation and Review Technique *(f)* **(PERT)**	programme evaluation and review technique (PERT)
Programm *(n)*	programme
	routine
Programm *(n)*: Absatz...	sales mix
Programm *(n)*: Computer...	computer program
Programm *(n)*: Dienst...	toolbox
Programm *(n)*: ein ... unabsichtlich auslöschen	crash a program (to)
Programm *(n)*: Entwicklungs...	development programme
Programm *(n)*: Führung *(f)* durch Vorgabe *(f)* von ...en *(pl)*	programmed management
Programm *(n)*: Investitions...	investment programme
Programm *(n)*: Produkt...	product mix
Programm (n) zum Drucken (n) persönlich adressierter Serienbriefe (mpl)	mail merge
Programmbefehl *(m)*	programmed instruction
Programmbudgetierung *(f)*	programme budgeting

Programmfehler *(m)*	bug
programmieren	program (to)
programmieren	programme (to)
Programmierer *(m)*	computer programmer
programmierter Lernprozeß *(m)*	programmed learning
programmiertes Lernen *(n)*	programmed learning
programmiertes Management *(n)*	programmed management
Programmierung *(f)*	programming
Programmierung *(f)*: dynamische ...	dynamic programming
Programmierung *(f)*: lineare ...	linear programming
Programmierung *(f)*: maschinelle ...	computer programming
Programmierung *(f)*: mathematische ...	mathematical programming
Programmierung *(f)*: nichtlineare ...	non-linear programming
Programmierung *(f)*: parametrische ...	parametric programming
Programmierung *(f)*: Planungs-, ...s- (und) Budgetierungssystem	planning, programming, budgeting system (PPBS)
Programmierung *(f)*: wissenschaftliche ...	scientific programming
Programminstruktion *(f)*	programmed instruction
Programmpaket *(n)*	programme package
Programmteil *(m)*	routine
Progression *(f)*: Gehalts...skurve *(f)*	salary progression curve
Progression *(f)*: Kosten...	diseconomy of scale
Projekt *(n)*: Bericht *(m)* über den Stand *(m)* eines ...(e)s	status report
Projekt *(n)*: ein ... in seine Einzelteile *(npl)* zerlegen	chunk a project (to)
Projekt *(n)*: integriertes ...-Management *(n)*	integrated project management (IPM)
Projekt-Management *(n)*	project management
Projektanalyse *(f)*	project analysis
Projektbewertung *(f)*	project assessment
Projektgruppe *(f)*	task force
Projektion *(f)*: Gewinn...	profit projection
Projektmanager *(m)*	project manager
Projektplanung *(f)*	project planning
Proportionalkostenrechnung *(f)*	direct costing
Provision *(f)*: Makler...	brokerage
provisorische Lösung *(f)*	quick fix
Prozeß *(m)*: Entscheidungs...	decision process

Prozeß *(m)*: iterativer ...	iterative process
Prozeß *(m)*: Produktions...	production process
prozeßgekoppelt	on line
prozeßgekoppelt: indirekt ...	off line
Prozeßkontrolle *(f)*	process control
Prozeßsteuerung *(f)*	process control
prüfen	audit (to)
	review (to)
	verify (to)
Prüfer *(m)*: Buch...	auditor
Prüfer *(m)*: Rechnungs...	auditor
	comptroller
Prüfung *(f)*: Bilanz...	balance sheet auditing
Prüfung *(f)*: Buch...	audit
Prüfung *(f)* der Ablaufsysteme *(npl)* einer Unternehmung *(f)*	management audit operations audit
Prüfung *(f)*: Eignungs...	aptitude test
Prüfung *(f)*: Rechnungs...	audit
Prüfung *(f)* und Bewertung *(f)* der Manager-Leistung *(f)*	management audit
Psychologie *(f)*: Betriebs...	industrial psychology
psychometrische Messung *(f)*	psychometric testing
psychometrische Untersuchungsmethodik *(f)*	psychometric testing
Public Relations *(pl)* (PR)	public relations (PR)
Puffervorrat *(m)*	buffer stock
Punkt *(m)*: Break-Even-...	break-even point
Punkt *(m)*: Deckungs...	break-even point
Punktbewertung *(f)*	points-rating method
Punktediagramm *(n)*	scatter diagram
Punktsystem *(n)*	points-rating method
Preisfestsetzung *(f)*	price determination
Pöstchenjägerei *(f)*	rat race

Q

Qualifikationen *(fpl)*: Stellen...	job competence
Qualifikationsprofil *(n)*	personnel specification
Qualität *(f)*: Führungs...en	leadership

Qualitätsbeurteilung (f)	quality assessment
Qualitätsbewertung (f)	quality assessment
Qualitätseinschätzung (f)	quality assessment
Qualitätskontrolle (f)	quality control (QC)
Qualitätskontrolle (f): umfassende ...	total quality control (TQC)
Qualitätsmanagement (n)	quality management
Qualitätssicherung (f)	quality assurance
Qualitätssteuerung (f)	quality control
Qualitätszirkel (m)	quality circle
Quality Circle (m)	quality circle
quantitative Analyse (f)	quantitative analysis
Quellenabzugsverfahren (n)	pay-as-you-earn (PAYE)
	pay-as-you-go
Quote (f): Absatz...	sales quota
Quote (f): Verkaufs...	sales quota
Quotenregelung (f)	positive discrimination
Quotient (m)	quotient

R

Raider (m)	corporate raider
Raider (m): Corporate ...	corporate raider
raiderabwehrender Investor (m)	white knight
Randmarkt (m)	fringe market
Rangeinteilung (f)	ranking
Rangfolge (f)	ranking
Rangordnung (f)	ranking
Rat (m): Aufsichts...	board of directors
Rat (m): Aufsichts...skontrolle (f)	board control
Rat (m): Aufsichts...ssitzung (f)	board meeting
Rat (m): Betriebs...	works committee
	works council
Rat (m): Verwaltungs...	board of directors
Rat (m): Verwaltungs...skontrolle (f)	board control
Rat (m): Verwaltungs...ssitzung (f)	board meeting
Rat (m): zu ...e ziehen	consult (to)
rationalisieren	rationalize (to)
	streamline (to)

Rationalisierung *(f)*	cost reduction
	rationalization
Rationierung *(f)*: Kapital…	capital rationing
räumen: das Lager *(n)* …	sell out (to)
Reaktion *(f)*: verspätete …	lag response
reaktiv	reactive
reaktive Strategie *(f)*	reactive strategy
Realeinkommen *(n)*	real income
realisierbar	feasible
	viable
realisierbar: leicht …e Aktiva *(pl)*	quick assets
realisieren (Gewinne *(mpl)*)	realize *(profit)* (to)
Realisierbarkeit *(f)*	viability
Reallohn *(m)*	real income
Realzeit *(f)*	real time
Rechenschaftspflicht *(f)*	accountability
Rechenzentrum *(n)*	computer centre
Rechnen *(n)*	number-crunching
Rechner *(m)*: Analog…	analog computer
Rechner *(m)*: Digital…	digital computer
Rechner *(m)*: Groß…	mainframe
Rechnerei *(f)*	number-crunching
rechnergestützte Schulung *(f)*	computer-based training (CBT)
Rechnung *(f)*: Betriebs…swesen *(n)*	management accounting
Rechnung *(f)*: funktionale Kosten…	functional costing
Rechnung *(f)*: Grenzkosten…	marginal costing
Rechnung *(f)*: Investitions…sverfahren *(n)*	capital project evaluation
Rechnung *(f)*: Konzern…	consolidated accounts
Rechnung *(f)*: Kosten- und Leistungs…	management accounting
Rechnung *(f)*: Kosten…	cost accounting
	costing
Rechnung *(f)*: Kosten… für Serienfertigung *(f)*	process accounting
Rechnung *(f)*: Kosten…art *(f)*	accounting model
Rechnung *(f)*: Plankosten…	standard costing
Rechnung *(f)*: Produktkosten…	product costing
Rechnung *(f)*: Standardkosten…	standard costing
Rechnung *(f)*: Verantwortungs…	responsibility accounting

Rechnungsjahr *(n)*	financial year
	fiscal year
Rechnungsperiode *(f)*	accounting period
Rechnungsprüfer *(m)*	auditor
	comptroller
	controller
Rechnungsprüfung *(f)*	audit
Rechnungswesen *(n)*: Betriebs...	management accounting
Rechtschreibprüfung *(f)*	spellcheck
rechtzeitig zu spekulieren aufhören	cut one's losses (to)
recyceln	recycle (to)
Recycling *(n)*	recycling
reduzieren	wind down (to)
Refa-Studie *(f)*	time and methods study
	time and motion study
regeln	regulate (to)
Regeln *(fpl)* zur Bestimmung *(f)* vom Mindestanteil *(m)* einheimischer Komponenten *(fpl)*	local content rules
Regelung *(f)*	regulation
Regelung *(f)*: Prämien...plan *(m)*	bonus scheme
Regressionsanalyse *(f)*	regression analysis
Regressionsanalyse *(f)*: Mehrfach-...	multiple regression analysis (MRA)
regulieren	regulate (to)
Regulierung *(f)*	regulation
Reihe *(f)*: Zeit...	time series
Reingewinn *(m)*	net margin
Reinvermögen *(n)*	net assets
reißerische Werbung *(f)*	hype
Rekonfiguration *(f)*	reconfiguration
rekrutieren	recruit (to)
Rendite *(f)*	rate of return
	return
	yield
Rendite *(f)*: angemessene ...	fair return
Rendite *(f)*: Anlagen...	return on assets
Rendite *(f)* des eingesetzten Kapitals *(n)*	return on capital employed (ROCE)

Rendite *(f):* Durchschnitts...	average yield
Rendite *(f):* Eigenkapital...	return on equity (ROE)
Rendite *(f):* Gewinn...	earnings yield
Rendite *(f):* Kapital...	return on capital
Rendite *(f):* Umsatz...	return on sales
Renner *(m)*	star product
Renner *(mpl)*	fast-moving consumer goods (FMG)
rentabel machen	turn around (to)
rentabel	viable
Rentabilität *(f)*	profitability
	viability
Rentabilität *(f)* des Kapitaleinsatzes *(m)*	return on investment (ROI)
Rentabilität *(f):* Anlagen...	return on investment (ROI)
Rentabilität *(f):* Eigenkapital...	return on equity (ROE)
Rentabilität *(f):* Produkt...	product profitability
Rentabilität *(f):* Umsatz...	profit-volume ratio (P/V)
	return on sales
Rentabilitätsanalyse *(f)*	profitability analysis
Rentabilitätsschwelle *(f):* die ... erreichen	break even (to)
Reorganisation *(f)*	reorganization
Reserve *(f)* für unvorhergesehene Ausgaben *(fpl)*	contingency reserve
Reservebestand *(m)*	safety stock
Reserven *(fpl):* stille ...	hidden assets
Ressort *(n):* Wahrung *(f)* des eigenen ...s	turf protection
Ressourcen *(fpl):* Bewertung *(f)* von ...	resource appraisal
Ressourcenmanagement *(n)*	resource management
Ressourcen *(fpl):* Bereitstellung *(f)* von ...	resource allocation
Restriktion *(f):* Kredit...	credit squeeze
restriktive Arbeitspraktiken *(fpl)*	restrictive practices (*industrial*)
restriktive Geschäftspraktiken *(fpl)*	restrictive practices (*legal*)
Revision *(f)*	audit
Revision *(f):* betriebsinterne ...	internal audit
Revision *(f):* Innen...	internal audit
Revisor *(m)*	auditor
revolvierender Kredit *(m)*	revolving credit
Revolvingkredit *(m)*	revolving credit
Rezession *(f)*	slump
Richtlinie *(f)*	guideline

Richtschnur *(f)*	guideline
Richtung *(f)* des Kursniveaus *(n)*	share price performance
Richtzahl *(f)*	benchmark
Risiken *(npl)* minimieren	minimize risks (to)
Risikoanalyse *(f)*	risk analysis
risikobereite Unternehmensführung *(f)*	venture management
risikobereite Unternehmensleitung *(f)*	venture management
Risikobewertung *(f)*	risk assessment
Risikoeinschätzung *(f)*	risk assessment
Risikokapital *(n)*	risk capital
	venture capital
Risikokapitalgeber *(m)*	venture capitalist
Risikomanagement *(n)*	risk management
Risikoprofil *(n)*	risk profile
Roboter *(m)*	robot
Roboter *(mpl)* einsetzen	robotize (to)
Robotertechnik *(f)*	robotics
robust	robust
Rohstoff *(m)*	commodity
	primary commodity
Rohstoffmarkt *(m)*	commodity market
rollende Landstraße *(f)*	piggyback
Rollenrepertoire (n) eines einzelnen (m)	role set
Rollenspiel *(n)*	role-playing
Rotation *(f)*: Job...	job rotation
Route *(f)*: Festlegung *(f)* der ...	routing
Routine *(f)*	routine
Rückgewinnung *(f)*: Informations...	information retrieval
Rückkopplung *(f)*	feedback
Rückstand *(m)*	backlog
Rückstellung *(f)* für	contingency reserve
Eventualverbindlichkeiten *(fpl)*	
Ruhestand *(m)*: in den ... treten	retire (to)
Ruhestand *(m)*: Versetzung *(f)* in den ...	retirement
rund: in ...en Zahlen *(fpl)*	in round figures
Rüstkosten *(pl)*	set-up costs

S

Sachvermögen *(n)*	tangible assets
Saldo *(n)*	bottom line
Sammlung *(f)*: Daten...	data gathering
sanieren	turn around (to)
Sanierung *(f)* eines Unternehmens *(n)*	company reconstruction
Sättigung *(f)*: Markt...	market saturation
Scanning *(n)*	scanning
Scanning *(n)*: Environmental ...	environmental scan
Schadensbegrenzung *(f)*	damage limitation
schätzen	appraise (to)
Schätzung *(f)*	appraisal
Schätzung *(f)*: grobe ...	guesstimate
Schaufensterdekoration *(f)*	window-dressing
Schichtarbeit *(f)*	shiftwork
Schiedsverfahren *(n)*	arbitration
Schleife *(f)*: geschlossene ...	closed loop
schlichten	conciliate (to)
Schlichtung *(f)*	conciliation
	mediation
Schlichtungsverfahren *(n)*	arbitration
	grievance procedure
Schmiergeldfonds *(m)*	slush fund
Schnelldreher *(mpl)*	fast-moving consumer goods (FMG)
Schnittstelle *(f)*	interface
Schreiblesespeicher *(m)*	random-access memory (RAM)
Schreibtischarbeiter *(m)*	white-collar worker
Schreibtischforschung *(f)*	desk research
schriftliche Vereinbarung *(f)*	written agreement
schrumpfen	slim down (to)
Schuldner *(m)*	debtor
Schuldtitel *(mpl)*: festverzinsliche ...	loan stock
Schuldtitel *(mpl)*: Finanzierung *(f)* durch die Emission *(f)* von ...n	debt financing
Schuldverschreibungen *(fpl)*	loan stock
Schulung *(f)*	training

Schulung *(f)*: innerbetriebliche ...	in-plant training
Schulung *(f)*: rechnergestützte ...	computer-based training (CBT)
Schulung *(f)*: zusätzliche ...	booster training
Schwarzarbeit *(f)*	moonlighting
Schwarzseher *(m)*	doomwatcher
Schwelle *(f)*: Gewinn...	break-even point
Schwelle *(f)*: Nutz...	break-even point
Schwerpunkt *(m)*	focus
Schwestergesellschaft *(f)*	affiliate company
Segment *(n)*: Markt...	market segment
segmentieren	segment (to)
segmentieren: herunter...	segment (to)
Segmentierung *(f)*	segmentation
Segmentierung *(f)*: Markt...	market segmentation
Sektor *(m)*: öffentlicher ...	public enterprise
Selbsteinschätzung *(f)*	self-appraisal
Selbstfinanzierung *(f)*	self-financing
Selbstmotivierung *(f)*	self-motivation
***Selbstständigkeit** (f): Prinzip der rechtlichen ... einer Tochtergesellschaft (f)*	arm's length
Selektion *(f)*: Medien...	media selection
senken: Preise *(mpl)* ...	cut prices (to)
Senkrechtstarter *(m)*	whiz-kid
Senkung *(f)*: Kosten...	cost reduction
sensibilisieren	sensitize (to)
Sensitivitätsanalyse *(f)*	sensitivity analysis
Sensitivitätstraining *(n)*	sensitivity training
Sequenzanalyse *(f)*	sequential analysis
***Serienbriefe** (mpl): Programm (n) zum Drucken (n) persönlich adressierter ...*	mail merge
Serienproduktion *(f)*	batch production
Service *(m)*	customer care
Setzung *(f)*: Ziel...	goal-setting
	objective
	target-setting
	targeting
sexuelle Belästigung *(f)*	sexual harassment
sich an einer Ausschreibung *(f)* **beteiligen**	tender (to)
sich besprechen mit	consult (to)

sich deutlich von Konkurrenzprodukten *(npl)* unterscheiden	product differentiate (to)
sich gegenseitig verstärkender Preisauftrieb *(m)*	price escalation
sich konzentrieren auf	focus (to)
sich pensionieren lassen	retire (to)
sich selbst abdeckend	self-liquidating
sich selbst abdeckender Kredit *(m)*	self-liquidating credit
sich Unvorstellbares *(n)* vorstellen	think the unthinkable (to)
sich zusammenschließen	amalgamate (to)
sich in Liquiditätsschwierigkeiten *(fpl)* befindend	cash-strapped
sich ins Zeug *(n)* legen	hustle (to)
Sicherheit *(f)*	collateral
Sicherheit *(f)*: Arbeitsplatz...	job security
Sicherheit *(f)*: Betriebs...	industrial safety
	industrial security
Sicherheit *(f)*: dingliche ...	collateral security
Sicherheit *(f)*: zusätzliche ...	collateral
Sicherheitslücke *(f)*	security leak
Sicherheitsmanagement *(n)*	safety management
Sicherheitsmarge *(f)*	margin of safety
Sicherungseinrichtung *(f)*	back-up facility
Sicherungsgegenstand *(m)*	collateral
Sicherungsgeschäft *(n)*	hedging operation
Sicherungsgeschäfte *(npl)*	hedging
Sicherungsgut *(n)*	collateral
Sichtfenster *(n)*	window
sieben	screen (to)
Simplex-Methode *(f)*	simplex method
Simulation *(f)*	simulation
Simulation *(f)*: Computer...	computer simulation
simulieren	simulate (to)
sinnvoll	meaningful
Sitten *(fpl)* und Gebräuche *(mpl)*	custom and practice
Sitzstreik *(m)*	sit-down strike
Sitzung *(f)*: Aufsichtsrats...	board meeting
Sitzung *(f)*: Verwaltungsrats...	board meeting
Sitzung *(f)*: Vorstands...	board meeting

Sitzungssaal *(m)*	board room
Skala *(f)*: gleitende ...	sliding scale
Softsell *(m)*	soft sell
Software *(f)*	software
Software *(f)*: Zwischenhändler *(m)* für ... -Vertrieb *(m)*	software broker
Software-Engineer *(m)*	software engineer
Softwareanwendung *(f)*	software application
Softwareanwendungsmöglichkeit *(f)*	software application
Softwarefirma *(f)*	software company
Softwarepaket *(n)*	software package
Soll-/Ist-Vergleich *(m)*	performance against objectives
Sollkosten *(pl)*	standard costs
Sortenfertigung *(f)*	batch production
Sortenproduktion *(f)*	batch production
Sortiment *(n)*	product range
Sourcing *(n)*	sourcing
Sozialdiagnose *(f)*	social analysis
Sozialleistungen *(fpl)*	fringe benefits
sozialwidrige Kündigung *(f)*	unfair dismissal
soziokulturell	socio-cultural
soziometrisch	sociometric
sozioökonomisch	socio-economic
Spanne *(f)*: Bruttogewinn...	gross margin (GM)
Spanne *(f)*: Gewinn...	profit margin
Spanne *(f)*: Kontroll...	span of control
Spanne *(f)*: Leitungs...	span of control
Spanne *(f)*: Nettogewinn...	net margin
Spanne *(f)*: Preis...	price range
Sparte *(f)*	operating division
Sparten *(fpl)*: in ... aufteilen	compartmentalize (to)
Spartenleitung *(f)*	divisional management
Spediteur *(m)*	forwarding agent
Spedition *(f)*	forwarding
	shipping
Speicher *(m)*	computer memory
	memory
Speicher *(m)*: Fest(wert)...	read-only memory (ROM)
Speicherplatz *(m)*	slot

Speicherung *(f)*	storage
Speicherung *(f)*: Daten...	computer storage
Spekulation *(f)*: Börsen...	jobbing
spekulieren: rechtzeitig zu ... aufhören	cut one's losses (to)
sperren	freeze (to)
Spesen *(pl)*: kleine ...	petty expenses
Spesenerstattung *(f)*	recovery of expenses
Spesenkonto *(n)*	expense account
spezialangefertigt	custom-made
Spiel (n), bei dem sich Gewinne (mpl) und Verluste (mpl) ausgleichen	zero-sum game
Spiel *(n)*: Führungs...	management game
Spiel *(n)*: Plan...	business game
	management game
Spiel *(n)*: Rollen...	role-playing
Spiel *(n)*: Unternehmens...	business game
Spieltheorie *(f)*	game theory
Spionage *(f)*: Industrie...	industrial espionage
Spitzen-	world class
Spitzenmanagement *(n)*	top management
Sponsoring *(n)*	sponsorship
Sponsorschaft *(f)*	sponsorship
Spontankaufen *(n)*	impulse buying
Sprache *(f)*: gemeinsame ...	common language
Sprache *(f)*: Maschinen...	computer language
	machine language
sprachlich: modische ...e Neuprägung (f)	buzz-word
sprungfixe Kosten *(pl)*	semi-variable costs
Sprungkosten *(pl)*	semi-variable costs
Stab *(m)* **und Linie** *(f)*	staff and line
Stablinienorganisation *(f)*	line and staff organization
Stabsassistent *(m)*	staff assistant
Stabsorganisation *(f)*	staff organization
Staffelung *(f)*	stagger
Stagflation *(f)*	stagflation
Stammbaum *(m)*	family tree
Stand *(m)*: auf den neuesten ... bringen	update (to)
Stand *(m)*: Bericht *(m)* über den ... eines Projekt(e)s *(n)*	status report

Stand *(m)* der Technik *(f)*	state of the art
Stand-alone-	stand-alone
Standard *(m)*	standard
Standard *(m)*: Lebens...	standard of living
Standardabweichung *(f)*	standard deviation
standardisieren	standardize (to)
Standardisierung *(f)*	standardization
	variety reduction
Standardkosten *(pl)*	standard costs
Standardkostenrechnung *(f)*	standard costing
Standardpreis *(m)*	standard price
Standardwerte *(mpl)*: erstklassige ...	blue-chip stock
Standardzeit *(f)*	standard time
ständiger Konkurrenzkampf *(m)*	rat race
Standort *(m)*: Unternehmens...	plant location
Stapelkontrolle *(f)*	batch control
Stapelverarbeitung *(f)*	batch processing
Startkosten *(pl)*	start-up costs
statistische Kontrolle *(f)*	statistical control
Status *(m)*: Erlangung *(f)* eines beruflichen ...	professionalization
Status *(m)*: Finanz...	financial position
Steckplatz *(m)*	slot
steigen: im Wert *(m)* ...	appreciate (to)
Steigerung *(f)*: Bemühungen *(fpl)* um Verkaufs...en *(pl)*	sales expansion effort
Steigerung *(f)*: gezielte Bemühungen *(fpl)* um Produktivitäts...	productivity drive
Steik *(m)*: offizieller ...	official strike
Steik *(m)*: inoffizieller ...	unofficial strike
Stelle *(f)*: Aufgliederung *(f)* des ...ninhalt(e)s *(m)*	operations breakdown
Stelle *(f)*: Interesse *(n)* an der ...	job interest
Stelle *(f)*: Kosten...	cost centre
Stelle *(f)*: mit einer ... verbundene Erwartungen *(pl)*	job expectations
Stelle *(f)*: Naht...	interface
Stelle *(f)*: Schnitt...	interface
Stelle *(f)*: systematischer ...nwechsel *(m)*	job rotation

Stelle *(f)*: Zweig...	branch office
Stelleinhalt *(m)*: **Aufgliederung** *(f)* **des ...(e)s**	operations breakdown
Stellenanalyse *(f)*	job analysis
Stellenanforderung *(f)*	job challenge
Stellenanforderungen *(fpl)*	job requirements
Stellenanforderungsprofil *(n)*	job specification
Stellenanhebung *(f)*	job improvement
Stellenaufschlüsselung *(f)*	job breakdown
Stellenbeschreibung *(f)*	job description
	job profile
	job specification
Stellenbesetzung *(f)*	staffing
Stellenbezeichnung *(f)*	job title
Stellenentwurf *(m)*	job design
Stelleninhalt *(m)*	job content
	work content
Stelleninhalt *(m)*: **Aufgliederung** *(f)* **des ...(e)s**	operations breakdown
Stellenklassifizierung *(f)*	job classification
Stellennachweis *(m)*	employment bureau
Stellenqualifikationen *(fpl)*	job competence
Stellenvereinfachung *(f)*	job simplification
Stellenvermittlung *(f)*	employment bureau
Stellung *(f)*: Markt...	market rating
Stellung *(f)*: Wettbewerbs...	competitive position
stellvertretender Direktor *(m)*	assistant director
	assistant manager
	deputy manager
stellvertretender Generaldirektor *(m)*	deputy managing director
stellvertretender Geschäftsführer *(m)*	deputy managing director
stellvertretender Manager *(m)*	deputy manager
	assistant manager
stellvertretender Vorsitzender *(m)*	deputy chairman
	vice-chairman
Steuer *(f)*: Einkommen...	income tax
Steuer *(f)*: Körperschafts...	corporation tax
	profits tax
Steuer *(f)*: Mehrwert...	value added tax (VAT)
Steuerbremse *(f)*	fiscal drag
steuerlich absetzbar	tax-deductible

steuerlicher Anreiz *(m)*	tax incentive
Steuernachlaß *(m)* aufgrund eines Doppelbesteuerungsabkommens *(n)*	double taxation relief
Steuerung *(f)*: Fertigungs...	manufacturing control
Steuerung *(f)*: Liquiditäts...	cash management
Steuerung *(f)*: Prozeß...	process control
Steuervergünstigung *(f)*	tax relief
Stichprobe *(f)*: Arbeits...n *(pl)*	activity sampling
Stichprobe *(f)*: Methode *(f)* der Arbeits...n *(fpl)*	random observation method
Stichprobenauswahl *(f)*: zufallsgesteuerte ...	random sampling
Stichtag *(m)*	cut-off point
	expected date
Stil *(m)* des Hauses *(n)*	house style
Stil *(m)*: Führungs...	managerial style
Stil *(m)*: Lebens...	lifestyle
stille Reserven *(fpl)*	hidden assets
Stillegung *(f)*	shut-down
Stillegungskosten *(pl)*	closing-down costs
Störung *(f)*	bug
Störung *(f)*: Funktions...	dysfunction
	malfunction
Strategie *(f)*: Benutzer...	user strategy
Strategie *(f)*: defensive ...	defensive strategy
Strategie *(f)*: Diversifikations...	diversification strategy
Strategie *(f)*: Durchführung *(f)* der ...	strategy implementation
Strategie *(f)*: Expansions...	expansion strategy
Strategie *(f)*: Finanz...	financial strategy
Strategie *(f)*: Formulierung *(f)* der Unternehmens...	stategy formulation
Strategie *(f)*: Führungskräfte...	executive manpower strategy
Strategie *(f)*: Geschäfts...	business strategy
Strategie *(f)*: Gewinn...	profit strategy
Strategie *(f)*: initiative ...	proactive strategy
Strategie *(f)*: Marken...	brand strategy
Strategie *(f)*: Marketing...	marketing strategy
Strategie *(f)*: Preis...	pricing strategy
Strategie *(f)*: Produkt...	product strategy
Strategie *(f)*: reaktive ...	reactive strategy

Strategie *(f)*: Überlebens...	survival strategy
Strategie *(f)*: Unternehmens...	company strategy
	corporate strategy
Strategie *(f)*: Verbraucher...	user strategy
Strategie *(f)*: Verhandlungs...	negotiation strategy
Strategie *(f)*: Wachstums...	expansion strategy
	growth strategy
Strategie *(f)*: Wettbewerbs...	competitive strategy
strategische Allianz *(f)*	strategic alliance
strategische Planung *(f)*	strategic planning
strategische Unternehmenseinheit *(f)*	strategic business unit
strategische Wechselbeziehung *(f)*	strategic interdependence
strategischer Plan *(m)*	strategic plan
strategisches Analyse (f) der wichtigsten Erfolgsfaktoren (mpl)	strengths, weaknesses, opportunities and threats (SWOT) analysis
Streben *(n)*: Gewinn...	profit motive
Streik *(m)*	walkout
Streik *(m)*: Bummel...	go-slow
	work-to-rule
Streik *(m)*: inoffizieller ...	unofficial strike
Streik *(m)*: offizieller ...	official strike
Streik *(m)*: Sitz...	sit-down strike
Streik *(m)*: Sympathie...	sympathy strike
Streik *(m)*: von einer Gewerkschaft *(f)* nicht genehmigter ...	unofficial action
Streik *(m)*: wilder ...	unofficial action
	wildcat strike
Streikbrecher *(m)*	blackleg
	scab
Streikmaßnahmen *(fpl)*	industrial action
Streikposten *(m)*	picket
Streß *(m)*: Arbeits...	work stress
Streubild *(n)*	scatter diagram
Streudiagramm *(n)*	scatter diagram
Ströme *(mpl)*: Kapital...	funds flow
Struktur *(f)*	structure
Struktur *(f)*: Führungs...	managerial structure
Struktur *(f)*: Gehalts...	salary structure

Struktur *(f)*: Gitter...	grid structure
Struktur *(f)*: Kapital...	capital structure
Struktur *(f)*: Kosten...	cost structure
Struktur *(f)*: Lohn...	wage structure
Struktur *(f)*: Markt...	market structure
Struktur *(f)*: Organisations...	organization structure
Struktur *(f)*: Preis...	price structure
Struktur *(f)*: Unternehmens...	corporate structure
strukturieren	structure (to)
strukturiert	structured
strukturiert: nicht ...	unstructured
Strukturierung *(f)*	structuring
Studie *(f)*: Arbeits...	work study
Studie *(f)*: Bewegungs...	methods study
	motion study
Studie *(f)*: Durchführbarkeits...	feasibility study
Studie *(f)*: Fall...	case study
Studie *(f)*: Markt...	market study
Studie *(f)*: Refa-...	time and methods study
	time and motion study
Studie *(f)*: Zeit- und Bewegungs...	time and methods study
	time and motion study
Stufe *(f)*: Gehalts...	salary grade
stufenweise einführen	phase in (to)
stufenweise einstellen	phase out (to)
stufenweise Finanzierung *(f)*	drip-feeding
Stundenzettel *(m)*	time sheet
Stützung *(f)*	support activity
Suboptimierung *(f)*	sub-optimization
Subsidiarität *(f)*	subsidiarity
Substanzwert *(m)*	asset value
Substitution *(f)* **von Bankkrediten** *(mpl)* **durch handelbare Wertpapiere** *(npl)*	securitization
Suche *(f)* **nach Führungskräften** *(fpl)*	executive search
suchen: nach Führungskräften *(fpl)*...	head-hunt (to)
Swap *(m)*	swap
Switch-Geschäft *(n)*	switch-trading
Sympathiestreik *(m)*	sympathy strike
Symposion *(n)*	symposium

Syndikat *(n)*	syndicate
Synergie *(f)*	synergy
Synergieeffekte *(mpl)*	synergism
Synergismus *(m)*	synergism
System *(n)*	system
System *(n)*: **Akkordlohn...**	payment by results
System *(n)*: **computerisiertes Informations...**	computerized information system (COINS)
System *(n)*: **elektronisches Buchführungs ...**	electronic accounting system
System *(n)*: **Experten...**	expert system
System *(n)*: **Informations...**	information system
System *(n)*: **integriertes Management...**	integrated management system
System *(n)*: **leistungsbezogenes Lohn...**	incentive scheme
System *(n)*: **Lohn...**	wage system
System *(n)*: **Management-...**	management system
System *(n)*: **Management-Informations...**	management information system (MIS)
System *(n)*: **nach ... geführtes Unternehmen** *(n)*	system managed company
System *(n)*: **Planungs-, Programmierungs- (und) Budgetierungs...**	planning-programming-budgeting system (PPBS)
System *(n)*: **Prämienlohn...**	bonus scheme
System *(n)*: **Punkt...**	points rating method
System *(n)* **vorbestimmter Zeiten** *(fpl)*	predetermined motion time system (PMTS)
System-Management *(n)*	systems management
Systemanalyse *(f)*	systems analysis
systematischer Stellenwechsel *(m)*	job rotation
systematisieren	systematize (to)
Systeme *(npl)* **und Verfahren** *(npl)*	systems and procedures
Systemgestaltung *(f)*	systems design
Systemingenieur *(m)*	systems engineer
Systemkostenvoranschlag *(m)*	estimating systems costs
Systemplanung *(f)*	systems engineering
	systems planning
Systemtheorie *(f)*	systems theory
systemunabhängig	off line
Systemverfahren *(n)*	systems approach
Systemverwaltung *(f)*	systems management

Systemvorgehen *(n)*	systems approach
Szenario *(n)*	scenario
Szenario *(n)*: **optimistischstes ...**	best-case scenario
Szenario *(n)*: **pessimistischstes ...**	worst-case scenario

T

Tabelle *(f)* **des kritischen Pfades** *(m)*	milestone chart
Tabelle *(f)*: **Input-Output-...**	input-output table
Tabellenberechnungsprogramm *(n)*	spreadsheet
Tag *(m)*: **letzter ...**	latest date
Tagesordnung *(f)*: **auf der ... stehen**	be on the agenda (to)
Tagschicht *(f)*	day shift
Tagung *(f)*	symposium
Taktik *(f)*: **Wettbewerbs...**	competitive tactics
taktische Planung *(f)*	tactical planning
taktischer Plan *(m)*	tactical plan
Talent *(n)*: **Hoch...**	high-flier
talentloser, nicht aufstrebender Mitarbeiter *(m)*	low-flier
Talsohle *(f)*: **die ... verlassen**	bottom out (to)
Tantieme *(f)*	royalty
Tarifkonflikt *(m)*	industrial dispute
Tarifpolitik *(f)*	wage policy
Tarifverhandlungen *(fpl)*	collective bargaining
	pay talks
Tarifverhandlungen *(fpl)*: **innerbetriebliche ...**	plant bargain
Tarifverhandlungen *(fpl)* **über Produktivitätszulagen** *(fpl)*	productivity bargaining
Tarifvertrag *(m)*	collective bargaining agreement
Tätigkeitsdiagramm *(n)*	activity chart
Tauschgeschäft *(n)*	trade-off
Tauschhandel *(m)*	barter trade
	countertrade
Team *(n)*: **Führungs...**	management team
Team-Bildung *(f)*	team-building
Teamchef *(m)*	team leader

teamfähiger Manager *(m)*	team player
Teammitglied *(n)*	team player
teamorientierter Manager *(m)*	team player
Technik *(f)*	engineering
Technik *(f)*: Betriebs...	industrial engineering
Technik *(f)*: Fertigungs...	product engineering
Technik *(f)*: Führungs...	management technique
Technik *(f)*: Konstruktions...	design engineering
Technik *(f)*: Management...	management technique
Technik *(f)*: Netzplan...	network analysis
Technik *(f)*: Produktions...	production engineering
Technik *(f)*: Roboter...	robotics
Technik *(f)*: Stand *(m)* der ...	state of the art
technische Abteilung *(f)* und Konstruktionsbüro *(n)*	engineering and design department
technischer Direktor *(m)*	technical manager
technischer Kaufmann *(m)*	sales engineer
Technologie *(f)*: Informations...	information technology
Technologietransfer *(m)*	technology transfer
technologisch: Prognose *(f)* der ...en Entwicklung *(f)*	technological forecast(ing)
Teil *(m,n)*: Ausbildung *(f)* in ...analysen	part-analysis training
Teile *(npl)* absondern	hive off (to)
Teilhaber *(m)*	partner
Teilzeitbeschäftigung *(f)*	part-time employment
Telefax-Gerät *(n)*	fax machine
Telefonmarketing *(n)*	telemarketing
Telefonverkauf *(m)*	telesales
Telefonwerbung *(f)*	telesales
Telekonferenz *(f)*	teleconference
Telematik *(f)*	telematics
Telexen *(n)*: Rückmeldung *(f)* beim ...	answerback code
Tendenz *(f)*: Markt...en *(pl)*	market trend
Tendenz *(f)*: Wirtschafts...en *(pl)*	economic trend
Termin *(m)*	deadline
	expected date
Termin *(m)*: äußerster ...	latest date
Termin- und Kapazitätsplanung *(f)*	scheduling
Termin-Swap *(m)*	forward swap

Terminal *(n)*	computer terminal
	terminal
Termingeschäfte *(npl)*	futures
Terminkontrakte *(mpl)*	futures
Terminkontrakte *(mpl)*: Finanz...	financial futures
Terminkontraktmarkt *(m)*	futures market
Terminmarkt *(m)*	forward market
Terminwaren *(fpl)*	futures
Test *(m)*: Eignungs...	aptitude test
Test *(m)*: Feld-...s *(pl)*	field testing
Test *(m)*: Markt...	market test
Test-Marketing *(n)*	test marketing
Testproduktion *(f)*	pilot production
	pilot run
Textverarbeiter *(m)*	word processor (WP)
Textverarbeitung *(f)*	word processing
Textverarbeitungseinrichtung *(f)*	word processor (WP)
Thema *(n)*: Werbe...	advertising theme
Theorie *(f)* des von oben nach unten durchsickernden Wohlstands *(m)*	trickle-down theory
Theorie *(f)*: Entscheidungs...	decision theory
Theorie *(f)*: Informations...	information theory
Theorie *(f)*: Kommunikations...	communications theory
Theorie *(f)*: Kontingenz...	contingency theory
Theorie *(f)*: Management-...	management theory
Theorie *(f)*: Organisations...	organization theory
Theorie *(f)*: Spiel...	game theory
Theorie *(f)*: System...	systems theory
Theorie *(f)*: Verwaltungs...	administrative theory
Theorie *(f)*: Wahrscheinlichkeits...	probability theory
Theorie *(f)*: Warteschlangen...	queuing theory
Think Tank *(m)*	think-tank
Tiefenanalyse *(f)*	depth analysis
Tiefeninterview *(n)*	depth interview
	in-depth interview
tilgen	pay off (to)
Tilgungsfonds *(m)*	sinking fund
Time-Sharing *(n)*	time-sharing
Tochtergesellschaft *(f)*	subsidiary company

Tochtergesellschaft (f): Prinzip (n) der rechtlichen Selbständigkeit (f) einer …	arm's length
Top-down-	top-down
Top-Management *(n)*	top management
Top-Management *(n): Verfahrensweise (f) des …s*	top management approach
Total Quality Management *(n)* (TQM)	total quality management (TQM)
TQM (Total Quality Management *(n))*	TQM (total quality management)
Träger *(mpl):* Werbe…	advertising media media
Training *(n)*	training
Training *(n):* Gruppen…	group training
Training *(n):* Sensitivitäts…	sensitivity training
Training *(n):* zusätzliches …	booster training
Transaktions-	transactional
Transaktionsanalyse *(f)*	transactional analysis (TA)
Transport *(m)*	transportation
Transport *(m):* Material…	materials handling
Trend *(m)*	trend
Trend *(m):* Aufwärts…	upswing upturn
Trend *(m):* exponentieller …	exponential trend
Trend *(m):* Konjunktur…	economic trend
Trend *(m):* Markt…	market trend
Treue *(f):* Marken…	brand loyalty
Troubleshooter *(m)*	troubleshooter
Turnaround-Zeit *(f)*	turnaround time
Typenrad *(n)*	daisy wheel
Typenraddrucker *(m)*	daisy wheel

U

über dem Nennwert *(m)*	above par
über pari	above par
Überalterung *(f)*	obsolescence
überbesetzt	overmanned

überbesetzt: personell ...	overstaffed
Überbesetzung *(f)*	overmanning
Überbesetzung *(f)*: **personelle ...**	overstaffing
Übereinstimmung *(f)*	consensus
Übergangs-	transitional
Überkapazität *(f)*	excess capacity
	overcapacity
überkapitalisiert	overcapitalized
Überlebensstrategie *(f)*	survival strategy
Überleiteinrichtung *(f)*	gateway
Übernahme *(f)*	buyout
	takeover
Übernahme *(f)*: **Kosten...**	absorption
Übernahme (f): von Fremdkapital (n) *unterstützte ...*	leveraged buyout (LBO)
Übernahmeangebot *(n)*	take-over bid (TOB)
Übernahmeangebot (n): mögliche *Mitbieter (mpl) abschreckendes ...*	pre-emptive bid
Übernahmeangebot (n): von Fremdkapital *unterstütztes ...*	leveraged bid
Übernahmen *(fpl)*: **Fusionen** *(fpl)* **und ...**	mergers and acquisitions (M&A)
übernehmen	buy out (to)
überprüfen	review (to)
	screen (to)
	verify (to)
Überprüfung *(f)* **der Finanzlage** *(f)*	financial review
Überprüfung *(f)*: **Finanz...**	financial review
Überprüfung *(f)* **im Feld** *(n)*	field testing
überschuldet	overextended
Übersicht *(f)*: **Gehalts...**	salary review
Überstunden *(fpl)*	overtime
überwachen	monitor (to)
	supervise (to)
Überweisungspolitik *(f)*	remittance policy
üblicher Satz *(m)*	going rate
umfassende Betriebsinstandhaltung *(f)*	total plant maintenance
umfassende Qualitätskontrolle *(f)*	total quality control (TQC)
Umfeldanalyse *(f)*	environmental analysis

Umfrage *(f)*: Markt…	market survey
umgehen	bypass (to)
umgruppieren	redeploy (to)
Umgruppierung *(f)* **der Arbeitskräfte** *(fpl)*	redeployment
Umlage *(f)*: Kosten…	allocation of costs
	cost allocation
	cost apportionment
Umlaufvermögen *(n)*	current assets
Umlaufvermögen *(n)*: Netto…	net current assets
Umsatz *(m)*	turnover
	volume
Umsatz *(m)*: Geschäfts…	sales turnover
Umsatz *(m)*: Kosten-/… -/ Gewinnananalyse *(f)*	cost, volume, profit analysis
Umsatz *(m)*: Verhältnis *(n)* von … zu Anlagen *(fpl)*	asset turnover
Umsatz *(m)*: Waren…	sales turnover
Umsatzrendite *(f)*	return on sales
Umsatzrentabilität *(f)*	profit volume ratio (P/V)
	return on sales
Umsatzvolumen *(n)*	sales volume
Umschlag *(m)*	turnover
Umschlag *(m)*: Lager…	inventory turnover
	stock turnover
Umschulung *(f)*	retraining
umstellen: auf Computer *(mpl)* umstellen	computerize (to)
Umstellung *(f)* **auf Container** *(mpl)*	containerization
umstrukturieren	restructure (to)
Umstrukturierung *(f)*	restructuring
Umstrukturierung *(f)* **einer Unternehmung** *(f)*	company reconstruction
Umwelt *(f)*	environment
Umweltfragen *(fpl)*	green issues
Undenkbares *(n)* **denken**	think the unthinkable (to)
unerwähnte Ziele *(npl)*	hidden agenda
unfertige Leistungen *(fpl)*	work in progress
unfertige Produkte *(npl)*	work in progress
ungefährer Betrag *(m)*	ballpark figure

ungelernte Arbeiter *(mpl)*	unskilled labour
ungenügend gedeckt	overextended
ungenutzte Kapazität *(f)*	idle capacity
Unkosten (pl): kleine ...	petty expenses
unlauterer Wettbewerb *(m)*	unfair competition
unmittelbar geleistete Arbeitszeit *(f)*	direct labour
unsichtbare Ein- und Ausfuhren *(fpl)*	invisibles
unstrukturiert	unstructured
unten: Theorie *(f)* **des von oben nach ...** **durchsickernden Wohlstands** *(m)*	trickle-down theory
unten: von ... nach oben	bottom-up
unter dem Nennwert *(m)*	below par
unter pari	below par
unter Preis *(m)* **anbieten**	underprice (to)
unterbesetzt	undermanned
unterbesetzt: personell ...	understaffed
Unterbesetzung *(f)*	undermanning
Unterbesetzung *(f)*: personelle ...	understaffing
unterbieten	undercut (to)
Unterbietung *(f)*: Preis...	price-cutting
unterbringen: im Haushaltsplan *(m)* **...**	budget (to)
unterkapitalisiert	undercapitalized
unterlegen: Kreditforderungen *(fpl)* **wertpapiermäßig ...**	securitize (to)
Unterlegung *(f)*: wertpapiermäßige ... von Kreditforderungen *(f)*	securitization
Unternehmen *(n)*	enterprise
Unternehmen *(n)*: börsennotiertes ...	quoted company
Unternehmen *(n)*: Einführung *(f)* neuer Mitarbeiter *(mpl)* in das ...	induction
Unternehmen *(n)*: Gemeinschafts...	joint venture
Unternehmen *(n)*: Geschäfts...	business corporation
Unternehmen *(n)*: nach System *(n)* geführtes ...	system-managed company
Unternehmen *(n)*: Organisation *(f)* eines ...s	business system
Unternehmen *(n)*: Sanierung *(f)* eines ...s	company reconstruction
Unternehmen *(n)*: verbundenes ...	associate company
Unternehmensaufkäufer *(m)*	predator

Unternehmensberater *(m)*	management consultant
Unternehmensberatung *(f)*	management consultancy
Unternehmensbereich *(m)*	operating division
Unternehmenseinheit *(f):* strategische ...	strategic business unit
Unternehmensergebnisse *(npl):* zurückliegende ...	track record
Unternhemenserfolg *(m)*	profit performance
Unternehmensforschung *(f)*	operational research (OR)
	operations research (OR)
Unternehmensführung *(f)*	business management
	management
Unternehmensführung *(f):* intuitive ...	intuitive management
Unternehmensführung *(f):* Organogramm *(n)* der ...	management chart
Unternehmensführung *(f):* risikobereite ...	venture management
Unternehmensführung *(f)* unter Beteiligung *(f)* nachgeordneter Führungsebenen *(fpl)*	multiple management
Unternehmensführung *(f):* wirksame ...	effective management
	managerial effectiveness
Unternehmensführung *(f):* wissenschaftliche ...	scientific management
Unternehmensgrundsätze *(mpl):* Erklärung *(f)* der ...	mission statement
Unternehmensgründung *(f)*	flotation
Unternehmensimage *(n)*	corporate image
unternehmensintern	in-company
Unternehmenskultur *(f)*	corporate culture
Unternehmensleitung *(f)*	management
Unternehmensleitung *(f):* Kontrollfunktionen *(fpl)* der ...	supervisory management
Unternehmemsleitung *(f):* Organogramm *(n)* der ...	management chart
Unternehmensleitung *(f):* risikobereite ...	venture management
unternehmungslustig	enterprising
Unternehmensmodell *(n)*	company model
	corporate model
Unternehmensneugründung *(f)*	start-up

Unternehmensneugründung *(f)*: **Kapital** *(n)* für eine ...	seed money
Unternehmensphilosophie *(f)*	company philosophy
Unternehmensplanung *(f)*	company planning
	corporate planning
Unternehmenspolitik *(f)*	company policy
	corporate policy
Unternehmenspolitik *(f)*: **Durchführung** *(f)* der ...	policy execution
Unternehmenspolitik *(f)*: **Formulierung** *(f)* der ...	policy formulation
Unternehmensprofil *(n)*	company profile
Unternehmensspiel *(n)*	business game
Unternehmensstandort *(m)*	plant location
Unternehmensstrategie *(f)*	company strategy
	corporate strategy
Unternehmensstrategie *(f)*: **Formulierung** *(f)* der ...	strategy formulation
Unternehmensstruktur *(f)*	company structure
	corporate structure
Unternehmenswachstum *(n)*	corporate growth
Unternehmenswerbung *(f)*	corporate advertising
Unternehmensziel *(n)*	company goal
	company objective
	corporate goal
	corporate mission
	corporate objective
Unternehmensziele *(npl)*: **gesamte** ...	overall company objectives
Unternehmenszusammenbruch *(m)*	failure *(of firm)*
Unternehmer *(m)*: **Eigentümer**...	owner-manager
Unternehmergeist *(m)*	entrepreneurial spirit
unternehmerisch eingestellt	enterprising
Unternehmertum *(n)*: **freies** ...	private enterprise
Unternehmung *(f)*	enterprise
Unternehmung *(f)*: **Ausschlachtung** *(f)* einer ...	asset-stripping
Unternehmung (f): Ausschlachtung (f) einer mittels Junk Bonds (mpl) übernommenen ...	unbundling
Unternehmung (f): eine mittels Junk Bonds (mpl) übernommene ... ausschlachten	unbundle (to)

Unternehmung *(f)*: Prüfung *(f)* der Ablaufsysteme *(npl)* einer...	management audit operations audit
Unternehmung *(f)*: Umstrukturierung *(f)* einer ...	company reconstruction
Unterricht *(m)*: computerunterstützter ...	computer-assisted teaching (CAT)
Unterrichtsmittel *(npl)*: audiovisuelle ...	audiovisual aids
Unterrichtung *(f)*	briefing
Unterrichtung *(f)* der Kundschaft *(f)*	customer orientation
unterscheiden	differentiate (to)
unterscheiden: sich deutlich von Konkurrenzprodukten *(npl)* ...	product differentiate (to)
Unterschied *(m)*: Preis...	price differential
Unterschiede *(mpl)*: Lohn...	earnings differential
unterschiedlich behandeln	discriminate (to)
unterschiedliche Preisgestaltung *(f)*	differential pricing
unterschwellige Werbung *(f)*	subliminal advertising
Untersuchung *(f)*: Arbeitsmethoden...	methods study
Untersuchung *(f)* der Betriebsanlagen *(fpl)*	plant layout study
Untersuchung *(f)*: Einstellungs...	attitude survey
Untersuchung *(f)*: Markt...	market study
Untersuchungsmethodik *(f)*: psychometrische ...	psychometric testing
Unterauftrag *(m)*: einen ... vergeben	subcontract (to)
unvorhergesehene Ausgaben *(fpl)*: Reserve *(f)* für ...	contingency reserve
Unvorstellbares *(n)*: sich ... vorstellen	think the unthinkable (to)
unzureichende Kapazität *(f)*	undercapacity
Updating *(n)*	update
Urlaub *(m)*: gestaffelter ...	staggered holidays
Ursprungsland *(n)*	home country

V

variable Kosten *(pl)*	variable costs variable expenses
Varianz *(f)*	variance
Veralten *(n)*	obsolescence

veränderliche Kosten *(pl)*	variable expenses
Verantwortlichkeit *(f)*	accountability
Verantwortlichkeit *(f)*: funktionale ...	functional responsibility
Verantwortung *(f)*: lineare ...	linear responsibility
Verantwortungsrechnung *(f)*	responsibility accounting
Verantwortungszentrum *(n)*: betriebliches...	responsibility centre
verarbeiten	process (to)
Verarbeitung *(f)*: automatische Daten...	automatic data processing (ADP)
Verarbeitung *(f)*: Daten...	data processing
Verarbeitung *(f)*: elektronische Daten...	electronic data processing (EDP)
Verarbeitung *(f)*: Informations...	information processing
Verarbeitung *(f)*: Stapel...	batch processing
Veräußerung *(f)*	divestment
verbale Kommunikation *(f)*	verbal communication
Verband *(m)*: Berufs...	trade association
Verbesserung *(f)*: Gewinn...	profit improvement
Verbesserung *(f)*: Produkt...	product improvement
verbinden: mit einem Netz *(n)* ...	network (to)
Verbindlichkeiten *(fpl)*	liabilities
Verbindlichkeiten *(fpl)*: kurzfristige ...	current liabilities
Verbraucher *(mpl)*: Akzeptanz *(f)* durch die ...	consumer acceptance
Verbrauchereinstellung *(f)*	user attitude
Verbraucherforschung *(f)*	consumer research
Verbrauchsgüter *(npl)*	consumer goods
Verbraucherpanel *(n)*	consumers' panel
Verbraucherpreisindex *(m)*	consumer price index
Verbraucherschutz *(m)*	consumer protection
Verbraucherschutzbewegung *(f)*	consumerism
Verbraucherschutzpolitik *(f)*	consumerism
Verbraucherstrategie *(f)*	user strategy
Verbraucherzufriedenheit *(f)*	consumer satisfaction
Verbraucherzurückhaltung *(f)*	consumer resistance
Verbrauchsgüter *(npl)*	consumer goods
	convenience goods
	non-durable goods
Verbrauchsgüter *(npl)*: langlebige ...	(consumer) durables

verbriefen	securitize (to)
verbundene Gesellschaft *(f)*	affiliate company
verbundenes Unternehmen *(n)*	associate company
vereinbar	compatible
Vereinbarung *(f)*: Arbeit *(f)* gemäß vertraglicher ...	work by contract
Vereinbarung *(f)*: Produktivitäts...	productivity agreement
Vereinbarung *(f)*: schriftliche ...	agreement *(written)*
Vereinfachung *(f)*	variety reduction
Vereinfachung *(f)*: Arbeits...	work simplification
Vereinfachung *(f)*: Stellen...	job simplification
vereinheitlichen	standardize (to)
Verfahren *(n)*	procedure
Verfahren *(n)*: administratives Kontroll...	administrative control procedure
Verfahren *(n)*: Aufteilungs... für Gemeinkosten *(pl)*	overheads recovery
Verfahren *(n)*: Beschwerde...	grievance procedure
Verfahren *(n)*: Investitionsrechnungs...	capital project evaluation
Verfahren *(n)*: iteratives ...	iterative process
Verfahren *(n)*: Kostenaufteilungs...	absorption costing
Verfahren *(n)*: logistisches ...	logistic process
Verfahren *(n)*: Produktions...	production process
Verfahren *(n)*: Quellenabzugs ...	pay-as-you-earn (PAYE) pay-as-you-go
Verfahren *(n)*: Schieds...	arbitration
Verfahren *(n)*: Schlichtungs...	arbitration grievance procedure
Verfahren *(n)*: System...	systems approach
Verfahren *(n)*: Systeme *(npl)* und ... *(pl)*	systems and procedures
Verfahren *(n)*: verwaltungstechnisches Kontroll...	administrative control procedure
verfahrensrechtlich	procedural
Verfahrensweise *(f)* des Top-Managements *(n)*	top management approach
Verflechtung *(f)*: Mandats...	interlocking directorate
verfügbare Betriebszeit *(f)*	uptime
verfügbares Einkommen *(n)*	disposable income
Verfügbarkeitsdauer *(f)*	uptime

Vergabe *(f)*: Auswärts...	outsourcing
	subcontracting
Vergabe *(f)* von Unteraufträgen *(mpl)*	contracting out
vergeben: einen Unterauftrag *(m)* ...	subcontract (to)
vergeben: einen Zulieferungsauftrag *(m)* ...	subcontract (to)
vergeben: in Franchise *(f)* ...	franchise (to)
vergeben: Unterauftrag *(m)* ...	contract out (to)
Vergleich *(m)*: Betriebs...	inter-firm comparison
Vergleich *(m)*: Soll-/Ist-...	performance against objectives
Vergleichsjahr *(n)*	base year
Vergütung *(f)*	remuneration
Vergütung *(f)* der Führungskräfte *(fpl)*	executive compensation
	executive remuneration
Vergütung *(f)* neben Gehalt *(n)* oder Lohn *(m)*	fringe benefits
Verhalten *(n)*: Einkaufs...	buying behaviour
Verhalten *(n)* in der Organisation *(f)*	organizational behaviour
Verhalten *(n)*: Kauf...	buying behaviour
Verhalten *(n)*: Konsumenten...	consumer behaviour
Verhaltensforschung *(f)*	behavioural science
Verhaltensgitter *(n)*, aus dem Führungsstile *(mpl)* abgeleitet werden	managerial grid
Verhaltensnormen *(fpl)* im Management *(n)*	management practices
Verhältnis *(n)*: Deckungs...	cover ratio
Verhältnis *(n)*: Kurs-Gewinn-...	price-earnings ratio (P/E)
Verhältnis *(n)* von Eigen- zu Fremdkapital *(n)*	debt-equity ratio
	leverage
Verhältnis *(n)* von Umsatz *(m)* zu Anlagen *(fpl)*	asset turnover
Verhältnis *(n)* von Verwaltung *(f)* zu Produktion *(f)*	administration-production ratio
Verhältnis *(n)* zwischen Fremd- und Eigenkapital *(n)*	gearing
	gearing ratio
verhandeln	negotiate (to)
Verhandlung *(f)*: gemeinsame ...	joint negotiation
Verhandlung *(f)*: innerbetriebliche Tarif...en *(pl)*	plant bargaining
Verhandlung *(f)*: Lohn...en *(pl)*	pay talks

Verhandlung *(f)*: Tarif...en *(pl)*	collective bargaining
Verhandlung *(f)*: Tarif..en *(pl)* über Produktivitätszulagen *(fpl)*	productivity bargaining
Verhandlungsstrategie *(f)*	negotiation strategy
Verkauf *(m)*	divestment
Verkauf *(m)*: Abdeckung *(f)* durch den ...	sales coverage
Verkauf *(m)*: Bemühungen *(fpl)* um ...ssteigerungen *(fpl)*	sales expansion effort
Verkauf *(m)*: Direkt...	direct selling
Verkauf *(m)*: Telefon...	telesales
Verkauf *(m)* von Impulswaren *(fpl)*	impulse sale
verkaufen	market (to)
	sell out (to)
Verkäufermarkt *(m)*	sellers' market
Verkaufsabteilung *(f)*	sales department
Verkaufsappeal *(m)*	sales appeal
Verkaufsaußendienst *(m)*	sales force
Verkaufsbezirk *(m)*	sales territory
Verkaufsbudget *(n)*	sales budget
Verkaufsdatum *(n)*: letztes ...	sell-by date
Verkaufserwartungen *(fpl)*	sales expectations
Verkaufsförderung *(f)*	sales promotion
Verkaufsförderungs-	promotional
Verkaufsförderungsmix *(n)*	promotional mix
Verkaufsförderungspolitik *(f)*	promotional policy
Verkaufsgebiet *(n)*	sales area
Verkaufsgespräch *(n)*	sales talk
Verkaufsingenieur *(m)*	sales engineer
Verkaufskampagne *(f)*	sales drive
Verkaufsleiter *(m)*	sales manager
Verkaufsleitung *(f)*	sales management
Verkaufsmanagement *(n)*	sales management
Verkaufsmethoden *(fpl)*: aggressive ...	hard sell
Verkaufsort *(m)*	point of sale (POS)
Verkaufspolitik *(f)*	sales policy
	selling policy
Verkaufspolitik *(f)*: aggressive ...	hard-sell
Verkaufsprognose *(f)*	sales forecast
Verkaufsquote *(f)*	sales quota

Verkaufsschlager *(m)*	star product
Verkaufstaktik *(f)*: aggressive ...	hard-sell
Verkaufstaktik *(f)*: weiche ...	soft-sell
verlangen: einen zu hohen Preis *(m)* ...	overprice (to)
Verläßlichkeit *(f)*	reliability
Verlauf *(m)*: Konjunktur...	economic trend
Verlauf *(m)*: Produktions...	production run
Verlaufsanalyse *(f)*	sequential analysis
verleasen	lease (to)
verlieren: an Wert *(m)* ...	depreciate (to)
Verlust *(m)*: Kapital...	capital loss
Verluste (mpl): aus zweifelhaften Forderungen (fpl) herrührende ...	bad-debt losses
verlustbringendes Produkt *(n)*	loss-maker
Verluste *(mpl)* abschreiben	cut one's losses (to)
vermarkten	market (to)
vermeiden	bypass (to)
vermitteln	mediate (to)
Vermittlung *(f)*	mediation
Vermittlung *(f)*: Arbeits...	employment bureau
Vermögen *(n)*: Anlage...	fixed assets
Vermögen *(n)*: Gesellschafts...	net worth
Vermögen *(n)*: Kapital...	capital assets
Vermögen *(n)*: Netto...	net assets
Vermögen *(n)*: Nettoumlauf...	net current assets
Vermögen *(n)*: Rein...	net assets
Vermögen *(n)*: Sach...	tangible assets
Vermögen *(n)*: Umlauf...	current assets
Vermögensertrag *(m)*	earnings on assets
Vermögenswert *(m)*	asset value
Vermögenswerte *(mpl)*	assets
Vermögenswerte *(mpl)*: kurzlebige ...	wasting assets
Vermögenswerte *(mpl)*: materielle ...	tangible assets
Vermögenswerte *(mpl)*: Neubewertung *(f)* von ...n	revaluation of assets
Vermögenswerte *(mpl)*: versteckte ...	hidden assets
verpackt: gut ...	well-packaged
Verpackung *(f)*	packaging
Verpflichtungen *(fpl)*: Finanzierung *(f)* von ...	debt financing

Verrechnungspreis *(m)*: fester ...	standard price
Verrechnungspreise *(mpl)*: Festlegung *(f)* der ...	transfer pricing
Verrechnungsstelle *(f)*	clearing house
Versand *(m)*	forwarding
	mailing
Versand *(m)*: Direkt...	direct mail
verschieben	put on the back burner (to)
Verschleiß *(m)*: eingeplanter ...	built-in obsolescence
Verschleiß *(m)*: geplanter ...	planned obsolescence
Verschuldungsgrad *(m)*	debt ratio
	debt-equity ratio
Verschuldungskoeffizient *(m)*	debt ratio
	debt-equity ratio
	leverage
Verschreibungen *(fpl)*: Schuld...	loan stock
Versetzung *(f)* der Mitarbeiter *(mpl)*	staff transfer
Versetzung *(f)* in den Ruhestand *(m)*	retirement
versöhnen	conciliate (to)
Versorgungsbetrieb *(m)*: öffentlicher ...	public utility
verspätete Reaktion *(f)*	lag response
versteckte Vermögenswerte *(mpl)*	hidden assets
Versuchsproduktion *(f)*	pilot production
	pilot run
verteilen	allocate (to)
	apportion (to)
verteilter Gewinn *(m)*	distributed profit
Verteilung *(f)*	apportionment
Verteilung *(f)*: Häufigkeits...	frequency distribution
Verteilung *(f)* von Kosten *(fpl)* auf Kostenstellen *(fpl)*	allocation of costs
	cost allocation
Verteilungsbogen *(m)*	spreadsheet
vertikale Integration *(f)*	vertical integration
Vertrag *(m)*: Tarif...	collective bargaining agreement
vertraglich: Arbeit *(f)* gemäß ...er Vereinbarung *(f)*	work by contract
Vertragsbedingungen *(fpl)*	conditions (*of a contract*)
Vertragsbetimmungen *(fpl)*	conditions (*of a contract*)

Vertrauensfrau *(f)*	trade union representative
Vertrauensfrau *(f)*: gewerkschaftliche ...	shop steward
Vertrauensmann *(m)*	trade union representative
Vertrauensmann *(m)*: gewerkschaftlicher ...	shop steward
Vertrauenswürdigkeit *(f)*	reliability
Vertraulichkeit *(f)*	confidentiality
vertraut: mit Computern *(mpl)* ...	computer literate
vertreiben	market (to)
Vertreter *(m)*: Allein...	sole agent
Vertreter *(m)*: Exklusiv...	sole agent
Vertretung *(f)* der Arbeitnehmer *(mpl)*	worker representation
Vertretung *(f)*: gemeinsame ...	joint representation
Vertrieb *(m)*	distribution
Vertriebsgebiet *(n)*	sales territory
Vertriebskosten *(pl)*	distribution costs
Vertriebsleiter *(m)*	distribution manager
Vertriebsnetz *(n)*	distribution network
Vertriebsplanung *(f)*	distribution planning
Vertriebspolitik *(f)*	distribution policy
Vertriebsweg *(m)*	distribution channel
Verwaltung *(f)*	administration
Verwaltung *(f)*: Finanz ...	financial administration
Verwaltung *(f)*: System...	systems management
Verwaltung *(f)*: Verhältnis *(n)* von ... zu Produktion *(f)*	administration-production ratio
Verwaltung *(f)* von Kapitalanlagen *(fpl)*	investment management
Verwaltungsgemeinkosten *(pl)*	administrative overheads
Verwaltungskosten *(pl)*	administrative expenses
Verwaltungsrat *(m)*	board of directors
Verwaltungsrat *(m)*: Mitglied *(n)* des ...(e)s	non-executive director outside director
Verwaltungsratskontrolle *(f)*	board control
Verwaltungsratssitzung *(f)*	board meeting
verwaltungstechnisches Kontrollverfahren *(n)*	administrative control procedure
Verwaltungstheorie *(f)*	administrative theory
Verwässerung *(f)* des Aktienkapitals *(n)*	dilution of equity
Verwässerung *(f)*: Kapital...	dilution of equity

Verzinsung *(f)*	rate of return
	return
	yield
Verzinsung *(f)* **der Aktiva** *(pl)*	return on assets
Verzögerung *(f)*	lag
Video-	video
Videotext *(m)*	teletext
Vision *(f)*	vision
Vision *(f)*: **Erklärung** *(f)* **der strategischen ...**	vision statement
Vizepräsident *(m)*	vice-president
vollautomatisch machen	automate (to)
Vollkostenprinzip *(n)*	full cost method
volle Kapazitätsausnützung *(f)*	full capacity
Volumen *(n)*	volume
Volumen *(n)*: **Absatz...**	sales volume
Volumen *(n)*: **Kredit...**	asset portfolio
Volumen *(n)*: **Umsatz...**	sales volume
vom Hörensagen *(n)*	grapevine
von Hand *(f)*	hands on
von Fremdkapital *(n)* **unterstützte Übernahme** *(f)*	leveraged buyout (LBO)
von Fremdkapital *(n)* **unterstütztes Übernahmeangebot** *(n)*	leveraged bid
von einer Gewerkschaft *(f)* **nicht genehmigter Streik** *(m)*	unofficial action
von unten nach oben	bottom-up
Voranschlag *(m)*: **Haushalts...**	budget forecast
Voranschlag *(m)*: **Systemkosten...**	estimating systems costs
Vorarbeiter *(m)*	foreman
vorausahnen	second guess (to)
Vorausberechnung *(f)*	projection
Voraussage *(f)*	forecasting
Voraussage *(f)*: **Konjunktur...**	business forecasting
voraussichtlicher Kunde *(m)*	prospective customer
Vorbereitung *(f)*: **Arbeits...**	production scheduling
	scheduling
vorbeugende Instandhaltung *(f)*	preventive maintenance
Vorgabe *(f)*: **Führung** *(f)* **durch ... von Programmen** *(npl)*	programmed management

Vorgabeleistung *(f)*	standard performance
Vorgehen *(n)*: System...	systems approach
vorhersagen	second guess (to)
vorläufig nich weiter bearbeiten	put on the back burner (to)
Vorlaufzeit *(f)*	lead time
Vorrat *(m)*: Puffer...	buffer stock
vorrätig: nicht ...	out of stock
Vorschau *(m)*: Liquiditäts...	cash forecasting
Vorschlag *(m)*: ernstgemeinter ...	value proposal
Vorschlag *(m)*: geschäftlicher ...	business proposition
Vorschlagswesen *(n)*: betriebliches ...	suggestion scheme
Vorschrift *(f)*	regulation
Vorschrift *(f)*: Dienst *(m)* nach ...	work-to-rule
vorsehen	schedule (to)
Vorsitzender *(m)*	chairman
Vorsitzender *(m)* und Generaldirektor *(m)*	chairman and managing director
Vorsitzender *(m)* und Geschäftsführer *(m)*	chairman and managing director
Vorsitzender *(m)*: stellvertretender ...	deputy chairman vice-chairman
Vorsprung *(m)*: Wettbewerbs...	competitive edge
Vorstand *(m)*	executive board
Vorstand *(m)*: Abteilungs...	departmental head
Vorstand *(m)*: Finanz...	financial director
Vorstandsmitglied *(n)*	executive director
Vorstandssitzung *(f)*	board meeting
Vorstandsvorsitzender *(m)*	chief executive
vorstellen: sich Unvorstellbares *(n)* ...	think the unthinkable (to)
Vorstoß *(m)*: Wettbewerbs...	competitive thrust
Vorteil *(m)*: Wettbewerbs...	competitive advantage
vorübergehend entlassen	lay off (to)
vorübergehende Entlassung *(f)*	lay-off
Vorwegnahme *(f)*	anticipatory response
vorzeitige Pensionierung *(f)*	early retirement

W

Wachstum *(n)*: organisches ...	organic growth
Wachstum *(n)*: Unternehmens...	corporate growth
Wachstumsbereich *(m)*	growth area
Wachstumsgebiet *(n)*	growth area
Wachstumsindex *(m)*	growth index
Wachstumsindustrie *(f)*	growth industry
Wachstumsindustrie *(f)*: junge ...	sunrise industry
Wachstumspotential *(n)*	growth potential
Wachstumsstrategie *(f)*	expansion strategy
	growth strategy
Wagniskapital *(n)*	seed money
	venture capital
Wagniskapitalgeber *(m)*	venture capitalist
Wahl *(f)*: in die engere ... ziehen	shortlist (to)
Wahl *(f)*: Medien...	media selection
Wahl *(f)* zwischen Eigenfertigung *(f)* und Kauf *(m)*	make-or-buy decision
wahlfreier Zugriff *(m)*	random access
Wahrscheinlichkeitstheorie *(f)*	probability theory
Wahrung *(f)* des eigenen Ressorts *(n)*	turf protection
Währung *(f)*: einheitliche ...	single currency
Währung *(f)*: gemeinsame ...	common currency
Währung *(f)*: Parallel...	parallel currency
Währungseinheit *(f)*: Europäische ... (Ecu, *m*)	European Currency Unit (ECU)
Währungssystem *(n)*: Europäisches ...	European Monetary System (EMS)
Währungsunion *(f)*: Europäische ...	European Monetary Union (EMU)
Wandel *(m)*: Management *(n)* des geordneten ...s	change management (management of change)
Ware *(f)*: fortlaufende ...nbestandsaufnahme *(f)*	continuous stocktaking
Warenmarkt *(m)*	commodity market
Warenumsatz *(m)*	sales turnover

Warenverteilung *(f)*	physical distribution management
Warenwerbung *(f)*: zwanglose ...	soft-sell
Warenzeichen *(n)*: eingetragenes ...	registered trademark
Warteschlangentheorie *(f)*	queuing theory
Wartung *(f)*: geplante ...	planned maintenance
Wartung *(f)*: Produktions...	productive maintenance
Wartung *(f)*: Produktiv...	productive maintenance
was man vorzuweisen hat	track record
waschen	launder (to)
Wechselbeziehung *(f)*	correlation
Wechselbeziehung *(f)*: strategische ...	strategic interdependence
Wechselkursgefüge *(n)*	Exchange Rate Mechanism (ERM)
Wechselkursmechanismus *(m)* im Europäischen Währungssystem *(n)*	Exchange Rate Mechanism (ERM)
Weg *(m)*: Absatz...	distribution channel
Weg *(m)*: Befehls...	chain of command
	line of command
Weg *(m)*: Instanzen...	chain of command
	line of command
Weg *(m)*: Vertriebs...	distribution channel
Wege *(mpl)*: Festlegung *(f)* der Handels...	routing
Wege *(mpl)*: Kommunikations...	channels of communication
weiche Verkaufstaktik *(f)*	soft-sell
weiße Gebrauchsgüter *(npl)*	white goods
Weisungsgewalt *(f)*: Aufteilung *(f)* der ...	authority structure
Weitbereichsnetz *(n)*	wide area network (WAN)
Weitblick *(m)*	vision
Weiterverfolgen *(n)*	follow-up
weiterverfolgen	follow up (to)
Weltklasse *(f)*	world class
weniger anspruchsvoll	down-market
Werbe: bewilligter ...etat *(m)*	advertising appropriation
Werbe: bewilligtes ...budget *(n)*	advertising appropriation
Werbeagent *(m)*	advertising agent
Werbeaussage *(f)*	advertising message
Werbebotschaft *(f)*	advertising message
Werbebudget *(n)*	advertising budget

Werbeerfolg *(m)*	advertising effectiveness
Werbeetat *(m)*	advertising budget
Werbeetat *(m)*: bewilligter ...	advertising appropriation
Werbefeldzug *(m)*	advertising drive
Werbeforschung *(f)*	advertising research
Werbekampagne *(f)*	advertising campaign
Werbeleiter *(m)*	advertising manager
Werbemanager *(m)*	advertising manager
Werbemedien *(npl)*	advertising media
Werbemittler *(m)*	advertising agent
werben (um)	canvass (to)
werben: durch Kundenbesuch *(m)* ...	canvass (to)
werbend	promotional
Werbetests (mpl): Durchführung (f) von ... *in regionalen Absatzmärkten (mpl)*	sales test
Werbethema *(n)*	advertising theme
Werbeträger *(mpl)*	advertising media
	media
Werbewirksamkeit *(f)*	advertising effectiveness
Werbung *(f)*: Köder...	switch selling
Werbung *(f)*: Lockmittel...	switch selling
Werbung *(f)*: POS-...	point-of-sale advertising
Werbung *(f)*: Produkt...	product advertising
Werbung *(f)*: reißerische ...	hype
Werbung *(f)*: Telefon...	telesales
Werbung *(f)*: Unternehmens...	corporate advertising
Werbung *(f)*: unterschwellige ...	subliminal advertising
Werksleiter *(m)*	plant manager
	works manager
Werkstatt *(f)*	shop floor
Werkstattprinzip *(n)*: Betriebsanlage *(f)* nach ...	process equipment layout
Wert *(m)*: an ... gewinnen	appreciate (to)
Wert *(m)*: an ... verlieren	depreciate (to)
Wert *(m)*: Ausschlachtungs...	break-up value
Wert *(m)*: Bar...	net present value (NPV)
Wert *(m)*: Buch...	book value
Wert *(m)*: Firmen...	goodwill
Wert *(m)*: im ... steigen	appreciate (to)

Wert *(m)*: im ... sinken	depreciate (to)
Wert *(m)*: immaterielle Anlage...e *(pl)*	intangible assets
Wert *(m)*: Kapital...	net present value ((NPV)
Wert *(m)*: Kurs...	market value
Wert *(m)*: Liquidations...	break-up value
Wert *(m)*: Markt...	market value
Wert *(m)*: Mehr...	added value
Wert *(m)*: Mehr...steuer *(f)*	value added tax (VAT)
Wert *(m)*: Methode *(f)* des Gegenwarts...es	present value method
Wert *(m)*: Mittel...	mean
Wert *(m)*: mündelsichere ...papiere *(npl)*	safety stock
Wert *(m)*: Substanz...	asset value
Wert *(m)*: Vermögens...	asset value
Wert *(m)*: Vermögens...e *(pl)*	assets
Wert *(m)*: Wiederbeschaffungs...	replacement costs
Wert *(m)*: Zentral...	median
Wertanalyse *(f)*	value analysis (VA)
Wertberichtigung *(f)*	depreciation allowance
Wertkette *(f)*	value chain
Wertkonzept *(n)*	value concept
wertlos: als ... abzuschreibende Sache *(f)*	write-off
Wertpapier *(n)*: erstklassiges ...	blue-chip stock
Wertpapiere *(npl)*	securities
Wertpapiere *(npl)*: erstklassige ...	gilt
	gilt-edged stock
Wertpapiere *(npl)*: mündelsichere ...	safety stock
wertpapiermäßig: Kreditforderungen *(fpl)* ... unterlegen	securitize (to)
wertpapiermäßige Unterlegung *(f)* von Kreditforderungen *(fpl)*	securitization
Wertpapierportfolio *(n)*	investment mix
Wertsteigerung *(f)*: Kapital...	capital appreciation
Wertzuwachs *(m)*	capital appreciation
Wertschöpfung *(f)*	value added
Wesen *(n)*: Betriebsrechnungs...	management accounting
Wettbewerb *(m)*	competition
Wettbewerb *(m)*: fairer ...	fair competition
Wettbewerb *(m)*: unlauterer ...	unfair competition

Wettbewerbsanreiz *(m)*	competitive stimulus
Wettbewerbsbeschränkungen *(fpl)*	restrictive practices *(legal)*
wettbewerbsfähig	competitive
Wettbewerbsfähigkeit *(f)*	competitiveness
Wettbewerbsposition *(f)*	competitive position
Wettbewerbsstellung *(f)*	competitive position
Wettbewerbsstrategie *(f)*	competitive strategy
Wettbewerbstaktik *(f)*	competitive tactics
Wettbewerbsvorsprung *(m)*	competitive edge
Wettbewerbsvorstoß *(m)*	competitive thrust
Wettbewerbsvorteil *(m)*	competitive advantage
wichtig	significant
wichtigster Erfolgsfaktor *(m)*	key success factor
wichtigster Kauffaktor *(m)*	key buying factor
Widerstand *(m)*: Käufer...	consumer resistance
widerstandsfähig	robust
Wiederbeschaffungskosten *(pl)*	replacement costs
Wiederbeschaffungswert *(m)*	replacement costs
Wiedererkennung *(f)*: Marken...	brand recognition
Wiedergewinnung *(f)*: Daten...	data retrieval
Wiedergewinnung *(f)*: Informations...	information retrieval
Wiedergewinnungszeit *(f)*	payback period
wiederholen	rerun (to)
wiederverwerten	recycle (to)
Wiederverwertung *(f)*	recycling
wilder Streik *(m)*	unofficial action
	wildcat strike
Winchesterplatte *(f)*	Winchester disk
Window *(n)*	window
wirksame Unternehmensführung *(f)*	effective management
	managerial effectiveness
wirksame Unternehmensleitung *(f)*	managerial effectiveness
wirksames Management *(n)*	effective management
	managerial effectiveness
Wirksamkeit *(f)*	effectiveness
Wirksamkeit *(f)*: Kosten...	cost-effectiveness
Wirksamkeit *(f)*: organisatorische ...	organizational effectiveness
Wirksamkeit *(f)*: Werbe...	advertising effectiveness
Wirt *(m)*: Betriebs...	business economist

Wirtschaft *(f)*: **Anlagen...**	asset management
Wirtschaft *(f)*: **Betriebs...**	business management
Wirtschaft *(f)*: **Betriebs...ler** *(m)*	business economist
Wirtschaft *(f)*: **Privat...**	private enterprise
wirtschaftliche Lebensdauer *(f)* **eines Produkt(e)s** *(n)*	product life (expectancy)
wirtschaftliche Fertigproduktmenge *(f)*	economic batch quantity
wirtschaftliche Losgröße *(f)*	economic order quantity
wirtschaftliche Nutzungsdauer *(f)*	economic life
wirtschaftliche Produktionsmenge *(f)*	economic manufacturing quantity
wirtschaftlicher Aufschwung *(f)*	take-off
wirtschaftlicher Auftrag *(m)*	economic mission
Wirtschaftsforschung *(f)*	economic research
Wirtschaftsgüter *(npl)*	capital assets
Wirtschaftsinformation *(f)*	economic intelligence
Wirtschaftsklima *(n)*	economic climate
Wirtschaftsprognose *(f)*	environmental forecasting
Wirtschaftstendenzen *(fpl)*	economic trend
wissenschaftliche Programmierung *(f)*	scientific progamming
wissenschaftliche Unternehmensführung *(f)*	scientific management
wissenschaftliches Management *(n)*	scientific management
Wohlwollen *(n)*	goodwill
Workstation *(f)*	workstation
Worst-Case-Szenario *(n)*	worst-case scenario
Wortprozessor *(m)*	word processor (WP)

Y

Yuppie *(m)* yuppie	

Z

Z-Diagramm *(n)*	Z-chart
Zahlen *(fpl)* **frisieren**	massage the figures (to)
Zeit *(f)*: **(Arbeits)...ermittlung** *(f)*	work measurement
Zeit *(f)*: **Ausfall...**	down time

Zeit (f): Echt...	real time
Zeit (f): Gleit...	flexitime
Zeit (f): Liefer...	lead time
Zeit (f): Normal...	standard time
Zeit (f): Real...	real time
Zeit (f): Standard...	standard time
Zeit (f): System (n) vorbestimmter ...en (fpl)	predetermined motion time system (PMTS)
Zeit (f): Turnaround-...	turnaround time
Zeit (f): unmittelbar geleistete Arbeits...	direct labour
Zeit (f): Vorlauf...	lead time
Zeit (f): Wiedergewinnungs...	payback period
Zeit (f): zulässige ...spanne (f) für unterdurchschnittliche Leistung (f)	time span of discretion
Zeit- und Bewegungsstudie (f)	time and methods study
	time and motion study
Zeitabstand (m)	lag
Zeitmanagement (n)	time management
Zeitplan (m)	work schedule
Zeitraum (m)	time frame
Zeitraum (m): Abrechnungs...	accounting period
Zeitreihe (f)	time series
Zeitspanne (f)	time frame
Zeitstudie (f)	time study
Zeitverzögerung (f)	time-lag
zellulares Mobiltelefon (n)	cellphone
Zentrale (f)	head office (legal)
Zentraleinheit (f) (ZE)	central processing unit (CPU)
Zentraleinkäufer (m)	chief buyer
zentralisieren	centralize (to)
Zentralisierung (f)	centralization
Zentralwert (m)	median
Zentrum (n): Datenverarbeitungs...	computer centre
Zentrum (n): Rechen...	computer centre
Zerfall (m)	disintegration
zerlegen	chunk down (to)
zerlegen: ein Projekt (n) in seine Einzelteile (npl) ...	chunk a project (to)
zerlegen: in Bruchteile (mpl) ...	fractionalize (to)

Zeug *(n)*: sich ins ... legen	hustle (to)
ziehen: in die engere Wahl *(f)* ...	shortlist (to)
ziehen: zu Rate *(m)* ...	consult (to)
Ziel *(n)*	objective
	target
Ziel *(n)*: Absatz...	sales goal
	sales target
Ziel *(n)*: Führung *(f)* durch	management by objectives
...vereinbarung *(f)*	(MBO)
Ziel *(n)*: gesamte Unternehmens...e *(pl)*	overall company objectives
Ziel *(n)*: Gewinn...	profit goal
	profit target
Ziel *(n)*: Produktions...	production target
Ziel *(n)*: Unternehmens...	company goal
	company objective
	corporate goal
	corporate mission
	corporate objective
Ziele *(npl)* identifizieren	target (to)
Ziele *(npl)*: unerwähnte ...	hidden agenda
zielen auf	target (to)
Zielfindung *(f)*	goal-seeking
Zielgruppe *(f)*	target market
Zielhierarchie *(f)*	hierarchy of goals
Zielidentifizierung *(f)*	targeting
Zielmarkt *(m)*	target market
Zielsetzung *(f)*	goal-setting
	objective
	objective-setting
	target-setting
	targeting
Zinsfuß *(m)*: interner ...	internal rate of return (IRR)
Zollfreigrenze *(f)*	non-tariff barrier (NTB)
Zollschranke *(f)*	tariff barrier
zu billig anbieten	underprice (to)
zu erreichen bemüht sein	target (to)
zu große Belegschaft *(f)*	overmanning
zu kleine Belegschaft *(f)*	undermanning
zu Rate *(m)* ziehen	consult (to)

zueinander passend	compatible
zufallsgesteuerte Stichprobenauswahl *(f)*	random sampling
Zufriedenheit *(f)* am Arbeitsplatz *(m)*	job satisfaction
Zufriedenheit *(f)*: Arbeits...	job satisfaction
Zufriedenheit *(f)*: Verbraucher...	consumer satisfaction
Zugang *(m)*: mehrfacher ...	multi-access
zugelassen: an der Börse *(f)* ... werden	go public (to)
zugreifen auf	access (to)
Zugriff *(m)* haben auf	access (to)
Zugriff *(m)*: wahlfreier ...	random access
Zukunftsplanung *(f)*	forward planning
Zulage *(f)*	bonus
	weighting
zulässige Zeitspanne *(f)* für unterdurchschnittliche Leistung *(f)*	time span of discretion
Zulieferungsauftrag *(m)*: einen ... vergeben	subcontract (to)
zum Nennwert *(m)*	at par
Zurechnung *(f)*: Kosten...	cost apportionment
Zurechnung *(f)* von Kosten *(pl)* auf die Kostenträger *(mpl)*	absorption
zurückbleiben: hinter den Erwartungen *(fpl)* ...	underperform (to)
zurückliegende Unternehmensergebnisse *(npl)*	track record
zurückschrauben	wind down (to)
zusammenarbeitend	collaborative
Zusammenbruch *(m)*	crash
Zusammenbruch *(m)*: Unternehmens...	failure *(of firm)*
Zusammenhang *(m)*: enger ...	correlation
zusammenschließen: sich ...	amalgamate (to)
Zusammenschluß *(m)*	amalgamation
Zusammenwirken *(n)*	synergy
Zusatzgeräte *(npl)*	add-on equipment
zusätzliche Schulung *(f)*	booster training
zusätzliche Sicherheit *(f)*	collateral
zusätzliches Training *(n)*	booster training
Zuschlag *(m)*: Gewinn...	mark-up
Zuständigkeit *(f)*	competency
	jurisdiction
Zuständigkeit *(f)*: instanzielle ...	line responsibility

Zuständigkeit *(f)*: **Zuweisung** *(f)* von ...sbereichen *(mpl)*	allocation of responsibilities
Zuständigkeitsbaum *(m)*	pertinence tree
zuteilen	allocate (to)
	apportion (to)
Zuteilung *(f)*	apportionment
Zuteilung *(f)*: **Aufgaben...**	job assignment
Zuverlässigkeit *(f)*	reliability
Zuverlässigkeit *(f)*: **Produkt...**	product reliability
zuvorkommen	second guess (to)
Zuwachs *(m)* **des Cash-flow** *(m)*	incremental cash flow
zuweisen	allocate (to)
	apportion (to)
Zuweisung *(f)*	apportionment
Zuweisung von Aufgabengebieten *(npl)*	allocation of responsibilities
Zuweisung *(f)* **von Zuständigkeitsbereichen** *(mpl)*	allocation of responsibilities
Zuweisung *(f)*: **Etats...**	budget allotment
Zuwendung *(f)*: **freiwillige ...**	*ex gratia* payment
zwanglose Warenwerbung *(f)*	soft sell
zweckfreie Forschung *(f)*	blue-sky research
zweifelhafte Forderungen *(fpl)*	bad debts
zweigleisige Beschaffung *(f)*	dual sourcing
Zweigstelle *(f)*	branch office
Zwischenhändler *(m)* **für Software-Vertrieb** *(m)*	software broker
zwischenmenschliche Beziehungen *(fpl)*	human relations
zwischenstaatliche Handelspraktiken *(fpl)*: **faire ...**	level playing-field
Zyklus *(m)*: **Arbeits...**	work cycle
Zyklus *(m)*: **Konjunktur...**	business cycle
Zyklus *(m)*: **Lebens... eines Produkt(e)s** *(n)*	life cycle of a product
	product life cycle